REAL ESTATE
EXCHANGE
DESK BOOK

JAMES SAYLOR

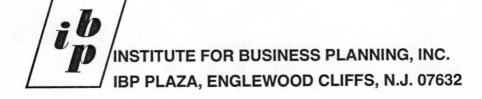

INSTITUTE FOR BUSINESS PLANNING, INC.
IBP PLAZA, ENGLEWOOD CLIFFS, N.J. 07632

ABOUT THE AUTHOR

James R. Saylor is a California Real Estate Broker who has specialized in real estate exchanges.

He has been a lecturer on topics of Real Estate Investments and Real Estate Exchanges before many Real Estate Boards and Associations. On the faculty of both Monterey Peninsula College and Hartnell College in California, he has taught courses in Real Estate Exchanges for several years.

Mr. Saylor is a Past President of the Pacific Exchange and Investment Counselors and is the current President of the Monterey Peninsula Exchange Counselors, both associations of real estate brokers who concentrate their activities in the exchange field.

His offices are now located in Carmel and Pacific Grove, California, where his business continues in Real Estate Consulting, and in Investments and Exchanges.

PREFACE

Real estate exchanging can result in many benefits for the owners. The first that we usually hear of are tax benefits. However, there is another equally important area of real estate, exchange for benefits. The Desk Book examines in depth both areas of real estate exchanging: the tax-deferred exchange of property held for investment, and the problem-solving exchange to move the owner into a property offering more benefits than the previous position.

Today, after a period of rapid gains in real estate values, the tax-deferred exchange is particularly significant. This kind of exchange results in *no tax* on any increase in the value of the property, no matter how much it has increased. Since the tax is deferred to a later date when a sale finally does occur, the owner has really received an interest-free loan from the government. This money is invested for a cash return *now* and further capital gains later.

In addition to the benefits of tax-deferred exchanges the book also explores the field of problem solving exchanges. This involves the handling of ''unsalable'' properties.

The proper place for these hard-to-sell properties is the exchange market place. By matching the real estate parcels, the owners' ages, occupations, tax situations, needs and desires, a better owner can be found for the various properties.

For example, a house builder may be ready to trade the last ''hard-to-sell'' home in a tract for a parcel of undeveloped land, since the land can be used for a future project. The former landowner, who knew nothing about land development, is happy with a completed house to live in, borrow money on, or rent out. Both are delighted with the results of the trade.

This book covers concepts in exchanging. The illustrations of real estate forms contain only the information and paragraphs written directly about the exchange example. This should make the concept easier to understand. In actual practice, other paragraphs would be included regarding pest-control inspections, possession dates, inspections of property, inventories, etc. These have been omitted in the book only to focus on the exchanging information.

What This Desk Book
Will Do For you

The REAL ESTATE EXCHANGE DESK BOOK cracks open a wide profit area for real estate investors and brokers. A prudent real estate exchange can not only defer taxes and earn money, it can turn a "worthless" or "unsalable" property into a very profitable situation.

The Desk Book is for brokers, sales people, investors, appraisers, lenders, and just about any real estate person who thinks he or she has an insoluble problem with real property.

In today's real estate world, rapid inflation has sent land values soaring. With the author's methods at your disposal, you will see how to avoid the heavy tax burden that usually plagues real estate investors. You'll also see how to get leverage to work to your advantage.

For the real estate broker, the Desk Book shows exactly how to match clients with properties so that instead of one commission, you earn two, as well as a pair of satisfied clients. It tells how to use multiple exchanges to secure better deals for clients who want to "exchange up."

In addition, you will find worked-out examples refreshingly simple to understand, as well as handy checklists to assist you every step of the way in working with an exchange.

The author also includes practical appendices which feature actual exchange forms and a complete glossary of real estate exchange brokers' language so that you will feel at ease in even the most complicated exchange procedure.

ACKNOWLEDGMENTS

I wish to thank my wife, Patti for her support during the long period of gathering the information and writing this book. Without her, it could not have been done.

Many of the examples used in the book are from exchanges that myself or one of my associates was familiar with. Since most real estate exchanges have another broker involved, I wish to thank the brokers who have worked with me in solving our clients' problems. The brokers who have been my teachers, particularly Chuck Chatham, Bill Broadbent and the late George Hoover, showed me that it could be done.

Thanks also to the California Association of Realtors and to Frank Weaver, Pony Express Co., for the permission to use their copyrighted Exchange Counselor Forms for the examples in the book.

CONTENTS

CONTENTS

CONTENTS

CONTENTS

CHAPTER 1

Why Exchange Real Estate?

[¶100]   AN OVERLOOKED OPPORTUNITY

In the United States today, there are hundreds of thousands of real estate brokers and salespeople. Most of the training given to all of these people is related to listing real estate, usually houses, and selling real estate, again usually houses. For money. Money is the common denominator, the measure of value, in almost all real estate transactions.

Volumes have been written, millions of hours of time spent training these salespeople to set up real estate purchases and sales, always using cash.

Why not cash? Is anything the matter with cash?

Nothing! Cash is the best understood and easiest medium of exchange to handle. Although money changes value constantly through inflation and other factors, almost everyone understands today's buying power of today's dollar.

With all of this emphasis on cash, is it any wonder that few real estate exchanges are ever made or even attempted? With all of the real estate people—the "experts" oriented toward cash, how can the public even hear of real estate exchanging?

So, here's the other question. Why *not* exchange real estate? Is anything wrong with exchanging real estate?

Nothing! *But* it is more complicated and more difficult. So, most real estate people discourage it. The public is not encouraged to think about it, so the possibility is usually ignored.

[¶101]   WHO EXCHANGES REAL ESTATE?

Most real estate exchanges today are made by property owners who are quite "sophisticated" or who have advisors who are.

The reasons are usually profit. Money. Cash. Spendable dollars.

When real estate is exchanged rather than sold for cash, it is possible,

1

under certain conditions, to defer all capital gains tax on the transaction.

Think about this. During a period of inflation such as we have experienced for many years, property goes up in value, "dollar" value, every day. Nearly everyone sells real estate for a dollar figure higher than the purchase price.

When the selling price has a higher dollar value than the purchase price, the difference is taxed at capital gains rates. This difference is taxed even though the increase may be totally due to inflation—the decrease in the value of the dollar.

Here's an example: Suppose Mr. Jones has purchased a $100,000 lot for cash. He intends to build a commercial building on it. After five years, his intentions have changed so he sells the lot. The selling price is $133,800.

Since the purchase price was $100,000 Mr. Jones has a gain of $33,800. Not bad, you might say. Well, this gain is taxable at long-term capital gains rates. So part of the gain or *profit* over the $100,000 purchase price has to be paid out in income tax.

Let's say that after computing all of his taxes for the year, that Jones pays a long-term capital gain tax of $8,450. on the gain on this sale. Now he has his $100,000 *plus* a gain of $25,350. after taxes.

Here's Mr. Jones' problem. During the five years that he owned the property, the inflation rate in the U.S. was about 6 percent per year. Now—6 percent inflation rate compounded for five years on $100,000 is approximately $33,800. Mr. Jones has had to pay income tax on a "profit" that really doesn't exist.

At the end of the five years, because of inflation, most everything else that Jones could have bought for $100,000. now costs around $133,800. So now Jones has *less* buying power after the sale and payment of tax than he had five years before. He has paid a tax of $8,450. on inflation.

The point of this example is that most sellers who have a capital gain pay tax if they sell. They sometimes pay tax on money that was only inflation dollars. Taxable gains are based on dollar increases with no regard for inflation.

We said *most* owners who have a capital gain pay tax if they sell. Some don't!

[¶102]   SALE OF AND REINVESTMENT IN A HOME

Most everyone who has owned a home is aware of the Internal Revenue Code Section that allows the sale of the home and reinvestment in another home without paying tax on the gain.

An owner does not have to recognize gain on the sale of his home if he purchases another principal residence within 18 months either before or after the sale of his old home. In order to qualify for this special treatment under Section 1034 of the Internal Revenue Code, the cost of the new home must be no less than the adjusted selling price of the old property.

Remember, the tax on the gain is not forgiven. It is merely deferred.

If the cost of the new home is the same as, or greater than, the adjusted selling price of the old home, none of the gain is taxed. If the cost of the new home is less than the adjusted selling price of the old home, the gain realized is taxed to the extent of the difference. (See IBP Real Estate Investment Planning 55,160.)

In regard to homes, there is no real news here. Nearly everyone is familar with these rules.

[¶103]   SALE OF NON-RESIDENCE PROPERTY

For all other classes of real estate, (any property owned other than the owner's principal residence), there is *no* period of 18 months for reinvestment. There is not a month—not a day. When the property is held for business, investment, speculation or for any other reason—even a vacation cabin used as a second home, the capital gains tax on any gain is incurred when the sale is made.

The tax becomes due in the tax year in which the sale is made. There have been countless people who have found this out after the sale, thinking that the reinvestment period was the same for other classes of property in addition to the owner's residence.

If their interest was in reinvestment, they should have exchanged! The Internal Revenue Code provides for tax deferment *only* if an *exchange* of properties is made. No sales!

[¶104]   THE TAX-DEFERRED EXCHANGE

All of the other property owned not as the owner's principal residence could be exchanged without incurring any *capital gains tax.*

Under Section 1031 of the Internal Revenue Code, it is possible to get very nearly the same tax treatment that Section 1034 allows for the homeowner. These properties cannot be sold without a tax on the gains, but they can be exchanged.

The Section will be covered in detail in the following chapter, but basically, if an owner exchanges his business, investment or other real estate that is not his personal residence for another business, investment or other real estate that is not his personal residence, the transaction is tax-free if:

1. The second property has a higher value than the first one;
2. He receives no cash or other non-real estate as "boot"
3. He closes the exchange of the properties at the same time.

[¶105]   **TAX-FREE EXCHANGING IN**
                         INCOME PROPERTIES—
                         ESTATE BUILDING

Inflation has a direct and unique effect on income properties. When prices increase, expenses, including taxes, also increase. Of course rents must also go up. Often, however, the income property is "leveraged" with a large mortgage that has fixed payments. The increase in rent then adds more spendable income to the owner. One of the largest "expenses" of the income property is the monthly mortgage payment which does not change.

This is the effect of leverage and the property will increase in value in relation to the increased cash flow. Since the total mortgage is also fixed, any increase in value of the property also is reflected directly in the owner's equity. It is possible that a small increase in the rent in an apartment property may result in doubling the owner's equity.

For example, an owner has a $100,000 apartment property that has a $90,000 mortgage. His equity is only $10,000. By a raise in the rent, the property increases its cash spendable, and the value goes up to $110,000. This small increase in value of the property (10%) has increased the owner's equity by 100 percent. Since the mortgage remains at $90,000 and the value is $110,000, the owner's equity has increased from $10,000 to $20,000.

Since income property can be exchanged "tax-free," an income property owner who is looking for the maximum leverage position might exchange this increased equity up into a larger property. With his larger equity of $20,000, he might be able to own a $200,000 apartment house.

Many apartment owners make a series of tax-deferred exchanges of income property for years, owning larger and larger complexes without ever making a taxable sale.

This is an efficient means of estate building.

**[¶106]   TAX DEFERMENT COMBINED WITH
             OTHER REASONS FOR EXCHANGE**

Since any investment or business property can be exchanged "tax-free," any other reasons for moving to a different property might be combined with a "1031" exchange. Here are a few examples of exchange motivations:

Exchange Properties to:

☐ Change locations.

☐ Increase income.

☐ Avoid a cash sale.

☐ Avoid a double move.

☐ An owner who wants no interruption of income may exchange income units for others without losing cash flow during the negotiations.

☐ Increase depreciation basis by "exchanging up" into a larger income property.

☐ Increase depreciation benefits by acquiring an older property with a shorter depreciation life.

☐ Increase depreciation benefits by acquiring a property with a different ratio between land and building.

☐ Restore depreciation which ran out entirely on the old property.

☐ Eliminate active management of income property by exchanging to a low-management type of investment.

☐ Reduce current cash flow by acquiring a property that has a large amortization instead.

☐ Enjoy capital appreciation instead of current income.

☐ Divide a large property into several smaller ones for diversification of risk.

☐ During a tight money market, benefit by exchanging instead of selling and carrying back a large mortgage.

☐ Exchange—leaseback a business property, to free frozen equity for a new investment.

☐ Defer "recapture" provisions of the Internal Revenue Code.

☐ Expand business or commercial premises.

☐ Acquire more speculative property for a higher cash return.

☐ Acquire a more conservative property for safety.
☐ Increase leverage or decrease leverage.
☐ Acquire a property that lenders will look more favorably upon for a new loan.
☐ Reduce overall holdings.
☐ Increase overall holdings.

[¶107]   THE REAL ESTATE EXCHANGE
TO SOLVE OWNERSHIP PROBLEMS

Among real estate brokers and salespeople, there is an example that is often used in "sales" training. The example describes the three elements that must be present in each "for sale" property when they take a listing. The property must be: (1) READILY SALABLE, (2) UNDER THE PRESENT OWNERSHIP, and (3) IN THE CURRENT MARKET.

These are important when a property is listed for sale. Taken one by one:

(1) READILY SALABLE. Isn't all real estate salable to *someone* at *some price*? Unfortunately, no it isn't! There are many parcels of property all over the country that have been on the market for years, for just about any price, with no takers. There are many properties in most counties in the country that are sold for taxes each year.

Examples: Many inner-city properties cannot be sold. These slum area buildings may be productive real estate with tenants and a positive cash flow. Given a choice, buyers with cash usually will pick something in another area with less potential trouble attached.

Land-locked real estate. After rapid development of a city or the suburbs, lots end up with houses, schools, streets and freeways on all sides. Usually they belong to a city, county, state, but sometimes remain in the hands of individuals.

Rural acreage and small town parcels. It's a little discouraging to have a 5-acre parcel for sale in an area with 100,000 parcels just like it all around, also for sale. The cash "deals" happen in the cities where the money is—where the banks look kindly on the near 100 percent loans for developments, and there is a certain demand for space at premium prices. In rural areas and small towns, even the local bankers are often reluctant to make loans on local real estate projects.

Recreational land. Buyers who have purchased land in mountain and desert and other "retirement" or highly promoted subdivisions find that the purchase was easier than any possible sale. While there might be some demand for the property, the original promoters are still in business. They usually have no interest in assisting a lot owner in selling his lot. After all, that is their business and they have their own huge inventory to dispose of.

(2) UNDER THE PRESENT OWNERSHIP. Suppose the property itself is readily salable. This alone, is not enough. The present owner must be *ready* and *able* to sell it and pass title to a buyer. A perfect example might be an owner who has a huge potential gain if he sells. He might have buyers standing by and bidding for the property, but he doesn't want to expose himself to the capital gains tax.

Another example might be multiple ownership. Several partners cannot decide on the right time, right terms, right price. Families often have a member who wants to "hold on a little longer" or wants to hold on for sentimental reasons.

If an owner is incompetent or is under the control of a court or trustee for any other reason, the otherwise salable property cannot be moved in either a sale or exchange.

(3) IN THE CURRENT MARKET. We have had "tight money" periods in recent years where few, if any, loans were available on any real estate. Market conditions regarding the availability of financing can take entire classes of real estate virtually out of the *sale* market place. Recently, during one of these periods, many banks and savings institutions reserved the small money supply for single-family home financing and re-financing. This stopped all of the action for a period of nearly two years in most construction and sales of any commercial or residential income properties. Wherever a new loan was needed, the transaction was not completed.

There could be a flooded market in any certain type of property in a local area. A manufacturing plant in a small town closes its doors. The area is suddenly depressed and 30 percent of all of the homes in the town go on the market. No one is a buyer—there are only sellers.

Since the "ideal" *sale* property is one that is READILY SALABLE, UNDER THE PRESENT OWNERSHIP, and IN THE PRESENT MARKET, then the definition of an "ideal" exchange property might be one that is *NOT* READILY SALABLE, IN THE PRESENT MARKET, and UNDER THE PRESENT OWNERSHIP. When an owner has been unable to sell a property, or feels that he can't pay the taxes on a large gain, or for any other reason can't go out of title in a sale, he might be the owner of a property that should be exchanged.

Once the idea of exchanging the property for another occurs to the owner, a new world opens up for him. If he looks around, he might see evidence of other properties all around him that have owners in the same predicament. By changing his thinking from a cash-only sale, the owner might find dozens of properties all around that might be just right for him to own. The only problem is getting the owner to take his property in trade.

So—all of the owners of the unsalable property just sit there with none of it changing hands. Most of them are discouraged and at this point are getting the feeling that no one in the world is ever going to want their property.

Not true! Usually there are hundreds, even thousands of people who would like to own that ''unsalable'' parcel of property. The only problem they have is—they have another ''unsalable'' parcel to dispose of first.

[¶108]   EXCHANGING HARD-TO-SELL
REAL ESTATE—
MATCHING PROBLEMS

In a medium-sized California community, an elderly couple had been trying to sell their home for several months. While there was nothing wrong with their house, it was not new. It was in competition with several nearby tracts of new homes that were being offered at good prices and excellent terms. The older home just was not even attracting any lookers.

The couple, the Smiths, had lived in the house for 20 years. They wanted to move into a condominium complex across town because Mr. Smith was having trouble keeping up with the yard work in the older home. He had suffered a heart attack and had to take it easier.

Even though the Smiths had twice lowered the price of the home, no interest had been forthcoming. They were about to give up their dream. It seemed as if their home was unsalable.

The Smith's broker discussed a change in terms with them. Like many sellers, they had been asking all cash for the home. After discussing it with him, they agreed that they might accept a small down payment and ''carry back'' part of the loan or all of it themselves. The change in terms, however, had to include some way to get into the condominium that they wanted. This was the first time the Smiths had discussed their future plans with the broker. Before, they had only talked about the house for sale, the terms, price and physical description. The broker questioned them at length. He finally found that since they had some other retirement income, they really wanted the proceeds of the house sale to (1) purchase the condominium for them, and (2) the balance to be invested in some safe investment—stocks, certificates of deposit or some like type of investment.

Now the broker immediately contacted the condominium developer. The developer had taken longer than he expected selling out all of his units. Most were gone, but several were left—he wanted to get on to building a new project, but was reluctant to leave this project until a few more were sold.

The builder did not wish to exchange a unit for the Smith's home. However, he told Smith's broker that he would certainly consider an exchange for some well-located land that was ready for development into tract homes or apartments.

Now the broker had an idea for an exchange. He went to work. By reviewing city records, within a few days he had a list of vacant land parcels in the city that might be suitable for the developer. By calling on each of the owners, he found a young couple who had inherited an R-4 lot, zoned for a small apartment property. They knew nothing about building apartments and would be willing to consider an exchange for a house. They were now occupying an apartment.

Now the broker had all of the elements of the three-way exchange in his hands. He knew the Smiths would take a condominium, and the developer might take the lot. The couple that owned the lot might take Smith's house. He showed the properties and each of the owners expressed an interest, if the terms could be worked out.

The first exchange offer was drawn, offering the vacant land for the Smith's house. The owners of the lot, the Jones' valued their lot at $50,000 and valued the house at the same price. The offer was for an equity for equity exchange as both properties were free and clear of any loans. The broker was careful to include a paragraph in the agreement that stated that the transaction was to be canceled if the Smiths could not exchange the lot for the condominium unit. The Smiths accepted the offer with that provision.

Now the broker prepared another offer—this time offering the lot. The Smiths now had the lot as "owners in acquisition" and signed the offer that offered the lot for the condo unit that they had picked. This offer had a clause that provided that the offer was canceled if the exchange between the Jones and the Smiths failed to close.

The two cancellation clauses in the two offers protected the Smiths two ways—if they couldn't get the lot to trade for the condo, it was canceled. If they couldn't get the lot in the first transaction, they had no obligation to take the condominium.

The Jones' needed no protection clause. They had examined the Smith's house and were willing to accept it. Their part of the offer was firm.

9

The condominium was valued at $30,000.00. The offer to the developer called for the condo unit to be transferred to the Smiths free and clear of loans. It also provided that the Smiths would carry back a loan secured by a mortgage or trust deed on the lot. The note would be for $20,000.00.

The developer accepted the offer. The escrows were opened and the properties were all transferred in a short time. None of the three parcels had to be financed by a bank or Savings and Loan so there was no delay for loans. The escrows closed within 30 days.

The Smiths were out of their home and into the condominium. They had moved their $50,000.00 house and for it received a $30,000.00 condo unit and a well-secured note for $20,000.00 on a prime development lot.

The developer was out of one more unit. He also acquired an excellent lot ready for his next venture.

The Jones, who knew nothing about property development got out of a piece of land that had worried them and into a free and clear home. While they were in negotiation with the broker, they had checked out the neighborhood and found that the home would rent for a good monthly rental figure.

After the close of escrow, the Jones contacted their bank and borrowed $30,000.00 cash secured by the house. They had calculated that the rent from the home would pay the monthly payments on the loan and leave something over for taxes and expenses. So now they had a property that would give them some tax shelter and also $30,000.00 in cash.

Shortly after the close of the exchange escrows, the Jones contacted the broker again. They purchased a 10-unit apartment property, using the $30,000.00 as the down payment. Now instead of the original lot that was just costing them taxes each year, they now owned a house and a 10-unit apartment.

The broker who had negotiated the three-way exchange had originally only one client, the Smiths with their house. He stood to collect only one real estate commission when and if that home sold. By trying to solve his client's problem of disposing of their home through a real estate exchange, he ended up with three happy owners. Incidentally, he also collected four real estate commissions, instead of just one. While negotiating with each of the owners of the three properties, he secured a listing agreement with each. In addition, he then sold a fourth property to the Jones, who wouldn't have had the money without having first made the exchange.

All of these owners might have waited much longer to dispose of their properties—if each had to wait for a cash buyer. Each received just what they wanted, and no cash changed hands in the transaction between the principals.

[¶108.1]   The Tax Results

The Smiths transferred from a $50,000.00 home to a $30,000.00 home. Their income tax was only on the difference, not on the entire gain. Since they had owned the property for many years, the tax was computed at long-term capital gains rates. They paid the same amount in taxes as they would have if they had sold and re-invested.

The developer was taxed in full on his gain. The condo was "dealer" property to him and as such, he could make no tax-deferred transaction. (This will be covered in detail, further in the book.)

The Jones made a totally tax-deferred exchange. They exchanged one property being held for business or investment for another to be held for business or investment. The values were the same. The transaction resulted in no tax on any gain on the lot. (Chapter 2 will cover the rules for a tax-deferred exchange.)

The Tax-Deferred Exchange

[¶200]   CONSEQUENCES OF THE CAPITAL GAINS TAX

When we refer to a "tax-deferred exchange" of real estate held for Investment, or trade or business, the tax being deferred is the *capital gains tax*. This is mentioned as many owners think of real estate taxes—assessments on the property by the city or county when the words, "taxes" and "real estate" are used together.

The capital gains tax is a tax on the gain or "profit" when certain real estate is sold for a price higher than the adjusted cost basis.

The capital gains tax consequences of the disposition of real estate are affected by the following:

1. The holding period.
2. The classification of the property.
3. The type of transaction.

[¶201]   HOLDING PERIOD

Long-term capital gains treatment is sought by most sellers of capital assets. The tax on the long-term gain is less, usually about 50 percent less than the short-term capital gain.

The necessary holding period for long-term capital gain and loss was lengthened to greater than one year starting in 1978. Prior to the Tax Reform Act of 1976, the holding period was greater than six months. There was a transitional increase to greater than nine months during 1977.

[¶201.1]   How to Measure the Holding Period

When measuring the holding period, remember that you are dealing in months rather than the same number of days that add up to a month. The holding period begins the day after the owner acquired the property. It ends when the property is sold.

For a long-term gain, starting in 1978, the property must be held for a period in excess of one year. So, if you bought a property on January 2, 1978 and held it until January 2, 1979, you have held it for one year. If you want long-term capital gains treatment, you should not sell it before January 3, 1979.

[¶202] CLASSIFICATION OF PROPERTY

The classification of the type of property as held by the owner going out of title also affects capital gains.

1. Residential property. This is property used by the owner as his primary residence. The taxable disposition of this property results in either a taxable capital gain or a non-deductible loss. Since the tax can be deferred on a sale or exchange in accordance with Section 1034 of the Internal Revenue Code, a sale is not always taxable.

2. Dealer property. Real estate held primarily for resale by a "dealer" is not a capital asset and gains or losses resulting from disposition are ordinary income or ordinary losses (fully deductible.)

3. Investment real estate. An investor in real estate acquires some property, usually land, to be held for investment as stocks and bonds are held for investment. Gain or loss realized from a disposition of this property gives capital gain or loss treatment.

4. Trade or business property. This is usually an income-producing property. Rental property is classified as trade or business property, even if never rented. Trade or business property often is real estate with depreciable improvements. A primary residence can be converted to this classification by using it as a rental before a sale or exchange.

Trade or business property is not a capital asset, and its disposition produces gains taxable at capital gains rates or a fully deductible ordinary loss. (Section 1231 of the code.)

[¶203] TYPE OF TRANSACTION

As previously shown, "dealer" property is taxed at ordinary rates whatever the transaction. Sales or exchanges that result in a gain are taxable.

Residence property, the owner's primary residence, can be sold or exchanged by the owner. Either transaction can be tax-deferred if the taxpayer acquires another home under certain conditions. (See Section 1034 of the code.)

Property held for *Investment* or for *Trade or Business*, if sold, is taxed as a capital gain. However, Section 1031 of the Internal Revenue Code provides for deferment of any gain or loss on these classifications of property in certain types of real estate *exchanges*.

[¶204]   HOW TO FIGURE TAX
ON A CAPITAL GAIN

After computing the gain or loss to be reported from the sale or exchange of a capital asset and determining whether it is long-term, the next step is to figure the tax.

(1) *Regular Way:* Short-and long-term gains must be included in your gross income. If you have a net long-term gain that exceeds your net short-term capital loss, you deduct 50 percent of such amount from your gross income. (Since the maximum tax bracket is 70 percent, the maximum tax rate on capital gains works out to half of that, or 35%). Here's an example:

Long-term capital gain	$14,000	
Long-term capital loss	11,000	
Net Long-term capital gain		$3,000
Short-term capital loss	$2,000	
Short-term capital gain	800	
Net Short-term capital loss		1,200
Excess net long-term capital gain		$1,800

Here the net long-term capital gain exceeds the net short-term capital loss by $1,800. Half of this amount ($900) may be deducted from your gross income. The other half is included in computing taxable income.

(2) *Alternative method:* If you're in an over-50 percent tax bracket, you can reduce the capital gain tax on the first $50,000 of gain by electing to compute the gain under the "alternative" method. Rather than deducting half of your gain in determining your tax, as under the regular method, the following is the method:

Under this section, the first $50,000 of long-term capital gain is taxed at 25 percent and the balance is taxed at 35 percent. (We must also consider the effect of the minimum tax on tax-preference income, since the untaxed portion of capital gains is counted as an item of tax-preference income subject to minimum tax.) (Sec. 1201 of the Code).

Capital Gains Tax for Corporations
Since the capital gains tax for corporations is 30 percent, it may be better to pay the regular tax on capital gains. Currently, corporations pay 20 percent on the first $25,000 of taxable ordinary income, 22 percent on the next $25,000 and 48 percent on ordinary income over $50,000. If the corporation has income of less than $50,000, the regular tax will be lower.

[¶204.1]   Minimum Tax

The tax law imposes a 15 percent tax (called the minimum tax) on tax preference income in excess of $10,000 or one-half the taxes paid for a year, whichever is greater. Included among the list of tax preference income items is the untaxed portion of capital gains. Therefore, if your capital gains plus your other tax preference income are high, you may be subject to the minimum tax.

[¶205]   RESIDENCES—SALE AND REINVESTMENT IS A FORM OF TAX-DEFERRED EXCHANGE

When a homeowner defers payment of capital gains tax by selling and reinvesting in a new home, it is covered by Section 1034 of the Internal Revenue Code. In general terms, it provides for deferring the capital gains tax if the taxpayer (1) sells his primary residence and reinvests in another within 18 months of the sale, or (2) begins construction on a new home within 18 months and completes it within 24 months of the sale.

If the owner invests in a new home which costs equal to or more than the adjusted sales price received for the first home, all of the capital gains tax is deferred. If the second home is valued less than the first, then the tax is on the (1) realized gain or, (2) the difference of the adjusted sales price and the amount invested, whichever is the lesser amount.

[¶206]   TAX-DEFERRED EXCHANGES ON BUSINESS OR INVESTMENT PROPERTY

The property owner can also get tax-deferred treatment on most other property that he owns—other than his primary residence. All real estate that he owns for business or investment purposes (excluding property owned for resale as ''dealer'' property), is covered by Section 1031 of the

Internal Revenue Code. This Section is about the *EXCHANGE* of property held for business or investment purposes.

It says in part:

> "No gain or loss shall be recognized if property held for productive use in trade or business or for investment (not including stock in trade or other property held primarily for sale, nor stocks, bonds, notes, Choses in Action, Certificates of Trust or beneficial interest, or other securities or evidences of indebtedness or interest) is exchanged solely for property of a like kind to be held either for productive use in trade or business or for investment."

It says simply that any property held for business or investment purposes may be exchanged tax-free for any other property held also for investment or business purposes.

Passed shortly after the First World War, this section has changed little since its origination.

The United States was changing after the Great War. People were moving to work in the industries in the cities. The cities were expanding quickly and pell-mell into the surrounding countryside and farms. Farmers were being forced out of the area on the edges of the cities, in the paths of the expansion. Other farmers and ranchers were moving Westward, acquiring much larger land holdings.

This was all happening just a few years after the passage of the Income Tax Amendment in 1913. No one had much experience with the capital gains tax—before the Internal Revenue Code, there was no such thing.

Some wise members of Congress determined that people who were moving from one location to another *and remaining in the same business* should be allowed to do so without being penalized by capital gains tax on the property that they were moving out of.

For purposes of figuring gain, it had been determined that the cost basis for capital gains tax was the cost of the property or the market value of the property on March 4, 1913. That was the effective date of the Income Tax Law. Property acquired subsequent to that date would have its cost basis computed from the acquisition cost. (A few individuals still have property with a 1913 cost basis. Many corporations, such as railroads, still own great amounts of property based on a cost basis prior to 1913.)

[¶207]   THE 1031 EXCHANGE

When Section 1031 was added to the tax law, most property owned by individuals was held free and clear. It was later in the century that financing, particularly long-term financing became common. In those days, it was quite simple to compute the tax aspects of an exchange. If the properties were valued the same and were of like kind (business or investment) then the transaction was tax-deferred or "tax-free" for both parties to the exchange. If the properties were not of equal value, then something was added as "boot" to even up the value. The "boot" was taxable to the one receiving it.

For instance, Mr. A exchanged his farm valued at $20,000 for a farm valued at $25,000 by Mr. B. Mr. A gave Mr. B cash in the amount of $5,000 as "boot." This amount was "unlike" property as it was not real estate, so it was taxable to Mr. B (providing that B had that much gain in the price).

Later, mortgages and trust deeds became very common and the exchange transactions were not so easy to compute. In some exchanges, one or more of the loans were assumed—others were paid off, and the owners "carried back" loans, contracts etc.

Following is an interpretation of current practice in computing tax-deferred exchanges under Section 1031 of I.R.C.

[¶207.1]   Like Property Under Section 1031

The code refers to "like kind" property which can be exchanged tax-free. This means that both the property *being exchanged* and the property *being received* by the taxpayer making the tax-deferred exchange must be held for investment or income-producing purposes. The property can be improved or unimproved.

It is of no consequence to the taxpayer making the tax-deferred exchange how the other party in the exchange holds the property. It must be "like" property to the party getting the tax deferment. (The other party might exchange his primary residence—this would be unlike property for him, but could be "like" property if the taxpayer receiving it treated it as an investment property.) *Example:* Mr. A trades a vacant commercial lot he holds for investment purposes. Mr. B exchanges his residence to Mr. A for the lot. The values of both properties are the same. This is a tax-deferred exchange for Mr. A, if he considers the second property, the house, as an investment property and treats it as such. It is an unlike exchange for B (Residence for business property.)

Like property also includes all fixtures included with the improvements that are considered real property under State law.

Finally a leased business or investment property which has at least 30 years to run on the lease at the time of the exchange is also considered "like" property.

The meaning of "like property" may be the most misunderstood and misinterpreted part of the code. It is meant to be very broad and means *any* property held for investment or business purposes can be exchanged for *any* other to be held for business or investment purposes.

Unimproved land may be exchanged for apartments. Apartments for commercial—commercial for farms or ranches, in all combinations.

Many good beneficial transactions have been postponed or canceled because an owner or his "advisors" did not believe that unimproved land and apartments were "like" property.

Note: Confusion about "like" property may be caused by the interpretation of "like" property for reinvestment after condemnation under Eminent Domain. This is covered by Section 1033 of the I.R.C. and has been far more restrictive than Section 1031.

[¶207.2]   Unlike Property Under Section 1031

The following are classified as "unlike" properties in an exchange.

1. The taxpayer's residence.
2. Property held primarily for sale. (Dealer property—often such as tract houses owned by the contractor.)
3. Cash.
4. Personal property such as furniture and other furnishings and chattel mortgages on the personal property.
5. Existing liens on the property.
6. Promissory notes from a third party owed to one of the parties in the exchange and transferred to the other party in the exchange as part of the consideration.

[¶208]   BOOT

Boot is a term to describe cash or other "unlike" property given in an exchange. There are two classifications of boot—cash boot and mortgage boot.

1. Cash boot is money or some other consideration of value that is transferred in the exchange. Cash boot can be, in addition to money—notes, automobiles, airplanes, furniture, or cash, note or other property given to a third party on behalf of either of the parties in the exchange. It is any item of value given in the exchange to "even up" equity

that is not classified as real estate or improvements being held by the recipient for business or investment purposes. Any *unlike* property given or received in the exchange is *cash* boot.

2. Mortgage boot is best described as "Being relieved of the obligation." All *net* existing liens (voluntary or involuntary) that the taxpayer is relieved of in the exchange are *mortgage boot*. The other party in the exchange assumes these liens or takes them over "subject to." (The taxable amount is the "net" mortgage relief.)

Example: Mr. A exchanges a lot with a small existing loan for another investment property with a smaller loan.

A's lot	$25,000	value
Loan	10,000	
Equity	$15,000	
B's property	$22,000	
Loan	7,000	
Equity	$15,000	

Mr. A was relieved of a $10,000 loan and took over a $7,000 loan when he accepted B's property. Although the exchange was an even "equity for equity" exchange, Mr. A had a "net" loan relief of $3,000. This is mortgage boot. (He would be taxed on this amount as a capital gain—or his total gain, whichever was the lesser amount.)

If the existing lien on the taxpayer's property, or any part of it, is paid off by the other party, during the transaction, it is *cash* boot to the taxpayer.

A mortgage or trust deed note on a third property, (or an unsecured note) not included in the exchange, is *cash* boot if given as an additional consideration in the exchange. (A note might be given to a real estate broker as a fee on behalf of one party by the other party in the exchange.)

[¶208.1]   Right to Offset Boot

This is a key rule of boot in an exchange. "Cash boot" given offsets "mortgage boot" received. However, "mortgage boot" given does *not* offset "cash boot" received.

Effect: No totally tax-deferred exchange can be made unless the taxpayer trades into a property with a market value equal to, or greater than the starting property, and an equity equal to or greater than his equity in the original property.

If the taxpayer receives some "boot" in an otherwise tax-deferred exchange, then the transaction becomes taxable to him only to the amount of the boot. (Assuming that he has a gain in value in the property being exchanged.)

The taxable amount in any exchange is either: the total gain or the total amount of the net boot received, whichever is the lesser amount.

[¶209] HOW TO FIGURE BASIS OF NEW PROPERTY IN EXCHANGE

Here is a formula for finding new basis in the second property after trading the first property for it.

Start with:	The adjusted basis of the old property,
Then, add:	The amount of mortgage loan on the property, liens, cash or other boot paid,
	Recognized gain
	Total
Then, subtract:	Amount of mortgage loan on old property, liens, cash or other boot received.
Result:	Basis of new property

The California Association of Realtors has an excellent form, the Form E, to assist in computation of basis and new allocation between land and buildings if the properties are improved.

Example: Suppose that Mr. Able and Mr. Baker exchange properties. The following is the known information regarding the original property of each:

	Mr. Able	Mr. Baker
Value:	$250,000	$320,000
Adjusted Basis:	125,000	250,000
Loan:	100,000	150,000
Equity:	150,000	170,000

Mr. Able agrees to give Mr. Baker the difference between the equities in cash. Mr. Able's equity is $150,000, and Baker's equity is $170,000, so Able will give Baker $20,000 in cash in the exchange.

Using the above information with the Form E (Figure 2.1), the exchange basis adjustment of each owner would show as follows:

EXCHANGE BASIS ADJUSTMENT

PROPERTY BASIS	
CAPITALIZED TRANSACTION COSTS	
ADJUSTED COST BASIS	

NAME _____ DATE ___/___/___

ROPERTY CONVEYED _____

			(1) PROPERTY ABLE		(2) PROPERTY		(3) PROPERTY BAKER		(4) PROPERTY		(5) PROPERTY		(6) PROPERTY		
INDICATED GAIN	1	Market Value of Property Conveyed	250	000			320	000							1
	2	Less: Adjusted Cost Basis	125	000			250	000							2
	3	INDICATED GAIN	125	000			70	000							3
BALANCE EQUITIES	4	Equity Conveyed	150	000			170	000							4
	5	Equity Acquired	170	000			150	000							5
	6	Difference	20	000			20	000							6
	7	Cash or Boot Received		-0-			20	000							7
	8	Cash or Boot Paid	20	000				-0-							8
	9	Old Loans	100	000			150	000							9
	10	Less: New Loans	150	000			100	000							10
DETERMINE RECOGNIZED GAIN	11	NET LOAN RELIEF		-0-			50	000							11
	12	Less: Cash or Boot Paid (L8)	20	000				-0-							12
	13	Recognized Net Loan Relief		-0-			50	000							13
	14	Plus: Cash or Boot Received (L7)		-0-			20	000							14
	15	TOTAL UNLIKE PROPERTY RECEIVED		-0-			70	000							15
	16	RECOGNIZED GAIN (LESSER OF L3 OR L15)		-0-			70	000							16

TRANSFER OF BASIS

TRANSFER OF BASIS	17	Adjusted Cost Basis (L2)	125	000			250	000							17
	18	Plus: New Loans (L10)	150	000			100	000							18
	19	Plus: Cash or Boot Paid (L8)	20	000				-0-							19
	20	Plus: Recognized Gain (L16)		-0-			70	000							20
	21	Total Additions	295	000			420	000							21
	22	Less: Old Loans (L9)	100	000			150	000							22
	23	Less: Cash or Boot Received (L7)		-0-			20	000							23
	24	NEW ADJUSTED COST BASIS	195	000			250	000							24

NEW ALLOCATION AND DEPRECIATION

ALLOCATION	25	Land Allocation													25
	26	Improvement Allocation													26
	27	Personal Property Allocation													27
	28	NEW ADJUSTED COST BASIS (L24)													28

			PP	IMP	PP	IMP	PP	IMP	PP	IMP	PP	IMP	PP	IMP	
DEPRECIATION	29	Estimated Life Term													29
	30	Depreciation Method													30
	31	ANNUAL DEPRECIATION IMPROVEMENTS													31
	32	ANNUAL DEPRECIATION PERSONAL PROPERTY													32

For these forms, address California Association of Realtors, 505 Shatto Place, Los Angeles, Calif. 90020   (11-68)

The statements and figures presented herein, while not guaranteed, are secured from sources we believe authoritative.
FORM E

Figure 2.1

21

EXCHANGE BASIS ADJUSTMENT

	PROPERTY BASIS	
	CAPITALIZED TRANSACTION COSTS	
	ADJUSTED COST BASIS	

NAME _____ DATE ___/___/___

ROPERTY CONVEYED _____

	LINE NO.		(1) PROPERTY ABLE		(2) PROPERTY		(3) PROPERTY BAKER		(4) PROPERTY		(5) PROPERTY		(6) PROPERTY		
INDICATED GAIN	1	Market Value of Property Conveyed	250	000			320	000							
	2	Less: Adjusted Cost Basis	125	000			260	000							
	3	INDICATED GAIN	125	000			60	000							
BALANCE EQUITIES	4	Equity Conveyed	150	000			170	000							
	5	Equity Acquired	170	000			150	000							
	6	Difference	20	000			20	000							
	7	Cash or Boot Received		-0-			20	000							
	8	Cash or Boot Paid	20	000				-0-							
DETERMINE RECOGNIZED GAIN	9	Old Loans	100	000			150	000							
	10	Less: New Loans	150	000			100	000							
	11	NET LOAN RELIEF		-0-			50	000							
	12	Less: Cash or Boot Paid (L8)	20	000				-0-							
	13	Recognized Net Loan Relief		-0-			50	000							
	14	Plus: Cash or Boot Received (L7)		-0-			20	000							
	15	TOTAL UNLIKE PROPERTY RECEIVED		-0-			70	000							
	16	RECOGNIZED GAIN (LESSER OF L3 OR L15)		-0-			60	000							

TRANSFER OF BASIS

TRANSFER OF BASIS	17	Adjusted Cost Basis (L2)	125	000			260	000							
	18	Plus: New Loans (L10)	150	000			100	000							
	19	Plus: Cash or Boot Paid (L8)	20	000				-0-							
	20	Plus: Recognized Gain (L16)		-0-			60	000							
	21	Total Additions	295	000			420	000							
	22	Less: Old Loans (L9)	100	000			150	000							
	23	Less: Cash or Boot Received (L7)		-0-			20	000							
	24	NEW ADJUSTED COST BASIS	195	000			250	000							

NEW ALLOCATION AND DEPRECIATION

ALLOCATION	25	Land Allocation													
	26	Improvement Allocation													
	27	Personal Property Allocation													
	28	NEW ADJUSTED COST BASIS (L24)													

			PP	IMP	PP	IMP	PP	IMP	PP	IMP	PP	IMP	PP	IMP
DEPRECIATION	29	Estimated Life Term												
	30	Depreciation Method												
	31	ANNUAL DEPRECIATION IMPROVEMENTS												
	32	ANNUAL DEPRECIATION PERSONAL PROPERTY												

For these forms, address California Association of Realtors, 505 Shatto Place, Los Angeles, Calif. 90020   (11-68)

The statements and figures presented herein, while not guaranteed, are secured from sources we believe authoritative.
FORM E

Figure 2.2

So, using the formula, Mr. Able has a new adjusted cost basis in the new property of $195,000. He has exchanged "up" in a totally tax-deferred exchange. Part of his new basis is from the $20,000 boot given (cash) and part is from the "net" amount of new loans assumed.

Mr. Baker has made a downward exchange that was entirely taxable to him. His indicated gain was originally $70,000 (value minus adjusted cost basis) and his recognized gain in the transaction was also $70,000. If he had sold the property, that amount would have been taxable as a capital gain. In the exchange, it was taxable in the same amount. However, the amount was taxable as a combination of $20,000 *cash* boot received and $50,000 *mortgage* boot received. He received $20,000 in cash and was relieved of $50,000 in mortgage (original loan $150,000 less $100,000 loan acquired).

Suppose Mr. Baker had an original adjusted cost basis of $260,000. His indicated gain on line 3 would then have been only $60,000.

Then, all of the information on the form E (Figure 2.2) would be as follows:

In the second Form E, Mr. Baker has a recognized gain of $60,000. His gain was the *lesser* of (1) The indicated gain, or the boot.

[¶210]   HOW TO HANDLE THE COSTS
IN A REAL ESTATE EXCHANGE

The Form E has no provision for brokerage fees or other expenses of the real estate transaction. *Rev. Rul. 72-456* (CB 1972-2, 468) shows how the arithmetic works out in three different situations in which boot is received in addition to like-kind property.

In the first example, Able has adjusted basis in the land he exchanges of $12,000. The property received has a value of $20,000. He also receives $10,000 in cash. His brokerage commission is $2,000, which he pays. In this example, the $2,000 commission reduces his taxable gain from $10,000 to $8,000.

In example two, Baker exchanges land with an adjusted basis of $29,500 for property of like kind with a value of $20,000. He also receives $10,000 in cash. He pays a $2,000 brokerage commission. Since he received cash boot in the exchange, he cannot get a current deduction for any loss on the transaction. But the basis in the property received is increased by the amount of the nondeductible loss. The effect is that the tax benefit of the loss is postponed until he makes a further disposition of the property.

In the third example, Crane exchanges land with an adjusted basis of $10,000 for property with a fair market value of $20,000, and there is a $2,000 brokerage fee paid. In this exchange, no boot is received, and there is no taxable gain even though there is $8,000 profit in the transaction. The commission paid increases Crane's basis for the new property received in the exchange. Later, there will be some deferred tax benefit from that commission when Crane disposes of the property by a sale.

EFFECTS OF BROKERAGE COMMISSION ON TAXABLE GAIN

	Example 1	Example 2	Example 3
Land — FMV	$20,000	$20,000	$20,000
Cash	10,000	10,000	—0—
Total	$30,000	$30,000	$20,000
Less:			
Brokerage Commission	2,000	2,000	2,000
Amount Realized	$28,000	$28,000	$18,000
Given up:			
Land—Basis	$12,000	$29,500	$10,000
Realized Gain (loss)	$16,000	$(1,500)	$ 8,000
Recognized gain (lessor of realized gain or net cash received.)	$ 8,000	$—0—	$—0—

EFFECT OF BROKERAGE COMMISSION ON BASIS

Basis:	Example 1	Example 2	Example 3
Land given up—basis	$12,000	$10,000	$29,000
Less Cash Received	(10,000)	—0—	(10,000)
Plus Recognized gain	8,000	—0—	—0—
Plus Brokerage Commission	2,000	2,000	2,000
Basis of land received	$12,000	$12,000	$21,500

[¶211]   COMBINATION TAX-DEFERRED EXCHANGE AND INSTALLMENT SALE

Another well known method of postponing the realization of taxable gain on the sale of real estate is through the installment sale. The general rules for an installment sale are as follows:

1. The purchase price must be paid in not less than two installments. Where *only* two installments are provided for, the two payments should not be in the same taxable year.

2. Not more than 30 percent of the total selling price can be paid to the seller (or to a third party on the seller's behalf) in the year of the sale. "Selling Price" is usually the gross contract price; commissions and other selling expenses are not considered, even though these do reduce the net profit.

Payments in the year of the sale include all payments made by the buyer in the year the sale is closed, whether in cash or *property*. (Other real estate can be exchanged as the consideration in the down payment.) The buyer's note or other evidence of obligation to pay the balance in a later year is merely a promise to pay, not a payment; consequently, it is not included.

The deferment of taxes in an installment sale works like this: The taxability of the gains recognized by the sale is deferred until the actual receipt of the purchase price. In addition, only a part of each payment received in payment of the purchase price is treated as the receipt of the taxable gain. The balance is treated as a non-taxable return of basis. (See IBP Real Estate Investment Planning 55,030—Installment Sales.)

Since a consideration, other than cash, can be the down payment, one party in an exchange can report a tax-deferred exchange and pay no tax on his gain. The other can report an installment sale and pay the taxes on his gain over a period of years.

Example: Mr. A offers to exchange his vacant lot as the consideration for a down payment toward Mr. B's 10-unit apartment building.

	A's vacant lot	B's apartment property
Value	$25,000	$100,000
Loan	—0—	10,000
Basis	10,000	50,000
Indicated Gain	15,000	50,000

Mr. B accepts the offer. He accepts the lot in exchange and carries back a $65,000 loan secured by a mortgage on the apartment property. The terms of the loan call for interest only, with monthly payments at 10 percent annual interest for the remainder of the year of the exchange. Starting in January of the following year, the balance is to be paid back in a fully amortized loan including 10 percent annual interest over a 10-year period. The monthly payments would be $859.02.

[¶211.1] Tax Treatment

Mr. A has made a totally tax-deferred exchange.

Mr. B can report an installment sale. He has received LESS THAN 30 percent of the total selling price in the year of the sale. He has contracted for MORE THAN ONE installment payable in more than one taxable year.

Mr. B would compute his tax on the gain as follows:

Gross selling price	$100,000.00	
Less adjusted basis	− 50,000.00	
Net Gain		50,000.00

Contract Price:

Gross selling price	100,000.00	
Existing loan	− 10,000.00	
Difference	90,000.00	
Excess of loan over basis	—0—	
"Contract Price"		90,000.00

Taxable Percentage:

$$\frac{\text{Net Gain} \quad 50,000.00}{\text{Contract Price} \quad 90,000.00} = 55.55 \text{ percent}$$

Result:

Consideration received	25,000.00
Taxable Portion (55.55% of $25,000)	13,887.50
Non Taxable Portion	11,112.50

The same proportion of the monthly payments in following years that were allocated to the principal would be taxable and non-taxable. Any interest would, of course, be ordinary income for the year it was received.

[¶212]   ABSENCE OF CHOICE AS TO TAX-FREE TREATMENT

Section 1031 of the I.R.C. does not give either the government or the taxpayer the right to choose to accept or reject this treatment. If a real estate exchange meets the requirements for tax-free treatment, no gain or loss will be recognized for tax purposes regardless of how the taxpayer or the government feels about it.

Care should be taken if a transaction is being structured as an exchange by a party who wishes to realize a *loss*. If the exchange follows the rules of Section 1031, *no gain* or *loss* can be recognized.

[¶213] "INTENT" OF TAXPAYER IS A FACTOR IN EXCHANGING

The second half of Section 1031 refers to the property received in the exchange. In addition to the property being exchanged, the property being received must be *"like kind to be held either for productive use in trade or business or for investment.."*

Example: An owner had his property for sale, listed with a real estate broker. After a long time with no purchase offers, an offer was received for an exchange. The owner checked out the property offered and felt that it was readily salable.

Since the values were about the same, he accepted the exchange offer and closed on the other parcel. Within a few days, the broker brought in an offer to purchase the second parcel on an installment sale. The owner accepted and everything was perfect. He had made a tax-free exchange, then an installment sale.

No, the owner had made a taxable exchange. In a case such as this, the tax court ruled that the exchange was not tax-free. It is obvious that the owner had no INTENT to use the property RECEIVED "to be held either for productive use in trade or business or for investment." He acquired that property only for the purpose of selling it.

[¶214] THE "UNBUILT BUILDING" EXCHANGE

Under certain conditions, an owner can exchange a property being held for use in trade or business or investment for another property that is "to be built." Here is an example:

The Baird Publishing Co. owned and occupied its own building in Nashville, Tennessee. The land had a basis of $2,000 and the improvements had been fully depreciated.

The Baptist School Board had been acquiring property in that area and on several occasions had approached Baird about a purchase of its property. Baird had always refused upon the specific ground that it did not want to incur the capital gains tax on the profit that it would realize on a sale.

An enterprising real estate broker, who had previously represented the Baptist School Board, proposed that he (the broker) construct a building and exchange it to Baird for the building now occupied by the publisher. The broker could then sell the Baird building to the School Board.

Baird agreed to this proposal and a contract was entered into giving the broker the right to sell the property subject to Baird's occupancy of it rent-free until the broker provided another building. The new building was to be constructed subject to Baird's approval and within a reasonable time. A price of $50,000 was put on Baird's original building.

The difference between the purchase price and the cost of the new building would be paid to Baird in cash.

The broker sold the Baird Building to the School Board for $60,000. Since Baird was owed $50,000, it was deposited in an escrow account. None of the money was paid to Baird until after the cost of the new building was established.

When the new building was completed, it was delivered to Baird. The cost was $33,000, so Baird also received $17,000. Since Baird's adjusted cost basis in the original property was only $2,000, the total gain on the transaction was $48,000.

Since boot is taxable up to the amount of gain realized, Baird reported as capital gain only the $17,000 that was received in cash.

The Treasury contended that the transaction was really a cash sale between Baird and the School Board, after which the broker constructed a building for Baird. Therefore, the entire $48,000 was capital gain. The test applied by the Treasury in determining if a transaction is a cash sale or an exchange is as follows: In an exchange, no fixed money price or value is placed on either property, while in a sale, there is either a money consideration or the equivalent in property. Since Baird placed a fixed price on its property, this was a sale.

Baird took the position that it had entered into an agreement with the broker to exchange properties and that it had no interest in what the broker would do with the property exchanged to him.

The court went along with Baird. The transaction was an exchange, for two reasons. First, Baird had consistently said that the only acceptable transaction would be one involving an exchange. Secondly, the relationship between Baird and the broker was not an agency one—that is, Baird did not in fact authorize the broker to sell the property on Baird's behalf. The agreement was really that Baird would sell its building to the broker in exchange for another building to be built by the broker. The broker had no duty to report or account to Baird for the price he received for selling Baird's property to anyone.

Further, the court did not agree with the Treasury's test to distinguish a sale and exchange. Giving dollar values to the respective properties does not always make the transaction a cash sale. Dollar values are involved whenever "boot" is exchanged and the statute permits this in a tax-free exchange.

Note on Build-to-suit Exchanges: under Rev. Rul. 75-291 (CB 1975-2, 332), IRS now says that in a situation such as that in *Baird*—a build-to-suit exchange—the transaction qualifies as a tax-free exchange. It makes no difference, says the Ruling, that the build-to-suit property was acquired solely for the purpose of exchanging it. However, the builder (the broker in *Baird*) would not be entitled to the same tax benefit since the property it bought was not held for productive use in a trade or business or for investment.

The Ruling points out that the party building to suit must not act on behalf of the party receiving the built-to-suit property. This, the Ruling emphasizes, is crucial to pulling off the deal successfully. *If the agency is found to exist, IRS will disqualify the exchange from the tax-free treatment.*

CHAPTER 3

Exchanging for Benefits

[¶300]   **REAL ESTATE AS A VEHICLE**

When a buyer acquires a parcel of real estate, there is usually a definite objective in mind for doing so. The property is going to do something for the owner. It might be his residence. It might be an income-producing property. These are benefits that everyone readily understands. In addition to obvious benefits, there are many others that are not as obvious. People acquire real estate for the less obvious reasons just as readily. Here is a short list of benefits to an owner for acquiring different properties.

1. Cash flow from rents for income.
2. Reduction of personal income tax because of overflow depreciation from the improvements.
3. Hope for future profits from increase in value.
4. Owner wants to develop undeveloped land.
5. Desire to preserve the land from developers.
6. Acquire a site for a business.
7. Pride of ownership.
8. Own as an inflation hedge.
9. Build an estate by having tenants pay expenses and loans.
10. Create a job for the owner.
11. Get away from a property that causes work for the owner.

There certainly could be many more reasons for an owner to acquire or own property. The list could be as long as the number of people we could interview. Each one of these reasons that an owner has for ownership can be classified as a BENEFIT to him, because he owns the property. Since everyone has different ideas of the set of benefits that he wants for himself, exchanges of all classes of properties become possible.

In the list above, an exchange of a piece of income property between owners #10 and #11 might be easy. Since #10 has a motivation to own a property that will keep him busy, he is a user for income property and is actively seeking it. Mr. #11 will be glad to move out of his—and if #10 owns something that will give him peace and quiet, we may have a perfect exchange.

There are others on the list that are opposites—but not necessarily exchange candidates with each other.

Owners usually have several *benefits* in mind when a property is purchased. Say that it is an investment property—an apartment. One buyer may have a "shopping list" like this. These are things that he wants when he gets the apartment property.

1. It must be new or near-new.
2. The land/improvement allocation must be favorable for depreciation.
3. After purchase, it must return 10 percent cash flow on the invested capital.
4. It must be located near a major highway.
5. It must be located near schools.
6. It must be near a large shopping center.

The longer the list of "wants" that a buyer develops, the less likely he is ever to find the property. If he hires a real estate professional to search for him, each possible investment may be rejected because one of the factors is missing. He may never find the "just right" property for investment. If the list is long enough, no property in existence could quality.

What this owner might be looking for is a set of benefits to him that he thinks will be satisfied by this shopping list. After all, in an income property, are all other factors really important—if there is a constant cash flow and no vacancies? Going through the shopping list and questioning the buyer, it might be possible to reach a mutual understanding on the *benefits* that he really wants from the income property. After an interview, looking at his list again, we might agree that he wants:

1. New or near-new. He may want one where maintenance will be low. Maybe other properties that are well maintained might be worth looking at. If we question this item, it could open up many other possibilities.
2. and 3. Land/improvement allocation and cash flow. The benefit sought here obviously is money. He wants it from cash flow and from favorable depreciation. Perhaps an older apartment might interest him—providing his depreciation period might be shorter in years.
4, 5, & 6. This might just be the insurance that he feels is needed to keep the property fully occupied so that the cash flow will be uninterrupted.

Interviewing this individual in depth might reveal that he wants to own an income property with a good, secure cash flow. If he can realize this, and accept that other factors might control these benefits, his search might be easier. There might be hundreds of properties that could suit him—properties that he might have rejected without inspection, because they did not conform to his shopping list.

[¶301]   INCOME PROPERTY

It is not our intention to write about the economics of owning income property. There are other excellent books and articles written about investing in income property. They cover cash flow, expenses, return on investment, internal rate of return, leverage and all of the other factors that contribute to a successful investment in income property.

Since this chapter is about benefits resulting from exchanges, we will assume that the reader has some knowledge or concept of his own regarding the ownership of income property. We will concentrate on the exchange aspects.

[¶301.1]   Benefits from Income Property

In an income property, there are three major benefits that relate to money. Most income property is bought, sold and exchanged because of these three. They are:

1. CASH FLOW from the property. After the direct expenses and the loans are paid, the money left over is cash flow or spendable income. This is usually known in advance by a new owner who has carefully inspected the income and expense statements before the acquisition.
2. DEPRECIATION of the improvements is a benefit that is available in improved income property. This is an *expense* that can be a write off from taxes. Since it doesn't cost money from the spendable, it can provide income from the cash flow that might have been paid in taxes from ordinary income—if the property wasn't owned.
3. LOAN REDUCTION is the third measurable benefit. Each month a portion of the monthly payment on the loan goes to the reduction of the mortgage. If the payments are being paid by rental income, and the rental income is sheltered by depreciation, then the loans are being paid off for the owner. Eventually the property could be free and clear, without the owner ever paying anything out of his pocket, other than the original down payment.

Note: Appreciation is sometimes called a benefit for owning a property. It certainly is a reason and may be the benefit that is the major one in choosing many properties. It was not included in the list above only because it cannot be measured in advance. The three above are known in advance and can actually be figured over the lifetime of the ownership. Cash flow from rents is the only one of the three that may vary from the information known in advance. Usually it is within the power of the owner to control it. An efficient, well-run business will increase cash flow. An inefficient, sloppy operation may quickly send the cash flow down.

The depreciation and loan reduction can be projected over their lifetimes. A lender can give an owner a statement showing the amount of loan reduction and interest for each payment during the entire payment cycle of 25 or 30 years. The depreciation is known in advance, based on the cost basis with the depreciation schedule and estimated life of the improvement.

Appreciation is a benefit after it happens, but it can't be planned in advance. It doesn't always happen.

Going back to the "objectives" that each of the buyers wanted in the beginning of this chapter, each could be classified as a benefit that the buyer was seeking.

When a property owner already has a property, or many properties, he might still be searching for a better set of benefits. Often, the owner stays right where is is—the capital gains tax might nullify any other benefit that he might get. That is, if he sells and uses the money to acquire another property.

Since we have the possibility of a tax-deferred exchange, exchanges can be made to place the owner into a better *benefit* position. Because of this fact, many exchanges are made by owners with only a passing interest in the price or value of the properties in the exchange. Of course, the value is certainly a consideration, but it may not be the *prime* consideration.

Here are some examples of tax-deferred exchanges for the benefit of the owner:

[¶301.2]   Depreciation Benefits

Depreciation is a tax benefit that directly affects cash flow. Depreciation allows us to recover the cost basis of the improvements in a real estate investment over the period of time we use the asset. The tax law gives an ordinary business deduction for the amount of this depreciation expense. Since the deduction reduces the tax we will have to pay, it increases our spendable income from the property. This tax deduction is an "expense" item of the property that requires no cash outlay.

Since the adjusted cost basis in the property is decreased by the amount of depreciation each year, that amount will be taxed as a capital gain when the property is sold again at a later date. So, one definition of depreciation we have heard is, "Depreciation is an allowable expense item that allows us to deduct ordinary income each year that we own an improved property, and convert it to long-term capital gain later."

[¶301.3]   Allocation for Depreciation

When an improved income property is acquired, the owner must allocate the value of the property between the improvements and the land. Since the land will always be there, it cannot be depreciated. For example, a duplex was purchased for $50,000. The land allocation was $10,000. The building allocation was $40,000, and since the owner decided to depreciate it over 20 years "straight-line," his depreciation expense was $2,000 per year. ($40,000 ÷ 20 = $2,000.)

[¶302]   EXCHANGING TO CHANGE ALLOCATION

Since the amount of the allocation to improvements is one control on the amount of the depreciation expense—the amount of allocation to improvements can control annual cash flow. A reason or benefit that an owner could have for an exchange might be for a reallocation between land and buildings.

Here is an example:

Mrs. Arthur had a commercial lot near the downtown of a medium-sized town. She had purchased the lot for $60,000 a few years before. It was now worth $100,000. There were no improvements on the lot, and she had nothing to depreciate—all of the basis of $60,000 was in the land. The lot was leased to a used-car dealer who paid $8,000 per year rent, just for the use of the land. This was a net, net, net lease, so the owner cleared the $8,000 after all expenses. She was in the 50 percent tax bracket.

Exchange #1

Mrs. Arthur exchanged the lot for a free and clear near-new four-unit apartment also valued at $100,000. It was an equity for equity exchange, with no boot given or received. Her basis of $60,000 in the lot was carried over to the new property. In allocating for depreciation, she ascertained that the building was worth $80,000, or 80 percent of the value, and the land $20,000 for 20 percent. She applied this ratio to her $60,000 basis. Mrs. Arthur allocated 80 percent of the basis to the improvement and chose to use a 20-year straight-line schedule for depreciation. The $60,000 × 80% = $48,000 as allocated to improvement for depreciation.

The exchange has given the owner the additional benefit of depreciation, not present in the other property. Using the 20-year straight-line gives $48,000 ÷ 20 = $2,400 a year as additional expenses that she can deduct for the next 20 years. Since this expense has no cash outlay, this is a definite benefit as income taxes will be reduced.

Exchange #2

Suppose that the four-plex acquired by Mrs. Arthur is on leased land. Now she owns the four-plex on land with, say, a 35-year lease. Since the land is leased, all of the allocation could go to the improvement. So the entire $60,000 basis could be depreciated. Using a 20-year SL schedule again, the annual depreciation benefit would be $60,000 ÷ 20 = $3,000 per year.

Exchange #3

If the apartment was on leased land and was a new property, Mrs. Arthur might also be able to use the *first user* benefit, 200 percent declining-balance depreciation. Probably she would have to use a longer life for the improvements under this schedule since the building is new. Using a 30-year life, for example, her first year's depreciation would be $60,000 ÷ 30 = $2,000 × 200\% = $4,000 per year.

If each of these example properties was available for exchange, Mrs. Arthur would have the choice of the amount of tax savings that she would like. Since she was in the 50 percent tax bracket, the savings might look like this for her during the first year:

	Gross Income (after expense)	Depreciation	Tax	Spendable Income (after tax)
Original Prop:	$8,000	—0—	$4,000	$4,000
Exchange #1	$8,000	$2,400	$2,800	$5,200
Exchange #2	$8,000	$3,000	$2,500	$5,500
Exchange #3	$8,000	$4,000	$2,000	$6,000

[¶303]   EXCHANGING UP

In the previous examples, Mrs. Arthur exchanged her free and clear $100,000 property for another $100,000 free and clear property. The only difference was the improvement on the second property which gave tax shelter through depreciation.

Using the same original property valued at $100,000 with a cost basis of $60,000 and no improvement, let's show an exchange for Mrs. Arthur up into a more valuable property. She will have to take on a loan—but her adjusted basis will increase in the same amount as the loan she assumes. Since the depreciation benefit is based on the adjusted cost basis, here is what might happen if she exchanges up to a $500,000 apartment property. For illustration, the loan will be shown as "interest only."

	Original Property	New Property
Value:	$100,000	$500,000
Loan:	—0—	400,000
Equity:	100,000	100,000
Basis:	60,000	460,000
Net Rental Income: after expenses:	8,000	40,000
Mortgage payment: 8 percent int. only.	—0—	32,000
Cash Flow:	8,000	8,000

In the new property, Mrs. Arthur allocates 80 percent of basis or $368,000 to the improvements and the balance of $92,000 to the land. She decides to use a 20-year straight-line depreciation schedule. Her depreciation "expense" is now $18,400 per year. ($368,000 ÷ 20 = $18,400).

In addition to her expenses, Mrs. Arthur now has loan payments on the new property. Since the property is larger, the income is more. Here's how the cash flow might look in comparison.

On the original property, Mrs. Arthur ended up with $8,000 after expenses. Since it was free and clear of loans, there were no loan payments. On the new property, the cash flow remained the same *after* loan expense.

Here is what the result of the cash flow for the building might look like after the tax factors (Income tax and depreciation) were applied:

	Original Property	New Property
Cash Flow:	$8,000	$8,000
Depreciation:	—0—	18,400
Tax free cash flow:	—0—	8,000
Taxable Cash flow:	8,000	—0—
Tax on taxable cash flow:		
50 percent Bracket	4,000	—0—
Net spend. after tax:	4,000	8,000
Overflow Depreciation:	—0—	5,200
Total after tax cash return:	$4,000	$13,200

In the new property, the entire cash for the property becomes spendable. The depreciation shelters that cash. In addition, it overflows and shelters another $10,400 of Mrs. Arthur's ordinary income. Since she is in the 50 percent tax bracket, the tax saving could be $5,200. ($10,400 ×

50% = $5,200) She is able to spend that amount of money which would have been paid in taxes, if she had not owned this property.

So now in addition to depreciation, we have added an additional benefit—leverage. In the previous examples, Mrs. Arthur owned a non-depreciable property, which was exchanged into three examples. Here's the original position and the three examples again, AND the fourth example, using leverage (borrowed money.)

	Cash Flow	Depreciation	Tax	Spendable Income
Original Property:	$8,000	—0—	$4,000	$4,000
Example #1	8,000	2,400	2,800	5,200
Example #2	8,000	3,000	2,500	5,500
Example #3	8,000	4,000	2,000	6,000
Example #4	8,000	18,400	—0—	13,200

Example #4 includes the amount from Mrs. Arthur's overflow tax shelter. Without owning this property, that amount would have been paid by her on her ordinary income—so the spendable can be attributed to the ownership of the property.

The benefits of leverage and depreciation contribute to the usual benefits sought by income property owners: cash flow.

In recent years, many income properties throughout the country have increased greatly in value. The "leverage" that most owners have when a property is purchased begins to erode just as soon as the transaction closes. Within a few months, or years, the value has increased and the loans have been reduced.

To get the best use of the equity, exchanges should be considered within a short period. Here is an example of an investment and the result after a few years of ownership:

	PROPERTY DURING FIRST YEAR	AFTER APPRECIATION AND DEPRECIATION
Value:	$75,000	$135,000
Loans:	45,000	25,000
Equity:	30,000	110,000
Analysis of Taxable Income: After Expenses		
Net Oper. Income:	6,700	12,185
Less Interest:	− 2,700	− 1,500
Less Deprec:	− 2,400	− 2,400
Taxable Income:	1,600	8,285

Spendable Income

Net Oper. Income:	6,700	12,185
Less Prin. & Int.:	− 6,000	− 6,000
Gross Spendable	700	6,185
Less Income tax:	− 480	− 2,485
(30 percent Bracket)		
Net Annual Spend.	220	3,700

Return on equity

Net Oper. Income:	6,700	12,185
Less Int. Payment:	− 2,700	− 1,500
Less Income Tax:	− 480	− 2,485
Net Equity Income	3,520	8,200
Net Equity Income Rate		
Net Equity Income ÷ Equity.	11.73 %	7.45%

This owner seems to have a much better property after a few years. His net spendable has increased from $220 to $3,700. As the rents have increased, so has the value of the property—and the *equity!* (We have assumed that the owner is in the 30 percent tax bracket and the property is allocated 75 percent to improvements—he is using 20-year straight-line depreciation.)

Since the benefits of leverage are based on a low equity position, look at the bottom line of the comparison—the Net Equity Income Rate has decreased from 11.73 percent to 7.45 percent. (The Net Equity Income ÷ by the current equity.)

Using the new equity that the owner has in the property after a few years, let's show the results of an exchange of *that equity* up into a better-leveraged position. (Equity is gained by both increasing the value of the property and by reducing loans. Value minus loans = equity.)

The following is an example of using the $110,000 equity in an exchange into a larger income property. Note that the equity is the same in each property. The first column is the *Now* for the property shown in the previous example—after it has been owned for a number of years.

	Present Property	New Property
Market Value:	$135,000	410,000
Loans:	25,000	300,000
Equity:	110,000	110,000

Analysis of Taxable Income: After Expenses

Net Operating Income:	12,185	36,900
Less Interest Payment:	− 1,500	− 19,500
Less Depreciation Allowance:	− 2,400	− 10,200
Taxable Income:	8,285	7,200

Spendable Income from properties:

Net Operating Income:	12,185	36,900
Less Principal & Interest:	− 6,000	− 27,792
Gross Spendable	6,185	9,108
Less Income Tax: (30 percent Bracket)	− 2,485	− 2,160
Net Annual Spendable	3,700	6,948

Return on Equity:

Net Operating Income:	12,185	36,900
Less Interest Payment:	− 1,500	− 19,500
Less Income Tax:	− 2,485	− 2,160
Net Equity Income:	8,200	15,240
Net Equity Income Rate:	7.45%	13.8%

Note the following: The owner's taxable income has slightly decreased. The *Net Annual Spendable* has nearly doubled. The net equity income rate has increased from 7.45 percent to 13.8 percent.

Without changing his equity (no cash added), the owner has moved to a larger property giving him an increase in all three of the benefits of income property. He has more: *cash flow, depreciation,* and *loan reduction.* His actual cash spendable increased 87 percent, (from $3,700 to $6,948).

He has deferred all tax on any gain in the smaller property when making the move.

Although APPRECIATION is not a measurable benefit in advance, it is measurable after it has taken place. The owner had received the benefit of $60,000 in appreciation on the first property. He successfully made an exchange without paying capital gains tax on the gain. Now he has the benefit of all of the amount of the gain invested in his new property.

This owner also classifies POTENTIAL APPRECIATION as a benefit. He feels that property is going up each year and he should figure that into his overall planning. As a rule of thumb, he feels that property has been increasing about 5 percent per year in value. This year, he owned a property valued at $135,000 and if it increased by 5 percent, next year the benefit would be $6,750 for him. ($135,000 × 5%). After the exchange, he controls a property valued at $410,000. So, his POTENTIAL APPRECIATION benefit he feels is worth $20,500 next year. ($410,000 × 5%)

[¶304]   OWNERS WHO SEEK BENEFITS

Real estate can be a more interesting investment to "trade" in than other types of investments. In addition to increase in value, tax losses, return or yield on invested capital, real estate can have other benefits to an owner than, say, stocks and bonds.

In addition to the money benefits, real estate can be used directly by the owner. Often he can upgrade the value of a building by painting it, changing its use or building on it. (Try that with your telephone stock.)

When making an exchange, the owner might be seeking a property that needs some of this attention. He might be thinking about what he might be willing to give up in property that is presently owned in order to have the opportunity to work on the one that needs help.

An exchange might be one way to salvage some good out of a disastrous investment. Here's one example:

Mr. Smith took a real flyer in a land investment. He calculated where a new expressway might be built and acquired a large parcel of rangeland along that route. As rangeland it might be worth $500 an acre. Smith's 25 acres cost him $75,000, all cash. The seller also guessed that the expressway might go by here also.

If Smith is right, he might make $500,000. If he was wrong, he could lose most of the $75,000.

He guessed wrong. The highway went 10 miles south of his property.

Smith listed his 25 acres for sale. The listed price: $12,500. He remarked to the broker, when they had established the value, that his cost was $75,000.

The broker suggested that Smith consider an exchange. Smith had one asset left in the property that was usable for him. No matter what the current value of the property, his basis was still based on the price he paid.

If Smith sold the land his loss would be $62,500. That capital loss could be used to offset ordinary income. Under the IRS formula, Smith could use the long-term capital loss to offset $3,000 per year of income. Using the 2:1 ratio for long-term losses, he would use $6,000 of the loss each year to offset the income limit of $3,000.

By this method, it would take Smith over 10 years to absorb the loss as an income tax write-off.

The broker arranged an exchange of the land, valued at $12,500, as a down payment on a duplex valued at $50,000. Smith would assume a first loan of $37,500 on the duplex property. The income on the duplex would be enough to service the loan, pay the taxes and give Smith a small monthly spendable income of $25.00.

Since Smith has a basis of $75,000 to carry forward, his new basis was computed as follows:

Old Basis	$75,000
Plus new loan	37,500
Total	112,500
Less old loan	—0—
New Basis	$112,500

Checking the tax bill on the duplex, Smith found that 75 percent of the bill was allocated to the improvement and 25 percent to the land. He used that ratio to allocate his basis for depreciation and chose 20-year straight-line as his schedule. His depreciation schedule was calculated as follows:

$$75\% \times 112,500 \text{ (basis)} = \$84,375$$
$$5\% \text{ (annual Depreciation)} \times 84,375 = \$4,218.75 \text{ (annual depreciation allowance)}$$

Smith chose the exchange after weighing the benefits and possible benefits that might accrue to him. He felt the benefits of selling the land for $12,500 vs. the exchange might be:

Sale:
(1) A fixed loss of $62,500 that could be written off over ten years.
(2) $12,500 cash that could be invested or spent.

Exchange:
(1) Basis in the improvement of $84,375 that could be written off over a period of 20 years.
(2) Small income from the property.
(3) Continuing his ownership in improved property, he could continue to get benefits of appreciation (at 6 percent, maybe $3,000 per year).
(4) Flexibility—his investment in real estate could be sold or exchanged to improve his position many times in future years.

Another example:

Mr. and Mrs. Thomas inherited a small commercial building in a small town about 100 miles from their home. The building was 50 years old, and it had a great deal of deferred maintenance. The building housed a drug store on the ground floor and three apartments upstairs. It needed some extensive roof repairs and various other less expensive repairs.

Mr. Thomas was employed as a bookkeeper and was tired of spending his weekends traveling to the building and working on it. Mrs. Thomas couldn't always go with him as they had three small children, one just an infant.

After a time, they listed the property for sale. On consulting with a broker, they decided on a price of $65,000. Since the building had a loan of $30,000 on it, they felt their equity was $35,000.

Months went by with no offers. Their broker said the property didn't attract buyers because of the location. Even if it had a positive cash flow, investors had not been interested in it. The investors wanted to see property in a community with a future—not a town going nowhere.

In addition, the broker explained, the age of the building made the lenders shy away from increasing the mortgage. The existing lender felt that $30,000 was as much a risk as he cared to have in that property. This meant that the buyer would have to make a sizable down payment or the Thomas' would have to carry back a large loan. The bank had agreed to allow assumption of the loan by a new buyer.

Suddenly, an exchange offer was received by Thomas' broker. It was delivered by another broker who was representing a property owner in the Thomas' home town. The offer was for a near-new residence in the best area of the community. The home was valued at $75,000 and had an existing loan of $60,000.

The owner of that home, named Jarvis, was offering the $15,000 equity in the home to Thomas. He was also offering a note for $20,000 which was to be secured by the commercial building that Thomas would exchange to him. The note would pay the Thomas' $200 per month.

Mr. and Mrs. Thomas inspected the home that was offered by Mr. Jarvis. They were impressed and delighted. The brokers checked for comparable sales near-by and showed them the figures. The value of $75,000 was justified. After a discussion of the values and the possible benefits of the exchange with their broker, the offer was accepted.

Mr. and Mrs. Thomas accepted because of these benefits to them:

1. They would be relieved of the responsibility of the property 100 miles away that was using their time and causing them worry.
2. The new home was larger than their present home. To the Thomas family, it would be a better residence in a more prestigious neighborhood. Since the latest child had arrived, they had been cramped in the smaller home.
3. Since they still had the smaller home that they had been living in, they could sell it (the equity was $25,000), rent it for income, or borrow money on it *and* rent it. (The home was valued at $50,000.)
4. They would be receiving payments of $200 per month from the note secured by the commercial building, so their income would not suffer (even with larger payments on the new home).
5. They would be receiving their entire equity out of the exchange ($15,000 equity in the home + a $20,000 note on the other property).

Benefits to Jarvis:

There has been no hint as to the motivation of Jarvis. He had listed his home for sale because it was near foreclosure. Jarvis was out of work and had recently been divorced. The home was one of his only remaining assets.

He had mentioned to his broker that he originally was from the town in which Thomas' commercial building was located and that some of his relatives still lived there. When the broker saw a property in that town on the market, particularly with the possibility of a trade, he showed the information to Jarvis.

He pointed out the benefits that might come to Jarvis:

1. Jarvis would be out of the obligation to make $500.00 a month payments on a home much too large for him.
2. More important, he would salvage the entire equity in the home and still have it invested for him. (The foreclosure was only a month away.)
3. Since the property being received had a positive cash flow, Jarvis would have time to help him get re-established in a job.
4. He could move to his hometown and live in one of the apartments if he wished.
5. If he didn't move to the property, his relatives in the community could easily help him with property management since they were right there.

Neither owner was concerned with the tax consequences. Both had high-cost basis in the property traded, so neither had much potential gain.

Both owners agreed to the exchange because of the benefits that would accrue to them. Neither had more than a passing interest in price.

The Thomas' had made an "unlike" exchange (investment property for residence property) that would have been taxable if there was a gain. However, since they had acquired a new principal residence, they had a period of 18 months to sell their previous home and defer all tax on any gain (IRC Sec. 1034).

Jarvis had also made an "unlike" exchange (residence for investment property). Since his gain was small, he was not concerned. His earned income for the year was low since he had been out of work. His income tax, if any, would be minor.

[¶305] THE "WANT-OUT CLIENT" VS. A "BUYER"

Many brokers representing exchange clients try to classify the clients to the degree of motivation. An extremely motivated client is classified as a WANT-OUT client. He may be quoted as saying when listing the property, "Just get me out of the ownership. I WANT OUT!" This owner usually has a motive that is bordering on desperation. He may be in foreclosure like

Jarvis in the previous example. Some have had such serious problems with tenants that they want nothing to do with another rental property. Others have serious tax situations that only an exchange can solve.

When a broker reaches the conclusion that his client may be a "Want-out" client, he may offer him a wider variety of properties than he would otherwise. The owner may have problems (real or imagined) with the property that can be solved mostly by getting hm away from that ownership as soon as possible.

"Want-out" owners have been known to exchange from a good cash-flow apartment property to rangeland. The benefit of a totally management-free investment seems like the best possible solution after years of tenant problems.

An exchange from a "Pride-of-Ownership" commercial building in the city to a run-down apartment in a small town might result from the owner's desire to get away from the problems of smog, congestion and crime in the metropolitan area.

Without knowing what is in the owner's mind, these exchanges may seem unreasonable to an observer oriented only to cash profit. The benefits sought by these owners just weren't apparent to others, and *were not measurable in dollars*.

When the broker classifies the exchange client as a "buyer" he means that the owner is just the opposite from a "want-out" owner. The client acts as if he is spending cash instead of equity. He is often so selective that it is impossible to come near to a solution for him. The benefits he seeks are very narrow. For example, he may want cash flow and tax shelter from an apartment complex—not too difficult—however, it must be in a certain part of town. To further complicate things, he may want a certain type of architecture, floor plans, etc.

The more selective a *cash buyer* is, the less chance we have of satisfying his needs. When this selectivity is added to a no-cash, exchange situation, it becomes nearly impossible. He is not just looking for a set of benefits, he wants too much. Since it is necessary to dispose of his property to someone else, who may not be offering cash either, his narrow choices just take him completely out of the exchange market place.

Most owners who are in the exchange market place would not fall into either of the classifications of "want-out" or "buyer." They would be somewhere between these extremes, and will accept the concept of a particular exchange if the benefits work for them. The more they lean toward the "buyer," the more difficult it is to please them. The more they resemble the "want-out" owner, the easier they will exchange their current property.

[¶306]   GEOGRAPHIC MOVES

Probably one of the prime reasons for passing Section 1031 of the Internal Revenue Code was to allow farmers to move to a new location. After World War I, with the cities rapidly expanding and the suburbs exploding, some farms were suddenly in town.

By making an exchange, the farmer could move his business, a farm, to a new location without paying a tax on any gain on the value of his land.

In the past decades many other businesses have had occasion to make geographic moves. Manufacturing companies have moved from the cities to the suburbs. Others have moved from northern states to the South to take advantage of lower labor costs.

Owners of investment properties have exchanged their apartment investment or commercial property investment to their new locations when they moved for health, retirement, job transfer or just for a change of scenery.

[¶307]   THE ALDERSON EXCHANGE

Following is the information about a geographic exchange that was taken to tax court.

Mr. and Mrs. Alderson lived in Orange County in Southern California. The Aldersons had negotiated for a sale of their land, 31 acres used for agriculture, to the Alloy Die Casting Co. A purchase and sale agreement was made in which the Aldersons agreed to sell the property for $172,000. Alloy deposited $19,000 as down payment into an escrow.

After the contract was made, Alderson located 115 acres of farm land in Salinas, Monterey County, California, that he wanted to exchange for the Orange County property.

Three months after the original escrow was executed, the Aldersons and Alloy amended the escrow to provide that:

1. Alloy would acquire the Salinas Property and exchange it for Alderson's property and,
2. if the exchange didn't take place before a certain date, the original sale would be made.

Alderson's daughter, Mrs. Howard, acting in behalf of Alderson, made arrangements for transfer of the Salinas property to Alloy Die Casting Co. and deposited $19,000 as a down payment. This amount represented the difference between the Salinas property and the price which Alloy had contracted to pay for the Alderson property.

Then, at simultaneous escrow closings, Alloy took title to the Salinas property, paying the balance of the purchase price, then exchanged it for Alderson's land in Orange County.

The tax court determined that this was a:

1. Sale by Alderson to Alloy for cash and,
2. A purchase of the Salinas property for cash.

The Ninth Circuit Court of Appeals reversed the decision. It held that this was:

1. A purchase by Alloy of the Salinas property for cash and,
2. An exchange between Alloy and Alderson.

The tax court had based its decision against Alderson primarily on the method used—namely, the negotiation for the Salinas property by Alderson (through his daughter, Mrs. Howard) rather than Alloy.

The Ninth Circuit Court of Appeals rejected that decision as being too narrow. It relied on *Intention* and *Legal Obligation*. It found that it was Alderson's intent to transfer the property in a tax-deferred exchange if at all possible since the beginning. It gave this finding great weight.

In addition, there never was a fixed obligation on the part of Alloy (since the amendment of the contract) to pay cash; Alloy merely had to exchange the Salinas property or pay cash. Since it did the former, it didn't have to do the latter.

The Court, in reversing the decision, and ruling for Alderson, made it clear that it is perfectly all right for one party to acquire property solely for purposes of an exchange to another party.

[¶308]   BENEFITS DERIVED FROM EXCHANGES OF
REAL ESTATE BETWEEN AGE GROUPS—
THE ESTATE BUILDER

Usually we think of an estate builder as young. Often it is a young couple, both working and investing all of their surplus money into real estate. The intent is to acquire or control the maximum amount of real estate, in the most leveraged position, to build the maximum estate in the shortest possible time.

If the estate builder uses tax-deferred exchanges, keeping all of the properties in the highest leverage possible, he will quickly build an estate. Of course, there is great risk too. Since all investments are always leveraged, there is little room left for error. A change in the economy can cause a wipe-out.

The possibility of going broke is the reason that we think of estate builders as young. Younger people in their twenties and thirties can gamble—they have plenty of time to do it again, if they lose it all.

A few years later, going into the middle years, our estate builders start to sound a little more conservative. Now they begin to talk about less leverage and more cash flow.

In middle years, the object becomes to consolidate the position into higher equity, throwing off good income that can be enjoyed. Now, perhaps both will either quit their jobs or take the earliest retirement possible.

Either by making less transactions or ones using larger equity, the estate builder now has changed into an *investor*. Using his large estate, he can concentrate on the highest, safest return on his equity in investments.

Over the years, mortgages on his properties have been reduced or paid off and little cash is going out other than direct expenses.

In earlier years, the young investor was very active in managing the estate. Toward retirement age, he may wish less personal management, less involvement. Perhaps some of the properties will be sold on installment sales, just to have a large monthly income from secured contracts and mortgages.

Because of the differences in philosophy during the different periods of life, exchanges of property between owners in different age groups might be arranged. Since each would be seeking a different set of benefits, each would get just what he wanted from the property that the other would prefer not to own.

The younger couple on the way up would be interested in exchanging a high-equity, high cash-flow property up into a property that would be highly leveraged with no cash flow at all. This exchange would fit into their plan.

The retired older couple would no longer be interested in owning a highly leveraged property. At this stage of life, cash flow would be much more important.

Since each would want the opposite benefits, an exchange would not be difficult to arrange.

[¶309]   RESIDENCE EXCHANGES

Often, when the children are grown and married, the parents find themselves with a large home with large grounds. They had put off moving to a smaller home until the youngest child was grown. Now the two of them live in a four-or five-bedroom home that is well located near schools, shopping—everything needed by a younger family.

This home could be sold through the usual sales marketplace. However, if the broker is alert, he may try to arrange an exchange.

The logical user for the home may be a couple with a growing family that has a smaller home or condominium on the market. They may not be actively searching for the new home until they receive an offer or sales contract on the present property. An exchange might be initiated between these owners by showing one or another a house. Both may be waiting for a sale of the existing house before seeking a new one.

[¶310]   UNITRUST AND ANNUITIES

The Unitrust or Charitable Remainder Trust will be covered briefly, although it is not a real estate exchange. However, the benefits may be similar to a tax-deferred exchange to many people of retirement age, so it bears mentioning.

Section 170 of the Internal Revenue Code covers charitable contributions and gifts. Within the limitations set out in this section, properties that have accrued capital gains may be contributed to charitable institutions.

Section 664 of the I.R.C. covers the CHARITABLE REMAINDER ANNUITY TRUST and CHARITABLE REMAINDER UNITRUST

Under these sections, an owner may contribute real estate with a large capital gain and in return may receive some or all of the following benefits:

1. Forgiveness of some or all of the capital gains tax.
2. Receipt of a deduction for charitable contribution to apply against other income for the year of the contribution.
3. Receipt of an ANNUITY paid for 20 years certain or for life of an amount equal to 5 percent *or more* of the fair market value of the property.
4. Relief from property taxes on the contributed property after the year of the contribution.
5. Exclude certain assets from probate.

Since many individual factors enter into this type of transaction, each should be investigated individually. The benefits listed above (and possibly many others) might mean substantial benefits in income and tax relief to certain taxpayers. It would be of particular interest to owners of assets such as the following:

1. Owner has low basis and large potential capital gain in an asset.
2. Owner may be nearing retirement age.
3. Owner may (or may not) have a large current income and be paying high taxes.

Since this chapter is about "Benefits," the *benefits* of *contributing* assets under our current tax laws should not be overlooked. Particularly when the taxpayer can arrange to receive an annual income for the rest of his or her life. This is an excellent *exchange*.

Individuals should investigate these possibilities through their attorneys and certified public accountants.

[¶311]   EXCHANGING HOUSES FOR BENEFITS—
BOTH OWNERS STARTING AS SELLERS

Exchanging for benefits works in a wide variety of properties. There are many benefits to almost everyone from owning or making an exchange of apartments, commercial buildings, lots, land, motels, recreational land or resorts. One exception seems to be houses—the most commonly owned real estate in the country.

Houses are where people live. When people own their own home, there are a different set of benefits that they enjoy. These benefits are very specific and personal. While an owner might be happy owning any number of different apartments, if the income is the same, his choice of a home must suit the whole family.

Privacy, pride of ownership, floor plan and flow of traffic, school district, proximity to churches, shopping are all important. In addition, size of yard, architecture, building materials, colors and many other benefits are considered in the home that people choose for their family.

Houses are difficult to exchange because of these personal needs (unless they are to be used as a rental).

[¶311.1]   Houses Can Be Exchanged—
Under Certain Circumstances

It we can break down the benefits an owner seeks—and they are *other* than the ones listed above—or outweigh them, houses can sometimes be exchanged.

Here's how houses are sold—and sometimes exchanged!

There is a usual formula for the sale of houses. After the property is listed, the owner is urged to place the property on the local Multiple Listing Service to give maximum exposure through the other real estate offices.

The multiple listing service is a cooperative program for the distribution of listing information on houses (and other property) among Realtors in a certain area. All brokers and salespeople in this area can work toward a sale on all properties listed with any office. There is a pre-determined percentage of the commission on the sale that is split between the "listing" and "selling" offices.

Cooperation between brokers, either on an established multiple listing service or on an informal basis is common throughout the country. It allows the maximum exposure between salespeople and is the most efficient way of selling houses.

In addition to this cooperation between brokers, the listing broker advertises the property for sale.

The advertising usually includes a sign on the property and newspaper and magazine advertising. The advertising may be in the local paper, in a near-by city paper, national publications such as *The Wall Street Journal*, depending on the value and size of the home. The more expensive and elaborate the property, the wider the exposure must be.

The broker and his salespeople know the local market, contacting all possible prospects for the sale of these homes.

The concentration of the broker and his salespeople is nearly always the same: (1) find a buyer, with money, who is looking for a home; (2) show him homes in the community; (3) when he shows some interest in one of the homes, use various closing techniques to get his signature on an offer; and (4) collect a commission.

The volume of recordings of sales in County Recorder's Offices and the number of SOLD signs in yards show that these simple steps work well in marketing houses. In fact, they are so simple that many owners do most of it themselves and save the commission.

Occasionally, the market for homes simply dries up. All at one time, everyone stops buying. This may be a local problem and it may be caused by local economic situations, such as plant lay-offs in a major local industry. It may be a nation-wide problem, with high interest rates, tight money, and all of the other symptoms of a recession period.

When this happens, the sales formula fails. No matter what amount of advertising, no matter how much drum-beating, the sale of homes falls off to a trickle—or stops completely. We have all seen this condition at one time or another.

Brokers beat the bushes for buyers. Someone must be out there with money. There has to be a motivated buyer someplace—someone has to want some of this property on the market! Cut prices—lower terms—these are the solutions that are suggested to the sellers.

The buyers are all around—it is just that no one sees them. Remember our formula for an exchange client. He may want to acquire another property—but he has to sell the property that he now has, in order to buy it.

Here's an example:

In a period of local economic problems in a small town in California, there were a number of homes for sale with no apparent buyers. Brokers were urging the owners to lower prices and extend better terms to help interest buyers.

One broker, Ms. Joan Brown had just attended an out-of-town seminar on real estate exchanging that was put on by another broker. They had covered income properties, land, commercial buildings, farms—all business-type properties. No mention was made of houses.

Joan remembered one thing that kept echoing back. One of the speakers had repeatedly emphasized, PEOPLE MAKE EXCHANGES—PEOPLE MAKE DECISIONS. THE PROPERTY IS LESS IMPORTANT THAN THE MOTIVATIONS OF THE OWNERS.

She looked over her listings. A few houses and lots. A duplex. They had been advertised thoroughly. She had made every effort to sell them. She had called the owners weekly to report her progress.

Vaguely she remembered why each was a seller. Two she particularly remembered. One family was moving because the husband had been transferred to a new job. Another was a growing family that needed a larger home.

[¶311.2]   Listing #1

Bob and Mary Jones had listed a 4-bedroom, 2-bath home located in a better neighborhood. The price of $42,500 seemed right—it was comparable to other sales in the area a few months ago. The home had a loan of $28,000 on it, so the Jones' had an equity in the property of $14,500.

Bob had been transferred to a factory 50 miles away when the local plant had closed six months ago. His job was permanent at the new location and he and Mary wanted to move the family to the new community as soon as possible. Bob was driving 100 miles round trip each day to and from work.

The house had been listed for sale for six months. There had been no offers. Bob and Mary had agreed to carry a second note of $4,200 if they could sell and get the balance in cash.

The Jones house was not the only one that was hard to sell. Since Bob's plant closed six months ago, little property had sold.

[¶311.3]   Listing #2

Jack and Ethel Smith had listed their 2-bedroom, 1-bath home several months ago. They had lived here for six years and were outgrowing the house. The Smiths had two boys, ages 2 and 4 years, and were expecting a baby in two months.

Their home was for sale at $18,000. It seemed like a fair market price, based on previous sales of other homes like it in the tract. The existing loan on the property was $10,600.

Jack worked for a utility company and had progressed in both salary and position during the past few years. He could quality for a much higher loan on a larger house.

Jack and Ethel wanted to move to a larger home, but needed to sell the smaller home for the down-payment money. They had only about $2,000 in savings.

In several months, there had been little interest in the home. One possible buyer had expressed an interest but with only $500 down payment. Ms. Brown could not get a new loan for the buyer with that offer.

[¶311.4] The Decision to Exchange

Joan Brown determined to try an exchange. She didn't quite see how it would turn out but felt that the Smiths might be the logical users for the Jones house.

Brown called Mrs. Smith and informed her that she wanted to show her a home that might work in exchange for her home. She made the appointment with Mrs. Smith for that afternoon and then called Mrs. Jones, to inform her of the showing of her home.

When Mrs. Smith saw the home, she was not too interested. She and Jack had always had a ranch-style home in mind as their "dream" home. This was a two-story Cape Cod. When the broker reminded her that this was the home that might be available for exchange, she looked again. It really was just right for them. She wanted it!

"It really is a lovely home," she thought.

After work that evening, Jack Smith saw the home and liked it.

Ms. Brown prepared an exchange agreement. She was offering the Smith's $7,400 equity in the small home toward the Jones home. Here is how the offer worked. First, here is the owners' original positions. (See Figure 3.1).

	ORIGINAL POSITIONS	
	SMITH	JONES
Value:	$18,000	$42,500
Loan:	10,600	28,000
Equity:	$ 7,400	$14,500

In the first paragraph of the terms and conditions, Smith applied for a new loan of $34,000 on the 4-bedroom home. This first step gives Jones $6,000 cash, so far in the transaction.

Since Jones is exchanging with Smith, he will go into title in the smaller home. It also can be refinanced. So, in the second paragraph, Ms. Brown calls for the re-finance of the smaller home. The proceeds of this loan also go to Jones. Remember, since he owns all of the equity in the smaller home, any re-finance goes to him.

An 80 percent new loan on the 2-bedroom would be $14,400. The difference between the old loan of $10,600 and that amount would be $3,800. Added to the $6,000 Jones was receiving from the other house, Jones now has $9,800 coming to him. The balance of his equity was represented in the smaller home.

In the third paragraph, Ms. Brown balanced the equity on the 4-bedroom house with a purchase-money second-trust deed and note payable to Jones. Since Smith had "purchased" the larger home with $7,400 as "down" and the new loan was $34,000, then Jones had not received his $42,500 yet. He had received only $41,400 ($7,400 equity + $34,000 loan = $41,400) So Smith is to give Jones a note secured by the 4-bedroom home for the amount of $1,100.

Following is a diagram of each owner's position after the proposed exchange:

NEW POSITIONS

	SMITH		JONES	
Value: (of homes)	$42,500	(4 Br.)	$18,000	(2 Br.)
Loans: (New loans)	34,000		14,400	
	1,100	(2nd Loan)		
Equity: (In homes)	7,400		3,600	
Cash: (To Jones from Loans)			9,800	
Note: (From Smith to Jones)			1,100	
Total Equity, home, note and cash:			$14,500	

Each has the same equity as before the exchange. Smith now has the same $7,400 equity, but in a new home.

Jones now has $9,800 in cash, $1,100 in a note and $3,600 in equity in a smaller home. While the properties were in escrow, Jones asked Ms. Brown, the broker, if the smaller house could be sold. He had accepted the exchange offer, planning to rent the home since the transaction gave them enough money to move.

Brown contacted the potential buyer who had previously offered $500 down for the smaller home. She revived the offer and submitted it to Jones. After a credit check on the buyer, Jones accepted the offer. The security would be a contract of sale, all due in five years.

EXCHANGE AGREEMENT

CALIFORNIA ASSOCIATION OF REALTORS STANDARD FORM

JOHN SMITH AND ETHEL SMITH, his wife

first party, hereby offers to exchange the following described property, situated in the city of Strawberry

County of Monterey California:

A two bedroom, one bath home located at 1130 Lincoln St. (Full legal description to be furnished in escrow.) Valued at EIGHTEEN THOUSAND and No/100 ($18,000.00) DOLLARS.

Subject to a 1st Trust Deed and note of approx. TEN THOUSAND SIX HUNDRED and No/100 ($10,600.00) DOLLARS, payable at EIGHTY-FIVE and No/100 ($85.00) DOLLARS monthly including interest at SEVEN (7%) annually.

For the following described property of ROBERT JONES and MARY JONES, his wife

second party, situated in

the city of Strawberry County of Monterey California:

A Four Bedroom, two bath home located at 2424 Bonnie Place. (Full legal description to be furnished in escrow.) Valued at FORTY-TWO THOUSAND FIVE HUNDRED and no/100 ($42,500.00) DOLLARS.

Subject to a 1st Trust Deed and note of approx. TWENTY-EIGHT THOUSAND and No/100 ($28,000.00) DOLLARS payable at ONE HUNDRED NINETY and No/100 ($190.00) DOLLARS monthly including annual interest at SIX (6%) PERCENT.

Terms and Conditions of Exchange:

1. This offer subject to FIRST PARTY (SMITH) securing a new loan secured by a 1st trust deed in the amount of THIRTY-FOUR THOUSAND and no/100 ($34,000.00) DOLLARS on the BONNIE PLACE property. Loan to pay off existing loan on property and balance to be paid to the SECOND PARTY (JONES).
2. Subject to SECOND PARTY (JONES) securing new loan and 1st Trust deed on LINCOLN ST. property for FOURTEEN THOUSAND FOUR HUNDRED and No/100 ($14,400.00) DOLLARS. Loan to pay off existing loan on property and balance paid to SECOND PARTY (Jones).
3. FIRST PARTY (SMITH) to execute and SECOND PARTY (JONES) to carry back a NOTE secured by a SECOND TRUST DEED on the BONNIE PLACE property. Note to be in the amount of ONE THOUSAND ONE HUNDRED ($1,100.00) DOLLARS, payable at TWENTY-FIVE and No/100 ($25.00) DOLLARS, or more, monthly including interest at NINE (9%) PERCENT annually. Balance of note due and payable in FIVE (5) YEARS.

The parties hereto shall execute and deliver, within Ten (10) days from the date this offer is accepted, all instruments, in writing, necessary to transfer title to said properties and complete and consummate this exchange. Each party shall supply Preliminary Title Reports for their respective properties. Evidences of title shall be California Land Title Association standard coverage form policies of title insurance, showing titles to be merchantable and free of all liens and encumbrances, except taxes and those liens and encumbrances as otherwise set forth herein. Each party shall pay for the policies of Title Insurance for the property to be acquired ☐ conveyed ☒ .

Figure 3.1

If either party is unable to convey a marketable title, except as herein provided, within three months after acceptance hereof by second party, or if the improvements on any of the herein named properties be destroyed or materially damaged prior to transfer of title or delivery of agreement of sale, then this agreement shall be of no further effect, except as to payment of commissions and expenses incurred in connection with examination of title, unless the party acquiring the property so affected elects to accept the title the other party can convey or subject to the conditions of the improvements.

Taxes, insurance premiums (if policies be satisfactory to party acquiring the property affected thereby), rents, interest and other expenses of said properties shall be pro-rated as of the date of transfer of title or delivery of agreement of sale, unless otherwise provided herein.

Brown Realty Co _____ of _____ Strawberry, _____ Calif. _____
Broker   Address   Phone No.

is hereby authorized to act as broker for all parties hereto and may accept commission therefrom. Should second party accept this offer, first party agrees to pay said broker commission for services rendered as follows:-
Six (6%) of exchange price.

Should second party be unable to convey a marketable title to his property then first party shall be released from payment of any commission, unless he elects to accept the property subject thereto. First party agrees that broker may cooperate with other brokers and divide commissions in any manner satisfactory to them.

This offer shall be deemed revoked unless accepted in writing within Five (5) days after date hereof, and such acceptance is communicated to first party within said period. Broker is hereby given the exclusive and irrevocable right to obtain acceptance of second party within said period. Time is the essence of this contract.

John Smith
Chas. Smith

Dated Oct 3, 1971

ACCEPTANCE

Second party hereby accepts the foregoing offer upon the terms and conditions stated and agrees to pay commission for services rendered, to:-

Brown Realty Co. _____ of _____ Strawberry _____ Calif. _____
Broker   Address   Phone No.

as follows:- Six (6%) of exchange price.

Second party agrees that broker may act as broker for all parties hereto and may accept commission therefrom, and may co-operate with other brokers and divide commissions in any manner satisfactory to them.

Should first party be unable to convey a marketable title to his property then second party shall be released from payment of any commission, unless he elects to accept the property of first party subject thereto.

Robert Jones
Mary Jones

Dated Oct 5, 1971

Figure 3.1 (continued)

Here is the final result for Jones at the close of escrow.

Cash:	$10,300	($9,800 from new loans + $500 down payment on the smaller home.)
	1,100	(Note secured by Trust Deed on 4-BR Home)
	3,100	(Note secured by Contract on 2-BR Home)
	$14,500	

Jones originally had his home for sale for terms that would have netted him $10,600 cash and a note for $4,200. His final results were very close to this. The cash was slightly less and the notes were on two properties, instead of just one.

Each owner had expenses in the transaction—commissions, etc. Jones paid these out of his proceeds from the transaction, in the usual way. Smith paid his from his savings.

Jones had one additional expense that he wouldn't have had in a sale. He had to pay a small loan origination fee (points) on the loan he placed on the smaller home. He wasn't concerned. As he said, "I paid points on that loan in the amount of $200. I might have accepted an offer of $41,000 on the house if someone had made one."

Ms. Brown felt that the exchange seminar had been worth the investment. She had two very happy clients and had earned two excellent commissions.

Both owners had received all of the benefits that they had been seeking when they had listed their properties.

CHAPTER **4**

Case Histories of Benefit Exchanges

[¶400] AN OVERVIEW

In some cases, owners go into the real estate marketplace with the specific intent of exchanging their property. From the beginning, they have no idea in mind of a cash sale. They have a realistic attitude about their property; it probably cannot be sold for cash. Their intent is to exchange the property, either for other real estate or for personal property, that they would rather own.

Their present attitude may be developed by previously trying to sell—perhaps for quite a long time. Perhaps the realization of the amount of taxes that would have to be paid on a sale influenced the decision. Whatever the reason, the intent is for an exchange, not a sale.

Most often, owners who have reached this realistic attitude are represented by brokers. The brokers may have helped them to face the real world.

[¶401] THE UNSALABLE PROPERTY

While some say that nothing in the world is "unsalable," there are parcels of real estate that seem to be. We have seen property offered for sale that was completely lost in other offerings that were just like it in every way.

Once the possibility of an exchange for other real estate is considered—the world opens up. Remember, for every person who will pay cash for your property, there are many others who will trade another property for it.

Here is an excellent example: the owner, Mr. Parker, had inherited a ten-acre parcel located in a desert area in Southern California. After owning it for several years, he decided to sell it.

Since Parker lived 100 miles away from the property, he traveled to the town nearest the land, about ten miles from it. In this small desert town, he contacted several real estate brokers who were running advertisments of local acreage for sale. Three of these agents were reluctant to look at the property. Each already had many listings of similar property for sale, and wanted no more listings like Parker's.

None of these brokers had much record of any sales recently, so it was difficult to place a value on a ten-acre parcel.

The fourth broker looked at the property with Parker. He offered to take a listing, but truthfully told Parker that there was little demand for this type of property. The price he mentioned was so low that the owner was discouraged. The property seemed worthless and unsalable.

Returning home, Parker decided to hold the property. Maybe some-day there would be a demand for property in that area. Meanwhile, the taxes were low.

A few weeks later, Parker mentioned the desert property and his trip to a friend at a party. The friend referred him to a broker, here in town, whom he identified as an *exchange specialist*.

When Parker contacted him, the broker suggested an appointment in the real estate office. He asked Parker for much information about the property, the surrounding area, the possible uses of the property.

By explaining these uses and information about the area—practically nil—Parker realized more than he did before that the property might have little value. A buyer must have some reason for wanting to acquire it. He couldn't think of a reason to give the broker other than a lame, "Well, someone may want it for a long-term investment for the future." The broker asked, "Who do you see as the new owner? What would he use it for, when he bought it? Why would someone buy it, if there were other properties that he might choose from?"

Parker now could put himself into the shoes of a buyer. He just could not see any reason for anyone spending cash for the property. He certainly wouldn't buy it himself.

Some of the other questions the broker asked were:

1. Where are you employed?
   (Self employed—painting contractor.)
2. What other property do you own?
   (A residence. Three rental houses.)
3. Do you consider yourself an investor in real estate?
   (Yes, a small investor.)
4. What was the appraisal on the desert property when it was in the estate at the time you acquired it?
   ($10,000, but that was years ago.)

5. Could you add another piece of real estate in with this property? Maybe we can exchange it along with a better property.
   (Yes. Any rental house, if the value is there.)
6. Can you add some cash to exchange with the property?
   (Yes. A very easily understood "can add.")

The owner was surprised when the broker accepted the listing on the property. He wrote the listing agreement "unpriced." No specific price was shown in the contract. He asked the owner, Parker, to agree to pay a fee of $1,000 if an exchange was found that Parker was willing to accept. Parker would have the right to turn down any offer. It would be his responsibility to evaluate all proposals and make up his mind whether the possible exchange made sense to him. Parker agreed.

The broker asked if Parker would consider taking a "problem" property, *if* he could see that it was a problem that he could solve. He explained that most of the offerings they might get would be other people's problems. However, maybe Parker could solve them more easily than the present owner.

All of this made sense. Parker agreed and signed the listing agreement. He felt confident that he was going to dispose of the desert property. He was interested in seeing what kind of challenge another property could give him.

The broker was also quite satisfied. He knew that Parker now had a better understanding of his position. He knew that Parker was willing to work with him, add cash if necessary or add a house. Parker was going to be a willing partner rather than a passive observer.

After a month, the broker called Parker. He asked him to come in to the office to see an offer.

Parker examined the offer. It was an equity-for-equity exchange offer, for six houses in a nearby town.

The present owner of the houses, the builder, would take over the desert land.

Parker would take over the six houses, subject to the existing loans. There was about $25,000 owing on each house, $24,000 in a long-term first loan and $1,000 in a second loan. The second loans had a due date that was just a month away. $6,000 cash would have to be paid in a month.

Parker and his broker went the few miles to the next town to examine the houses. Here is what they found:

1. The houses were the last six unsold houses in a tract of 50 homes that had been completed 18 months before.
2. Three of the homes were rented. The other three were vacant and showed neglect. There were broken windows and other signs of vandalism.

3. Looking over the local situation, the town seemed overbuilt in this price range. The six homes were being offered at the original price of $30,000 despite the neglected look. Some of the other homes in the tract were for sale at lower prices.
4. Each home had the original construction note of $24,000 on it. This could be converted to a permanent loan with a small fee to the lender. The second note of $1,000 was a separate loan that had been made this year to pay two year's taxes.

Parker accepted the offer. The transaction was quickly closed. Parker's broker had pointed out the benefits:

1. The land of questionable value was exchanged.
2. Parker could put a painting crew quickly into the vandalized houses and refurbish them for rental or sale.
3. Parker had the cash to solve the second loan payoff.
4. The rental income from the six houses, if all were rented, would put Parker into a small spendable income position. If he kept the houses, there would be depreciation benefits also.

Parker had a good understanding of his position when the listing was signed with his broker. He had no illusions about the value and use of the desert land. He moved quickly when the offer was received because he was able to see more benefits in owning the houses than the desert land. His only question was why the builder wanted to make the exchange into the land of unmeasurable value.

The broker told him the following problem that faced the builder. He had taken most of the profits out of the tract of houses and made a land purchase for his next project—a large shopping center. He was nearly ready to begin the project.

The land for the shopping center was not free and clear. The builder had made a down payment. His bank had placed a loan for the balance.

His banker told him that the loan committee had suggested that the builder "clean up some liabilities on his personal financial statement," before the new construction loan was funded. He was referring to the $150,000 outstanding on the remaining tract houses. It was a small thing, but it was holding up a large building project.

At about that time, Parker's broker contacted the broker who usually worked with the builder. He heard about the houses. He pointed out the "benefits" that the builder would have with an exchange with Parker.

1. Immediately, the $150,000 liability would be removed from the financial statement.
2. He would not have to pay the $6,000 due in 30 days.
3. He could start his new project—a highly profitable shopping center, with no delay.

4. His equity in the houses of questionable value (remember the vandalism) would be transferred to free-and-clear land. His broker would have time to work on the disposal of the land later.
5. Since the land was free and clear it would show only on the asset side of the financial statement.

When these benefits were explained to the builder, he was quick to sign an offer to exchange.

Both of these owners considered the property that they owned as unsalable or nearly so. Both had tried to sell. The land owner had trouble even trying to list his property.

The solution to both problems was only in new ownership. The properties each took on a new "value" to the new owner.

[¶402]   ICE BOX LAND AS A SOLUTION
(PUTTING EQUITY ON ICE)

When we talk about real estate as an investment, each investor has a different idea of what the "investment" is to him.

Some owners feel an investment in real estate is a highly leveraged residential income property. No other real estate investment has any interest for them. Just as soon as they begin to build equity through an increase in value and loan reduction, an exchange must be made. (Go after more leverage—it's the only thing!)

Others want the improved property, but want no residential income. The possible tenant problems are too much for them. *They* only want leased commercial property. A bank, a grocery chain, an office building are the only investment properties—and the only tenants worth considering.

Some others will consider only single-family homes and duplexes as investment property. These are the only things that give them the flexibility that they want. Sometimes they own dozens of them.

Each of these investors also has a "Comfort Zone" about loans. The leverage seeker wants the biggest loans possible. Others have been brought up to never owe money to anyone. They must have property free and clear of any loans. Most of us have a loan comfort zone somewhere between these extremes. Nearly everybody accepts the idea of some sort of mortgage. The use of OPM (other people's money) makes sense to most of us.

Land is the only investment for some. They want no improvements, only the land. The only investment they will ever consider in real estate is land. They will only consider a commercial property if you have another buyer standing by to purchase the improvements.

Let's consider some of the benefits that are available to an investor in bare land:

1. There are usually no tenant problems. There may be a lease for farming or grazing but seldom many contacts between lessor and lessee. Often, the land lies unused.
2. Well chosen land for a long-term investment can result in huge profits. We have all heard stories of owners who have sold for millions land that was purchased for just a few dollars an acre. (The key is "well chosen." Many land parcels have gone down in value during many years of ownership.)
3. Land is a secure investment. Even in the worst economic situations, the land is still there. Value might fluctuate, but the investment won't disappear.
4. Land represents wealth. It can be a quick source of cash for an owner for another short-term investment. Land looks good on a financial statement. It adds permanence and stability to an applicant for loans or a line of credit.

Since land is the best possible investment at any time for *some people*, it might be a consideration for *anyone*, given the right set of circumstances.

Here's an example:

One couple, Mr. and Mrs. Streeter, had been building quite a large estate by investing in small inexpensive houses, duplexes and lots in their city. They had been accumulating these properties since they were married 20 years before. They now owned *eighteen* parcels, most either free and clear, or with small loans. They had *twelve* rental houses *three* duplexes, *a three-unit* building and *two* vacant lots.

Since most were single-family houses, management had been fairly easy. Both of the Streeters had helped with the rentals, cleanup and other management. However, Mrs. Streeter had done most of it as Mr. Streeter was employed as a manager in a large manufacturing corporation.

Many of the couple's properties had increased substantially in value over the years. The Streeter's equity was about $600,000.

Mr. Streeter was offered an interesting opportunity by his company. He was picked to manage the company's new plant being built in a foreign country. It was an exciting challenge, but would take them out of the country for at least six years.

The Streeters intended to accept the position. Something would have to be done with their real estate investments.

They rejected the idea of turning the properties over to a manager. Since the investments were scattered, they feared the manager might let the properties down. They could lose value quickly if not handled properly.

A sale of the investments was also considered. After looking at the possible capital gains tax, that possibility was also rejected. The tax would be huge. It was the Streeter's plan to sell their investments later, after his retirement, scattering the sales over several tax years.

Their broker suggested an exchange into a neutral investment that would take little or no management. An investment that would continue to increase in value, but with no problems, and about which they would never have to worry. They agreed with the idea, but what was it?

He explained the tax-deferred exchange, and suggested that they consider land as a storage place for their equity during the six-year period that they would be away.

When they returned, their equity would be intact. There would be neither problems with tenants nor with a property manager. The property could not be hurt by neglect.

If the property was reasonably well chosen, there could be some very substantial gains during the six years.

The Streeters agreed.

The broker negotiated a series of exchanges of the 16 improved properties for the Streeters into five large land parcels on the outskirts of the city. They retained the two lots that they already owned.

After the exchanges, the Streeters owned seven unimproved properties. They had effectively placed all of their equity into an "ice box" position. There would be little or no problems with the investments while they were out of the country. When they returned, they could consider exchanges back into improved, cash-flow properties or go on with the long-term liquidation, selling off parcels spread over different tax years to minimize the taxes.

[¶403]   FAMILY BENEFITS

Joint ownership by partners who are not related may result in disagreements and problems. Partners may have changes in their lives or changes in their objectives after property is acquired.

Sometimes partners in property have had serious problems even before a property is acquired. Real estate is often inherited by relatives in joint ownership as a result of a will. The relatives may have nothing in common except the property they own together. They sometimes do not even know each other. They may not like each other and may be separated socially, financially. They may live in different ends of the country.

Property owners who cannot get along—cannot agree on what to do with a property—can tie up a fortune in property while fighting over the problem. No matter what one may suggest, the other will want to do something else.

For instance, two brothers might be heirs to a house that is being used as a rental property. One, John, needs cash. The other, Peter, doesn't need cash and would like to continue owning the property because of the tax shelter benefits. They are in a stalemate position. They have now owned it for several years, so there would be a significant tax to be paid on capital gains on a sale.

John could force a legal partition of the property. Their interests could be separated by force of the court, if one started a legal action. Since this might result in a forced sale, both could be losers.

A third-party relationship with an attorney or real estate broker might assist these relatives to split the ownership in several ways. They might need this outside influence to help since a face-to-face negotiation between them has become strained.

Here are some methods of solving the problem:

1. John might sell his half of the property to Peter. Peter could place a loan on the property equal to 50 percent of the equity, and buy John out with the proceeds. John gets the cash, Peter keeps the same equity as before in the house. (Instead of John owning the other half, the bank would own it with a mortgage.)
2. They could sell the house and each take one-half of the proceeds. Peter could then buy another property for himself. (Both would be subject to capital gains tax.)
3. Peter could execute a note and mortgage payable to John, secured by the house. The note would be equal to one-half of the value. John deeds his share to Peter in return for the mortgage on which he will receive regular monthly payments. (John is in effect in the same position as the bank in example #1.)

All of these solutions could cause a tax problem for one or both depending on the adjusted cost basis that they have in the property.

Using a real estate exchange, the problem might be solved so that each gets what he wants and a minimum amount of tax liability would be created. Here are examples:

1. An exchange might be arranged to exchange the house for two smaller houses, in a tax-deferred exchange. Peter then owns his own separate house. John does also and can sell it or borrow money on it. (Since borrowing is tax-free, no tax would be due from either brother in capital gains.)
2. They might exchange down into one smaller house. Peter goes into sole

ownership. John carries back a loan on the home that they previously owned. (John has converted his equity into a note valued at 50 percent of the original house.)

3. They might exchange with an owner who has a portfolio of investments, who wants to consolidate his holdings into one real estate parcel. They could exchange into stocks, existing mortgages, personal property or different kinds and other parcels of real estate. The various parts of the portfolio could be divided equally between them, the real estate to Peter and the readily negotiable personal property to John.

Since John is really seeking "unlike" property—cash or notes, almost every plan is taxable for him. It is not difficult to work it out so that Peter does not get hit with income tax on the gain also.

[¶404]　　　SPLITTING MULTIPLE OWNERSHIP

Like the previous example where two owners wanted to split their interests, the same type of creative transaction can be handled using many owners. There may be two or three owners of a real estate parcel, several, or as in large real estate syndications or Real Estate Investment Trusts, up to hundreds or more.

The very large multiple ownerships are more like a securities investment than a real estate investment. An exchange of the property owned by this type of owner—a syndicate—can be just like the exchange of a property for any other owner. The real estate can be exchanged for another piece of real estate, perhaps giving the owners a new set of benefits. The ownership, as to the people, remains the same. If it is a partnership, corporation or whatever the business entity, it is the same in the new property as in the old.

Splitting out the different owners in a very large entity with many owners could be a mammoth undertaking. It would probably be better to sell the property and give everyone a share of the cash.

Properties owned by smaller groups of owners might be helped by an exchange just as the brothers in a previous example.

Here is an example with three owners:

These owners jointly owned a free-and-clear commercial lot valued at $120,000. Their basis was $20,000. They didn't know how to develop the property, which had been purchased as an investment. They now wished to separate their ownership, and to defer the capital gains tax.

A builder offered six duplexes in exchange for the lot. Each duplex was valued at $60,000 with a $40,000 loan on it.

The three owners accepted the offer and went into title in the duplexes. It was a tax-deferred exchange for each, as each of them went into title alone in two duplexes. Since each took over $80,000 in new loans, each was able to increase his cost basis by that amount. It was an excellent beneficial exchange that put each owner into a pair of properties that gave spendable income and depreciation that was not available in the lot.

The same type of transaction could easily be arranged for six or ten owners. The exchange could be made into a type of property wanted by the majority of the owners. The others could go with them and then be cashed out by a sale of whatever property had been accepted.

In this way, the owners who wanted a tax-deferred exchange would receive that benefit and those who wanted to be cashed out would do that without affecting the others.

[¶405]　　　　　BENEFITS TO A CORPORATION

Since this book is about real estate exchanges, corporations will not be covered in detail except in relation to exchanges. They are mentioned separately because corporations own much real estate. Some of these corporations own real estate that could be exchanged to benefit the company.

Corporations may have an existence far longer than people. While a corporation can do almost anything that people can do, it can also live a perpetual life. So, some older corporations have real estate that has been owned for longer than the average lifetime of a man. We heard of one railroad that had a large office building that it carried on its books at a value of one dollar.

All owners of businesses should always look at real estate as a source of wealth. Boards of directors of corporations may sometimes think of their real estate only in terms of its primary use—a factory or retail site. Doing creative things with their real estate can often change the profit and loss statement appreciably.

Owners of smaller businesses, either as sole owners or corporations, have spent a lifetime working in and building up their business to support themselves, their families, and to leave an estate. Many have found that the business had little value after many years, but the real estate that it was situated on was worth millions.

So, while business owners toil over orders, merchandise, manufacturing and profit-and-loss statements, they should also pay some attention to what is happening to the real estate and buildings used in the business. This might be the real source of money for now and for the future.

One motion picture production company, after many years of movie production, found that its back lots were among the company's most valuable assets.

Since the land may have been purchased at low prices many years ago and the buildings and other improvements completely depreciated, the adjusted cost basis of business property may be extremely low. This low basis is often the reason that the owners fail to utilize these assets. The problem, again, is capital gains taxes.

Some of the things that an owner of low basis business property might do are:

1. Borrow money on the property. This is a tax-free event and frees up assets for current business expansion or investments.
2. If the real estate is extremely valuable, consider a move to a less valuable site, cashing out the original property. (A taxable event.)
3. Make a tax-deferred exchange to a different location.
4. Exchange the real estate up into a non-related investment property that will give the owner new benefits of depreciation and cash flow. Lease back the current site. Lease payments for a current site might be paid for out of cash flow from the newly acquired property.

[¶406]   THE EXCHANGE-LEASEBACK

Suppose the owner of a corporation has a retail location on a major intersection in the downtown of a city. The building has been owned for over 20 years.

When the property was purchased, the price was $50,000. After depreciation of the improvements, the current adjusted cost basis is only $10,000. The property has been appraised at $550,000. The corporation wishes to keep a store on this site, but is also interested in expansion to the suburbs.

While negotiating for an additional business lease in a shopping center in the suburbs, the vice-president finds that the shopping center is for sale for $2,000,000. It is newly constructed and has an existing loan of $1,250,000.

The vice-president proposes that the corporation negotiate for the purchase of the shopping center. The board agrees that this would be an excellent move.

Since the downtown location, although still good, lacks a few modern amenities, a proposal is made to exchange the downtown property up into the shopping center. This could be an excellent move, providing that a good lease can be worked out on the downtown location.

The board reasons that if the downtown area deteriorates within the next few years, as many cities have, then it certainly would be better to already have the equity in the property moved out. The lease can be beneficial in two ways. The payments are a business expense and when the lease is up, the company has no investment in that location.

The owner of the shopping center is represented by a broker and an attorney. With the corporation attorney, a written proposal for the exchange was worked out. The offer was generally as follows:

1. The downtown site was offered in exchange as a "down" on the shopping center. The downtown building was valued at $550,000. The shopping center at $2,000,000.
2. The corporation would assume the existing loan of $1,250,000 on the shopping center.
3. The builder of the shopping center would "carry back" a loan of $200,000 as a second loan on the center. This would be paid interest only quarterly, for two years, then paid off in full. The interest rate would be 9¾ percent.
4. The offer was made contingent on the corporation being able to negotiate a lease on the downtown location that would be satisfactory to them.

The builder of the center accepted the offer, providing that he could sell the downtown location within 30 days of accepting the offer.

The builder's broker went into his files and contacted several possible buyers for the downtown property. He could offer an excellent investment to a buyer:

1. An excellent downtown location.
2. Good financing available to a qualified buyer.
3. An excellent tenant already in the building.

An investor signed an offer to purchase the downtown site for $550,000. This offer was contingent on:

1. Paying $150,000 down payment.
2. Getting a new loan of $400,000 from his bank.
3. Negotiation of a satisfactory lease with the present occupant of the building within thirty days.

The contingicies were quickly removed. Within two weeks, a good lease was worked out, financing arranged, and the transaction was closed within 60 days.

The participants ended with:

1. The retail corporation owned the $2,000,000 shopping center. It had a $550,000 equity and owed $1,450,000. ($1,250,000 assumed bank loan and a $200,000 note to the builder.)

2. The builder of the shopping center received $550,000 cash and a note for $200,000 for his $750,000 equity in the center. ($550,000 cash was from his sale of the downtown property that had been accepted in trade.)
3. The new investor purchased an excellent downtown comercial building. He put up $150,000 down payment and secured a $400,000 loan from his bank.

[¶407]   THE EXCHANGE-BUYBACK

In the previous example, what if there was no third-party investor available to purchase the downtown building? Since the retail corporation wanted very much to acquire the shopping center, they decided to purchase the downtown property back themselves.

If that transaction was set up, the following benefits *might* follow:

1. The corporation would transfer the old adjusted cost basis to the new location. The new basis would be $1,460,000 (old basis of $10,000 plus new loans of $1,450,000 less old loan of zero).
2. Since they were purchasing the downtown site from another party, for $550,000, they would consider that as the new basis and begin a new depreciation schedule.

If any such transaction is planned, it should be carefully cleared in advance with a tax attorney. The government might decide that no exchange and repurchase took place. The same ownership would result from a refinance of the downtown location and a purchase of the shopping center with the money.

[¶408]   THE SALE-LEASEBACK

A similar transaction to the exchange-leaseback is the sale-leaseback. It is also an excellent way to free capital that is tied up in real estate.

When a company has a *high* adjusted cost basis in property, there will be little tax consequences from a sale. Little gain means little tax liability.

The lease payments that the company makes on the property are a deductible expense—if the original sale was at "arms length."

Take care. In one case, a corporation sold real estate to an "arms length" buyer and immediately leased the property back, deducting all of the rent.

The lease was interesting reading to the I.R.S. The corporation agreed to pay all the property taxes, maintenance expenses, liability for damages to the property, losses from possible government condemnation, etc.

The I.R.S. held that the seller retained so many of the powers and obligations of ownership, that it hadn't made a real sale at all. All of the expense deductions for rent were disallowed.

[¶409]   TAX-FREE CASH THROUGH EXCHANGES

The sale-leaseback gets the entire amount of cash out of the transaction. If the lease is written correctly, then all of the rental payments are expenses, deductible as a normal business expense.

In the previous example, the property had a *high* adjusted cost basis, resulting in little tax on the sale.

If the basis is very low, the sale-leaseback could be quickly forgotten—it won't be beneficial. But consider again the exchange-leaseback.

In the exchange-leaseback example, the corporation exchanged into a new location, then leased back the original location. It was going to be a "user" for both properties. What about a property that is acquired only for the possibility for getting a loan on it?

As an example, the property owned by the company is a storage yard, valued at $100,000, Construction equipment, lumber and vehicles are stored there at a location remote from the other facilities of the company. The only improvement on the property is a chain-link fence. Although the real estate is owned free and clear of loans, the bank will lend only $50,000 secured by a mortgage on the property, about 50 percent of the value. It is their policy on unimproved real estate to keep the ratio of loan to value quite low.

An exchange is worked out, exchanging the land at the storage yard for several small houses. The company then leases back the storage yard and continues to use it as before.

The four houses, also worth $100,000 are now used as security for the loan. The company gets $80,000 as the lender's policy of residential property is to make loans at 80 percent of the value.

The exchange was tax-deferred, equity for equity. The company exchanged business property for investment property. After the exchange was completed, another tax-free transaction was arranged. They refinanced the houses.

The houses were already rented to tenants. The rents amounted to an amount approximately equal to the monthly payments and taxes. The management of the rentals was handled by a local Realtor.

So, the company had $80,000 in cash. Since the tenants in the houses were paying back the loan, the company had money that didn't really have to be paid back. They do have to pay rent on their storage yard which is now owned by another investor. The lease payments are a business expense.

Any time that a tax-deferred exchange can be worked out exchanging property that has a low loan ratio to value for property with a high loan ratio, it can result in tax-free cash, usable now.

[¶410] EXCHANGE OF REAL ESTATE INTO A CORPORATION

Section 351 of the Internal Revenue Code in part states as follows:

> No gain or loss shall be recognized if property is transferred to a corporation by one or more persons solely in exchange for stock or securities in such corporation and immediately after the exchange such person or persons are in control (as defined in section 368 (c)) of the Corporation. For purposes of this section, stock or securities shall not be considered as issued in return for property.

Section 368(c) defines "control" as meaning the ownership of stock possessing at least 80 percent of the total combined voting power of all classes of stock entitled to vote and at least 80 percent of the total number of shares of all other classes of stock of the corporation.

Section 351 is another section that allows the exchange of real estate (and other property) without the recognition of gain or loss. This governs the transfer of things of value into a corporation in return for shares of stock in the corporation.

For instance, an owner forms a "close corporation" and starts it with contributions of real estate and money. In return he owns more than 80 percent of the stock of the corporation. There is no capital gains tax on any gain that the owner may have on the real estate. However, the owner's adjusted cost basis in the property is carried over and is the corporation's basis in the property.

When the property is subsequently sold by the corporation, the gain would be taxed to the corporation.

[¶411] SPLITTING THE LIMITED PARTNERSHIP— GOING DIFFERENT WAYS

Many real estate syndications have been started during recent years, putting groups of investors together to purchase real estate. Most were to purchase income property as a "tax shelter" for the members. Others purchased land, houses, groves, farms and other types of property.

One of the most popular types of ownership used has been the limited partnership. Using this, the investors were limited partners, their liability limited only to their investment. Therefore, the partnership could "pass through" tax shelter benefits and income to the limited partners.

When the objectives of the partnership are achieved, the property is usually sold, and the profits or loss passed on to the owners.

Since anything of value can be sold or exchanged, in a few cases these limited partnership shares have been exchanged for real estate. However, the limited partnership owner did not actually own the real estate; he owned just the share of the partnership. Since the limited partnership share then is a security, it cannot be exchanged for real estate without becoming taxable. It is not "like" property under the rules of Section 1031.

Unless the property falls into the unsalable category and would be worked on as a situation to solve a problem, then limited partnership interests might as well be sold for cash.

[¶412]   CHECKLIST OF IMPORTANT CONSIDERATIONS IN NEGOTIATING AND DRAFTING A SALE-LEASEBACK AGREEMENT

A sale-leaseback usually involves a valuable property with a substantial amount of cash changing hands. No two are exactly alike except that all involve a number of factors that require intensive study and evaluation. A mistake cannot be easily remedied. Here are some of the important factors that should be given serious study and consideration.

☐ At what amount should the selling price be fixed? This requires more than evaluating a current value. Both parties generally are tied to the property for a long period.

☐ For economic and tax reasons, the seller may be reluctant to take a loss on a sale, but a loss sale may be called for due to the value of the property.

☐ The amount of rental and length of the lease require evaluation of intangibles. A change in economic circumstances, the neighborhood, or property values can hurt either party.

☐ The seller should compare the sale-leaseback with other methods of financing. Even if a sale-leaseback as agreed on by the parties seems advantageous, it may not be advisable for a particular seller-lessee. Other methods of financing may offer greater benefits.

☐ State law has to be considered, too. There may be: (a) restrictions on purchases, (b) mortgage restrictions in such deals or the transaction may be considered a mortgage and a recording tax sought, and (c) a question of legal title if the seller has an option to repurchase.

☐ The lease, aside from rental amount, length of time, and options, must include provisions covering: (a) the effect of condemnation of the property, (b) subleasing and lessee's primary obligation for rent, (c) building alterations and security to the lessor against loss, (d) repair covenants, (e) insurance coverage, (f) destruction of the property regardless of insurance coverage, (g) restoration of the property in case of casualty and use of insurance recovery, and (h) default and escape clauses for both parties if one fails to live up to the agreement.

CHAPTER **5**

Multiple Exchanges

[¶500]   **THE TWO-WAY EXCHANGE
                    AND SELL-OUT**

The most common form of real estate exchange is the two-way made between a "seller" and an exchange-motivated owner of another property.

The seller wants cash for his property.

The exchange-motivated owner wants to exchange his property for the property owned by the seller. Often, the exchange-motivated owner may wish to avoid capital gains tax on the sale of his real estate. Usually, he has a cash buyer lined up, ready to buy his property with cash.

The third party in the exchange transaction is the cash buyer. He provides the money for the seller.

Example:

Mr. A has a duplex apartment valued in today's market at $50,000. He owes $20,000 on it, so has a sizable equity of $30,000.

A paid $35,000 for the duplex a few years ago, so that figure was his original basis or cost. During his ownership, the depreciation on the building for tax purposes has been $7,500. At the present time, Mr. *A* has a depreciated cost basis of $28,500 (original cost, $35,000 less the $7,500 of depreciation). If Mr. *A* sells for $50,000, his capital gain will be $22,500 ($50,000 selling price less adjusted basis of $28,500).

Mr. *A*'s neighbor has asked several times about purchasing the duplex. The neighbor said he is willing to pay the $50,000, providing he can get a new loan on the property for $40,000.

Mr. *A* knows of a four-plex apartment that he would like to own. It belongs to Mr. *B*.

Mr. *B* has his four-plex for sale for $100,000. Since he currently owes $60,000 on it, his equity is $40,000. His terms for the sale are all cash to the present loan. He wants a buyer to pay him $40,000 cash and assume the existing loan of $60,000 with the bank. Since B is moving out of the state, he is reluctant to carry even a small loan on the property.

A approaches B with the following proposal:

A offers his $30,000 equity in to B for B's four-plex with the following terms:

1. B accepts the $30,000 equity in the duplex ($50,000 value less the $20,000 loan).
2. Mr. A to get a new loan on the four-plex for $70,000. Loan to pay off existing $60,000 loan and balance of $10,000 cash to Mr. B.
3. The offer is contingent on Mr. B's sale of the duplex to A's neighbor for $50,000. It is further contingent on both transactions closing escrow simultaneously.

After A's explanation of a cash-out sale of the duplex, a written offer was prepared with the above terms and B accepted. Since the offer was contingent on the sale of the duplex, B had no obligation to close the exchange escrow unless he received all cash for the duplex. The entire transaction would be canceled if the sale on the duplex was not completed.

Now, Mr. A's neighbor signed an offer to purchase the duplex from B. The offer for the duplex was as follows:

1. Neighbor pays $10,000 cash as down payment.
2. Offer is contingent upon the buyer securing a new bank loan of $40,000 on the duplex; the loan to pay off the existing loan of $20,000 on the property and the balance of $20,000 to the seller.
3. Offer was also contingent on the simultaneous close of escrow of the exchange between A and B.

With paragraph #3 written into the offer to purchase the duplex, Mr. B could accept the offer as "owner in acquisition" or "contingent owner" of the duplex property, since when the exchange between A and B closes, B owns the duplex.

[¶500.1]   Results of the Exchange

All the contingencies were met and the two escrows were closed. Here is how the owners and the buyer ended:

1. Mr. A started with a $30,000 equity in a duplex (value of $50,000 less a loan of $20,000).
   Mr. A ended with a $30,000 equity in a four-plex (value of $100,000 less a new $70,000 loan).

2. Mr. *B* started with $40,000 equity in a four-plex (value of $100,000 less a $60,000 loan).

Mr. *B* ended with $40,000 cash.

a. $10,000 from proceeds of new loan on the four-plex.

b. $10,000 from down payment paid on the duplex by the neighbor.

c. $20,000 from the proceeds of the new loan on the duplex.

Benefits to the owners:

The neighbor of *A* purchased the duplex for $10,000 down payment as he wanted.

Mr. *A* received the benefit of a tax-deferred exchange. Any tax that he would have paid on the capital gain of $22,500 on a sale of the duplex was now invested in his new property. He stepped up his basis for depreciation on the new property from his old basis of $28,500 to $78,500.

Mr. *B* received all cash as he originally wanted. His tax on the gain remains the same as if he sold the original property. *(Rule:* He is taxed in an exchange for the *gain* or *boot,* whichever is the lesser.

Note: This exchange could also be worked two other ways and still get Ackerman his tax deferment.

1. Neighbor could purchase the Four-Plex from Baker, then exchange it to Ackerman.

2. A fourth party (a friend) could purchase the Four-Plex, exchange with Ackerman, then sell the duplex to Neighbor.

Either of these will work. Often, the second party, (Baker) will not cooperate. He refuses to help anyone. In practice, the second choice is usually used. The "friend" is often one of the brokers. Neighbor usually cannot afford to purchase the second property—otherwise he wouldn't be in the market for the smaller one.

Examples of the Prepared Exchange Agreement between *A* and *B* and the Purchase Agreement by the neighbor are shown in Figures 5.1 and 5.2.

[¶501] THE MULTIPLE EXCHANGE— ANY NUMBER CAN PLAY

A multiple exchange is an exchange with three or more properties under three or more ownerships exchanging properties so that each ends the transaction with a different property.

In practice, owners may occasionally make a two-way exchange or a two-way with a buy-out as previously described without the assistance of a broker. Usually, a broker guides them through the transaction.

In a multiple exchange of several properties or "legs" in the transaction, I have never seen or heard of owners handling it without professional help. The knowledgeable broker is absolutely necessary. He exerts his "third party" influence to negotiate as many as 40 or 50 different terms, conditions and prices in a many-partied exchange. Often, each owner is represented by a broker.

The owners in a multiple exchange usually are moving from only one present position to one different position. However, since there are many owners, only the broker coordinating the transaction has the interest of all the owners in mind. He sees the overall problem of solving each owner's *problem* with another property.

EXCHANGE AGREEMENT
CALIFORNIA ASSOCIATION OF REALTORS STANDARD FORM

ANDREW A. ACKERMAN
....

first party, hereby offers to exchange the following described property, situated in...the city of Strawberry
....County of........Monterey........................California:
A duplex apartment located at 1103 Charles Street (Lot 3, block 25, Townsend Tract) valued at FIFTY THOUSAND AND No/100 ($50,000.00) DOLLARS.
Subject to a note secured by a first trust deed in the approximate amount of TWENTY-THOUSAND and No/100 ($20,000.00) DOLLARS.
Also subject to current property taxes, covenants, conditions, reservations, restrictions, easements and rights of way of record.

For the following described property of.................BERTRAM B. BAKER

the city of Strawberry.................County of........Monterey.........................second party, situated in
....California:
A four unit apartment located at 157 Main Street (Lot 15, block 6, Carlsbad tract) valued at ONE HUNDRED THOUSAND and No/100 ($100,000.00) DOLLARS.
Subject to a note secured by a first trust deed in the approximate amount of SIXTY THOUSAND and No/100 ($60,000.00) DOLLARS.
Also subject to current property taxes, covenants, conditions, reservations, restrictions, easements and rights of way of record.

Terms and Conditions of Exchange:
1. Subject to FIRST PARTY (ACKERMAN) being able to get a new institutional loan on the MAIN Street property in the amount of SEVENTY THOUSAND and No/100 ($70,000.00) DOLLARS. Loan to be distributed as follow: (a) Loan to pay off existing loan on Main Street property, and (b) balance to be paid to SECOND PARTY (BAKER).
2. Subject to the sale of the CHARLES Street property for SECOND PARTY (BAKER) within THIRTY (30) days of acceptance of this offer, at terms acceptable to him.
3. The close of this exchange escrow will be subject to the concurrent close of the escrow of the sale of CHARLES street property for SECOND PARTY (BAKER).

The parties hereto shall execute and deliver, within...Ten (10)...days from the date this offer is accepted, all instruments, in writing, necessary to transfer title to said properties and complete and consummate this exchange. Each party shall supply Preliminary Title Reports for their respective properties. Evidences of title shall be California Land Title Association standard coverage form policies of title insurance, showing titles to be merchantable and free of all liens and encumbrances, except taxes and those liens and encumbrances as otherwise set forth herein. Each party shall pay for the policies of Title Insurance for the property to be acquired ☐ conveyed ☒ .

Figure 5.1

77

If either party is unable to convey a marketable title, except as herein provided, within three months after acceptance hereof by second party, or if the improvements on any of the herein named properties be destroyed or materially damaged prior to transfer of title or delivery of agreement of sale, then this agreement shall be of no further effect, except as to payment of commissions and expenses incurred in connection with examination of title, unless the party acquiring the property so affected elects to accept the title the other party can convey or subject to the conditions of the improvements.

Taxes, insurance premiums (if policies be satisfactory to party acquiring the property affected thereby), rents, interest and other expenses of said properties shall be pro-rated as of the date of transfer of title or delivery of agreement of sale, unless otherwise provided herein.

N/A
Broker .... of .... Calif. ....
                                                    Address   Phone No.
is hereby authorized to act as broker for all parties hereto and may accept commission therefrom. Should second party accept this offer, first party agrees to pay said broker commission for services rendered as follows:-

N/A

Should second party be unable to convey a marketable title to his property then first party shall be released from payment of any commission, unless he elects to accept the property subject thereto. First party agrees that broker may cooperate with other brokers and divide commissions in any manner satisfactory to them.

This offer shall be deemed revoked unless accepted in writing within Five (5) days after date hereof, and such acceptance is communicated to first party within said period. Broker is hereby given the exclusive and irrevocable right to obtain acceptance of second party within said period. Time is the essence of this contract.

Dated .... 19 ....

ACCEPTANCE

Second party hereby accepts the foregoing offer upon the terms and conditions stated and agrees to pay commission for services rendered, for

N/A
Broker .... of .... Calif. ....
                                                    Address   Phone No.

as follows:- ..... N/A

Second party agrees that broker may act as broker for all parties here to and may accept commission therefrom, and may co-operate with other brokers and divide commissions in any manner satisfactory to them.

Should first party be unable to convey a marketable title to his property then second party shall be released from payment of any commission, unless he elects to accept the property of first party subject thereto.

Dated .... 19 ....

FORM E 14   REVISED APRIL 1972

Figure 5.1 (continued)

CALIFORNIA REAL ESTATE ASSOCIATION STANDARD FORM

REAL ESTATE PURCHASE CONTRACT AND RECEIPT FOR DEPOSIT

THIS IS MORE THAN A RECEIPT FOR MONEY. IT MAY BE A LEGALLY BINDING CONTRACT. READ IT CAREFULLY.

Strawberry, _____, California, _____ January 15, ____ 19 78

Received from _____ NORMAN N. NEIGHBOR _____ herein called Buyer,

the sum of _____ FIVE HUNDRED AND No/100——————————————— Dollars ($ 500.00)

evidenced by cash ☐, personal check ☒, cashier's check ☐, or _____ as deposit on account of

purchase price of _____ FIFTY THOUSAND and No/100——————————————— Dollars, ($ 50,000.00)

for the purchase of property, situated in ___ the city of Strawberry ___, County of ___ Monterey ___,

California, described as follows: ___ Lot 3, Block 25, Townsend Tract, commonly known as

1103 Charles Street.

1. Buyer will deposit in escrow with ___ a reputable title co. ___ the balance of purchase price as follows:

   A. ___ TEN THOUSAND and No/100 ($10,000.00) DOLLARS down payment including

      the deposit shown above.

   B. ___ Offer subject to buyer securing a new institutional loan in the amount

      of FORTY THOUSAND and No/100 ($40,000.00) DOLLARS on the property at

      terms acceptable to him, within THIRTY (30) DAYS of the acceptance

      of this offer.

   C. ___ This offer is also subject to the concurrent close of the exchange

      escrow between A. A. Ackerman, 1103 Charles St. / B.B. Baker, 157 Main

      Street, Strawberry.

Set forth above any terms and conditions of a factual nature applicable to this sale, such as financing, prior sale of other property, the matter of structural pest control inspection, repairs and personal property to be included in the sale.

2. Title is to be free of liens, encumbrances, easements, restrictions, rights and conditions of record or known to Seller, other than the following: ___ None.

Seller shall furnish to Buyer at ___ Seller's ___ expense a standard California Land Title Association policy issued by

___ a reputable title ___ Company, showing title vested in Buyer subject only to liens, encumbrances, easements, restrictions, rights and conditions of record as set forth above. If Seller fails to deliver title as herein provided, Buyer at his option may terminate this agreement and any deposit shall thereupon be returned to him.

3. Property taxes, premiums on insurance acceptable to Buyer, rents, interest, and ___ prepaid rents and deposits ___ [insert in blank any other items of income or expense to be prorated] shall be prorated as of (1) the date of recordation of deed or (2) _____

[Strike (1) if (2) is used]. The amount of any bond or assessment which is a lien shall be ~~assumed~~ paid [Strike one] by ___ seller ___. Seller shall pay cost of documentary stamps on deed.

4. Possession shall be delivered to Buyer [Strike inapplicable alternatives] (a) on close of escrow, or ~~(b) on xxxxxxxxxx x xxxx~~ ~~days after close of escrow, or xxx~~

Figure 5.2

5. Escrow instructions signed by Buyer and Seller shall be delivered to the escrow holder within ___30___ days from the Seller's acceptance hereof and shall provide for closing within ___30___ days from the Seller's acceptance hereof, subject to written extensions signed by Buyer and Seller.

6. Unless otherwise designated in the escrow instructions of Buyer, title shall vest as follows: ___to be determined by buyer before the close of escrow.___

[The manner of taking title may have **significant legal and tax consequences. Therefore, give this matter serious consideration.**]

7. If the improvements on the property are destroyed or materially damaged prior to close of escrow, then, on demand by Buyer, any deposit made by Buyer shall be returned to him and this contract thereupon shall terminate.

8. If Buyer fails to complete said purchase as herein provided by reason of any default of Buyer, Seller shall be released from his obligation to sell the property to Buyer and may proceed against Buyer upon any claim or remedy which he may have in law or equity; provided, however, that by placing their initials here. Buyer: ( ) Seller: ( ). Buyer and Seller agree that it would be impractical or extremely difficult to fix actual damages in case of Buyer's default, that the amount of the deposit is a reasonable estimate of the damages, and that Seller shall retain the deposit as his sole right to damages.

9. Buyer's signature hereon constitutes an offer to Seller to purchase the real estate described above. Unless acceptance hereof is signed by Seller and the signed copy delivered to Buyer, either in person or by mail to the address shown below, within ___Five (5)___ days hereof, this offer shall be deemed revoked and the deposit shall be returned to Buyer.

10. Time is of the essence of this contract.

Real Estate Broker ___N/A___

Address ___N/A___   By _____

                                               Telephone _____

The undersigned Buyer offers and agrees to buy the above described property on the terms and conditions above stated and acknowledges receipt of a copy hereof.

Address _____   Buyer _____

Telephone _____   Buyer _____

ACCEPTANCE

The undersigned Seller accepts the foregoing offer and agrees to sell the property described thereon on the terms and conditions therein set forth.

The undersigned Seller has employed _____ as Broker(s) and for the Broker(s) services agrees to pay Broker(s) as a commission, the sum of _____ Dollars ($_____) payable as follows: (a) On recordation of the deed or other evidence of title, or (b) if completion of sale is prevented by default of Seller, upon Seller's default, or (c) if completion of sale is prevented by default of Buyer, only if and when Seller collects the damages from Buyer, by suit or otherwise, and then in an amount not to exceed one half that portion of the damages collected after first deducting title and escrow expenses and the expenses of collection, if any.

The undersigned acknowledges receipt of a copy hereof and authorizes Broker(s) to deliver a signed copy of it to Buyer.

Dated: _____   Seller _____

Telephone _____   Seller _____

Broker(s) consent to the foregoing. Broker _____ Broker _____

Dated: _____ By _____   Dated: _____ By _____

A REAL ESTATE BROKER IS THE PERSON QUALIFIED TO ADVISE ON REAL ESTATE. IF YOU DESIRE LEGAL ADVICE CONSULT YOUR ATTORNEY.

FORM NO. D-14 (Rev. 6-71)

Figure 5.2 (continued)

Since the broker has the complete transaction and how it will work in his mind, he is able to persuade individual owners to make small allowances in terms, prices, etc. to complete the entire exchange.

[¶501.1] How the Broker Fits In

An example might be the owner of an apartment property. He is moving up to a larger property in a multi-partied exchange involving five other owners and five other properties. When the tentative contract is presented to him, the interest rate on a note he is executing on the new property is ½ percent higher than he paid on his previous property. He refuses to continue until he gets the interest he wants.

This might work in a buy-sell transaction between two people. In a multi-partied transaction, the broker may show the owner how it will affect the overall agreements already signed by three or four other owners. Since the others have already agreed to these terms, if this owner will not accept the terms, the others may substitute another owner and another property to replace him. If the benefits of the exchange to the reluctant owner are a large saving of taxes or a large increase in income, he is urged to weigh these benefits against either remaining in his present position or accepting the higher interest rate.

Often, owners may disagree on prices of the properties in the exchange. As we all know, everyone wants to buy low, sell high. But since an exchange often results in increased income, increased depreciation benefits, deferment of capital gains taxes, etc., the price shown on a property in an exchange is often of little importance. Sometimes, brokers suggest that all owners use the same method of valuing the properties. This might be using a "times gross" rule, a capitalization rate or some other method.

When prices are quite close, an owner can be persuaded to make a small adjustment in price if the benefits in the overall transaction to him far outweigh the price difference. He may be deferring $50,000 in taxes by making an exchange. His new property may increase his spendable income by $5,000 a year. If the difference in prices is just a few thousand dollars, the benefits to him would far outweigh the small disagreement on values.

[¶502] THE "IN LIEU OF" CONTINGENCY

Multiple exchanges all close escrow at the same time. All of the deeds are recorded in order, one after the other, to transfer the properties to each new owner. Therefore, when the first few property owners are brought in during early negotiations, any offers and acceptances between owners must be "contingent" on the owner being able to exchange the property offered for the property he wants.

See the following example:

Owner:	A	B	C
	10-Unit Apartment	20-Unit Apartment	40-Unit Apartment

Owner *A*, who has a 10-unit apartment wants to move up to B's 20 units. Owner *B*, in turn, wants to move up also. He wants to trade up to C's 40 units.

Therefore, when *A* offers his property to *B*, Mr. *B*'s acceptance must be contingent on being able to secure the property he wants. Above his signature, in the acceptance, the following phrase is written:

"THIS OFFER IS ACCEPTED PROVIDING, WITHIN 90 (OR 30, 60, etc) DAYS, ANOTHER PROPERTY (OR CASH) IS FOUND FOR THE UNDERSIGNED IN LIEU OF THE PROPERTY BEING OFFERED BY MR. A."

[¶503]   EXAMPLE OF A FIVE-WAY EXCHANGE FOR TAX BENEFITS—HOW IT ALL BEGINS

Real estate broker John Brown owned a firm that specialized in the sale and exchange of income properties. Brown was in contact with most of the owners of apartments and commercial properties in his community on a periodic basis. He always explained the possibility of an exchange to each property owner that he contacted. He had found previously that some owners offered income property for sale in order to get cash to invest in a larger property. Often, they failed to mention that fact to the broker. The sale resulted in a tax liability that might have been avoided with an exchange.

Brown was working with three owners who had employed him to "exchange up" their property.

[¶503.1]   The First Owner

Brown's first client was Arthur Able. Able was the owner of a vacant lot that was priced at $10,000. The lot was located in the city that Brown and Able lived in and it was zoned R-1, single family residence only.

Able had listed the lot for sale with Brown's office for a cash sale. He mentioned to the broker that he wanted to invest the proceeds of the sale in an income property. On questioning Able, Brown found out that he had purchased the lot for $5,000 a few years ago as an investment. It was free and clear of loans.

Since there would be a taxable gain of $5,000 on a sale, Brown suggested that Able exchange the lot for a rental property such as a duplex. He explained the simple step of offering it to a duplex owner, subject to the sale of the lot, or even after a buyer had been found.

Brown also ascertained that Able had the cash to pay the small expenses and Brown's fee. There would be no cash coming to Able if the property was exchanged.

[¶503.2]   The Second Owner

Brown's second client was a married couple, Billy and Betty Bravo. The Bravos had a six-unit apartment that they had just recently refurbished. They had purchased the property six months before.

The apartments had been sadly neglected by the previous owner. The Bravos bought it when it had only three tenants paying rent. The other three units couldn't be rented because of the poor condition of the property.

The Bravos had spent time and money painting the units inside and out, installing new carpeting and plumbing fixtures. The front yard, which had been weeds, was newly landscaped.

The purchase price of the property was $75,000. After spending $10,000 and time on the property, the Bravos rented all six units, and at twice the previous rent.

Brown and the owners decided that the six-unit apartment was now worth $120,000, based on the current income and expenses of the property. The apartments were listed with Brown at that price. The existing loan on the six units was $60,000.

Since the owners had a large potential gain on the property, they preferred to exchange for a larger apartment house. They wanted a better-leveraged position, preferably a "problem" property that would require upgrading.

[¶503.3]   The Third Owner

The third exchange client who had listed property with the office was Charles Carter. He had a 16-unit apartment, purchased five years ago for income and tax shelter.

Carter was a local businessman and had managed the apartments himself in his spare time. He was anxious to move up to as large a property as his equity would allow. Because his business was across town, he had not spent as much time as he would have liked on the apartments. There was deferred maintenance and the rents were lower than some comparable-size apartments nearby.

While Carter wanted a larger property for income, his main objective was to have a large enough property that could support professional management. He was tired of dealing directly with tenants.

Based on the current income, and taking into consideration the deferred maintenance, Broker Brown and Carter decided on a listed value of $270,000. Carter's current loan was only $70,000.

[¶503.4]   Planning the Exchange

Brown could see the possibility of Bravo exchanging up to Carter's 16-unit apartment. However, since Carter also wanted an "upward" exchange, he knew a multiple exchange was necessary. Carter obviously would not trade with Bravo in a "two-way" exchange. Brown set out to find the larger property for Carter.

At the next meeting of the Real Estate Board's trading club, Brown told the other ten brokers who attended about his problem.

Several other properties were posted by brokers looking for an exchange. They were:

BROKER	PROPERTY	VALUE	WANTS
Jackson	5 acreas desert land	$10,000	Income property
Jones	2 houses, local prop.	35,000	Wants larger income.
Williams	Commercial lot, downtown	50,000	Sale or exchange
Harrington	360-acre farm	2,000 (acre)	Income property

Of the properties presented, Brown asked for further information from Jones about the two houses that he had listed. They were two adjoining houses owned by a man named Woods. Brown decided to look at the houses on the way back to his office. He thought they might be a good investment property for Mr. Able.

None of the other properties interested Brown.

As the meeting ended, another broker, Smith, mentioned to Brown that he had a client, Zerbo, who had a 30-unit apartment, nearly completed, for sale for $600,000. Smith had hesitated to mention it at a trader's club meeting because Zerbo had no intention of exchanging the property. It was for sale only. Since Zerbo was a "dealer" in real estate, there could be no tax benefits in an exchange. Besides, his need was for cash.

The existing loan on Zerbo's property was the construction loan of $400,000, so the owner's equity was $200,000. He had agreed to carry back a second loan of $50,000 himself on the property, if he could get a $150,000-cash down payment.

[¶503.5]   The Solution

Brown got the idea for a five-way exchange using the listings in his own office and the other offices. The following day, he contacted brokers

Smith and Jones and made an appointment with them in his office.
   At the meeting, Brown diagrammed his idea for the exchange:

	1.	2.	3.	4.	5.
Owner:	Able	Woods	Bravo	Carter	Zerbo
Property:	Vacant lot	2 houses	6 unit apt.	16 unit	30 unit
Value:	$10,000	$35,000	$120,000	$270,000	$600,000
Loan:	—0—	—0—	60,000	70,000	400,000
Equity:	$10,000	$35,000	$60,000	$200,000	$200,000
Wants:	Income property	Larger income property	Larger income property	Larger income property	Cash sale

Brown proposed that each owner move up to the next property except
Zerbo. The equities could be balanced with new loans on properties 2, 3,
and 4.
   Brown proposed that the exchange contracts be written as follows:

1. CARTER OFFERS 16-UNIT TO ZERBO FOR 30-UNIT.
   ZERBO ACCEPTS CONDITIONALLY.
      A. Subject to exchanging 16 units to another owner.
   RESULT: Carter moves up to 30 units with his $200,000 equity in a tax-
      deferred exchange.
      Zerbo exchanges down into 16 units with $200,000 equity.

2. BRAVOS OFFER EQUITY ($60,000) IN 6-UNIT APARTMENT TO ZERBO
   AS OWNER IN ACQUISITION OF THE 16 UNITS, SUBJECT TO:
      A. Bravos to secure maximum loan of $190,000 on the 16-unit property.
         Loan to pay existing loan off ($70,000) and balance of $120,000 cash
         paid to Zerbo.
      B. Bravos to execute a purchase money note to Zerbo for $20,000 to be
         secured by the 16-unit apartment.
      C. Zerbo being able to exchange equity in 6-unit apartment to someone
         else.
   RESULT: Bravos exchange their $60,000 equity up into the 16-unit apartment
      in a tax-deferred exchange.

	Bravos' new position:	16-unit apartment	$270,000
		First loan	190,000
		Second loan	20,000
		Equity	$60,000
	Zerbo's new position:	6-unit apartment	$120,000
		Loan on 6-unit	60,000
		Equity	$60,000

      Zerbo also has: $120,000 cash and a $20,000 note secured by the
      16-unit apartment.

3. WOODS OFFERS EQUITY ($35,000) IN TWO HOUSES TO ZERBO (OWNER IN ACQUISITION) FOR 6-UNIT APARTMENT, SUBJECT TO:
   - A. Woods to secure new loan on 6-unit in amount of $85,000. Loan to pay off existing loan on property ($60,000) and balance of $25,000 paid to Zerbo.
   - B. Zerbo being able to exchange two houses to another owner.

   RESULT: Woods exchanges his $35,000 equity in two houses up to 6 units in a tax-deferred exchange.

Woods' new position:	6-unit apartment	$120,000
	Loan	85,000
	Equity	$35,000

   Zerbo exchanges down into two houses.
   Zerbo's new position. He has: 2 houses $35,000
   He also has $145,000 cash ($120,000 from Bravos plus $25,000 from Woods) and a $20,000 note on the 16-unit apartment.

4. ABLE OFFERS EQUITY ($10,000) IN LOT TO ZERBO (OWNER IN ACQUISITION) FOR TWO HOUSES, SUBJECT TO:
   - A. Able to secure new loans on houses totaling $25,000. Proceeds of loans to be paid to Zerbo, bringing his cash total to $170,000.

   RESULT: Able exchanges his lot ($10,000) up into 2 houses in a tax-deferred exchange.

Ables new position:	2 houses	$35,000
	Loans	25,000
	Equity	$10,000

   Zerbo exchanges down into the lot. His final position:

1. Vacant lot—Value	$10,000
2. Note on 16-unit apt.	$20,000
3. Cash	$170,000

For each owner in the exchange, except the "seller," Zerbo, there is a simple two-way exchange contract. Since Able, Woods, Bravo and Carter each only sees his part of the transaction, the explanation of each contract is simple. *Although they are part of a five-way exchange, each only needs to see his own two-way exchange contract.*

Mr. Zerbo's broker, Smith, stated that Zerbo had previously exchanged an income property down into a smaller property which was sold for cash. The proposed transaction would just take a little longer explanation. Smith felt the builder would accept the idea and the transaction as his total cash received would be $170,000. He had only been asking $150,000 cash plus the balance in a note.

Smith also felt that Zerbo would accept the lot owned by Able. The lot was well located and the builder was always on the lookout for a good lot to purchase.

[¶503.6] Preparing the Offers

Since Brown represented three of the owners, he volunteered to prepare the exchange agreements on all five of the properties. The brokers had agreed that the contracts would be prepared in advance. When the owners were shown the properties, the exchange agreements could be shown as a possible way of working out the details of the trade.

The exchange agreements were prepared and the properties shown to the principals. Within a few days, all of the agreements were signed. Figures 5.3, 5.4, 5.5 and 5.6 show sample exchange agreements that could cover this transaction.

In each of the agreements, there was an exchange between two parties. Each owner "exchanging up"—Able, Woods, Bravo and Carter only needed to sign one form and consider and inspect one property.

William Smith, Zerbo's broker, had to explain only the following to Zerbo:

1. The cash, note and vacant lot that Zerbo would receive at the end of the exchange.

2. The protection for Zerbo written into the offers. Each offer, except the last, had the "in lieu of" clause written into it. If another property was not found "in lieu of" the one Zerbo accepted, each previous "leg" of the transaction was canceled. If any other owner decided not to go through with the recommended terms, the other "legs" were canceled. Further, each new offer was written "subject" to the concurrent close of escrow of the previous offer. If anything happened to stall or cancel any part of the five-way exchange, all of it was stalled or canceled.

Zerbo also had to inspect just one property. He inspected the lot and agreed to accept it. The five-way exchange was complete.

[¶503.7] Escrowing the Exchange

The escrow documents for the exchange would reflect the instructions for the transaction. Each party exchanging up will be deeded the property being acquired by him. Zerbo will be deeded into each property in sequence, then in turn deed the property out. In this way, all parties exchanging up make only one transaction, an exchange. Zerbo, exchanging down, collects the funds from each new loan in each of the properties being financed and re-financed in the transaction.

[¶503.8] Expenses and Commissions in the Exchange

In the agreements, title insurance and other expenses for each property were each to be paid by the party conveying the property. (This is negotiable in all transactions.)

EXCHANGE AGREEMENT

CALIFORNIA ASSOCIATION OF REALTORS STANDARD FORM

CHARLES CARTER

first party, hereby offers to exchange the following described property, situated in........the city of Strawberry

County of........Monterey ....California:

A SIXTEEN (16) Unit apartment property located at 505 Knott Street. (Legal: Lot #25, Block 3, Highland Tract.)
Subject to a note secured by a First Trust Deed in the current amount of SEVENTY THOUSAND and No/100 ($70,000.00) DOLLARS.
PROPERTY IS VALUED AT TWO HUNDRED SEVENTY THOUSAND and No/100 ($270,000.00) DOLLARS.

For the following described property of........VICTOR ZERBO

........second party, situated in

the city of Strawberry ....County of........Monterey ....California:

A THIRTY (30) Unit apartment property located at 26 Polk Street (Legal: Lot #3, Block 6, Serra Tract.)
Subject to a note secured by a First Trust Deed in the current amount of FOUR HUNDRED THOUSAND and No/100 ($400,000.00) DOLLARS.
PROPERTY IS VALUED AT SIX HUNDRED THOUSAND and No/100 ($600,000.00) DOLLARS.

Terms and Conditions of Exchange:

1. FIRST PARTY (Carter) to take title to Polk Street property and assume existing loan of FOUR HUNDRED THOUSAND and no/100 ($400,000.00) DOLLARS.

2. SECOND PARTY (Zerbo) to take title to Knott Street property subject to existing loan of SEVENTY THOUSAND and No/100 ($70,000.00) DOLLARS.

3. Offer subject to FIRST PARTY'S inspection and written approval of financial records of Polk Street property within TEN (10) days of SECOND PARTY acceptance.

The parties hereto shall execute and deliver, within........Fifteen (15)........days from the date this offer is accepted, all instruments, in writing, necessary to transfer title to said properties and complete and consummate this exchange. Each party shall supply Preliminary Title Reports for their respective properties. Evidences of title shall be California Land Title Association standard coverage form policies of title insurance, showing titles to be merchantable and free of all liens and encumbrances, except taxes and those liens and encumbrances as otherwise set forth herein. Each party shall pay for the policies of Title Insurance for the property to be acquired ☐ conveyed ☒ .

Figure 5.3

MULTIPLE EXCHANGES

If either party is unable to convey a marketable title, except as herein provided, within three months after acceptance hereof by second party, or if the improvements on any of the herein named properties be destroyed or materially damaged prior to transfer of title or delivery of agreement of sale, then this agreement shall be of no further effect, except as to payment of commissions and expenses incurred in connection with examination of title, unless the party acquiring the property so affected elects to accept the title the other party can convey or subject to the conditions of the improvements.

Taxes, insurance premiums (if policies be satisfactory to party acquiring the property affected thereby), rents, interest and other expenses of said properties shall be pro-rated as of the date of transfer of title or delivery of agreement of sale, unless otherwise provided herein.

John C. Brown   of   147 15th St. Strawberry   Calif.

       Broker   Address   Phone No.

is hereby authorized to act as broker for all parties hereto and may accept commission therefrom. Should second party accept this offer, first party agrees to pay said broker commission for services rendered as follows:-

      as agreed in the terms of a separate listing agreement.

Should second party be unable to convey a marketable title to his property then first party shall be released from payment of any commission, unless he elects to accept the property subject thereto. First party agrees that broker may cooperate with other brokers and divide commissions in any manner satisfactory to them.

This offer shall be deemed revoked unless accepted in writing within   Ten (10)   days after date hereof, and such acceptance is communicated to first party within said period. Broker is hereby given the exclusive and irrevocable right to obtain acceptance of second party within said period. Time is the essence of this contract.

Dated   Jan 15,   78   19

A C C E P T A N C E

Second party hereby accepts the foregoing offer upon the terms and conditions stated and agrees to pay commission for services rendered,

to:- William Smith   of   62 Light St., Strawberry   Calif.

       Broker   Address   Phone No.

as follows:-   as agreed in the terms of a separate listing agreement.

Second party agrees that broker may act as broker for all parties hereto and may accept commission therefrom, and may co-operate with other brokers and divide commissions in any manner satisfactory to them.

Should first party be unable to convey a marketable title to his property then second party shall be released from payment of any commission, unless he elects to accept the property of first party subject thereto.

This offer is accepted providing, within THIRTY (30) days, another property is found for the undersigned in lieu of the SIXTEEN (16) Unit apartment at 505 Knott St.

Dated   Jan 16,   78   19

FORM E 14   REVISED APRIL 1972

Figure 5.3 (continued)

EXCHANGE AGREEMENT

CALIFORNIA ASSOCIATION OF REALTORS STANDARD FORM

BILLY AND BETTY BRAVO
----

first party, hereby offers to exchange the following described property, situated in......the city of Strawberry
_____ County of......Monterey_____ California:

A SIX (6) Unit apartment property located at 156 Lincoln Street. (Legal: Lot 21, Block 14, Country Club Tract)
Subject to a Note secured by a First Trust Deed in the current amount of SIXTY THOUSAND and No/100 ($60,000.00) DOLLARS
PROPERTY IS VALUED AT ONE HUNDRED TWENTY THOUSAND and No/100 ($120,000.00) DOLLARS.

For the following described property of......VICTOR ZERBO (owner in acquisition)
_____ second party, situated in

the city of Strawberry _____ County of_____Monterey_____ California:
A SIXTEEN (16) Unit apartment property located at 505 Knott Street. (Legal: Lot #25, Block 3, Highland Tract.)
Subject to a note secured by a First Trust Deed in the current amount of SEVENTY THOUSAND and No/100 ($70,000.00) DOLLARS.
PROPERTY IS VALUED AT TWO HUNDRED SEVENTY THOUSAND and No/100 ($270,000.00) DOLLARS.

Terms and Conditions of Exchange:

1. Offer is subject to FIRST PARTY (Bravo) securing a new institutional loan on the Knott Street property in the amount of ONE HUNDRED NINTY THOUSAND and No/100 ($190,000.00) DOLLARS, at terms acceptable to them. Loan to pay off existing loan on property, then balance to be paid to SECOND PARTY (Zerbo).

2. FIRST PARTY (Bravo) to execute and SECOND PARTY (Zerbo) to carry back a purchase money SECOND trust deed and note in the amount of TWENTY THOUSAND and No/100 ($20,000.00) DOLLARS on the KNOTT STREET property. Payments to be TWO HUNDRED and no/100 ($200.00) DOLLARS, or more, monthly including NINE (9%) PERCENT annual interest, all due and payable EIGHT (8) years from close of escrow.

3. This offer also subject to the CONCURRENT close of escrow of the EXCHANGE between Carter, 505 Knott Street/Zerbo, 26 Polk Street.

The parties hereto shall execute and deliver, within...Fifteen (15)...days from the date this offer is accepted, all instruments, in writing, necessary to transfer title to said properties and complete and consummate this exchange. Each party shall supply Preliminary Title Reports for their respective properties. Evidences of title shall be California Land Title Association standard coverage form policies of title insurance, showing titles to be merchantable and free of all liens and encumbrances, except taxes and those liens and encumbrances as otherwise set forth herein. Each party shall pay for the policies of Title Insurance for the property to be acquired ☐ conveyed ☒ .

Figure 5.4

If either party is unable to convey a marketable title, except as herein provided, within three months after acceptance hereof by second party, or if the improvements on any of the herein named properties be destroyed or materially damaged prior to transfer of title or delivery of agreement of sale, then this agreement shall be of no further effect, except as to payment of commissions and expenses incurred in connection with examination of title, unless the party acquiring the property so affected elects to accept the title the other party can convey or subject to the conditions of the improvements.

Taxes, insurance premiums (if policies be satisfactory to party acquiring the property affected thereby), rents, interest and other expenses of said properties shall be pro-rated as of the date of transfer of title or delivery of agreement of sale, unless otherwise provided herein.

John C. Brown _____ of. 147 15th St., Strawberry _____ Calif. _____
　　　　Broker　　　　　　　　　　　　　　　　　　Address　　　　　　　　　　Phone No.

is hereby authorized to act as broker for all parties hereto and may accept commission therefrom. Should second party accept this offer, first party agrees to pay said broker commission for services rendered as follows:-
　　as agreed in the terms of a separate listing agreement.

Should second party be unable to convey a marketable title to his property then first party shall be released from payment of any commission, unless he elects to accept the property subject thereto. First party agrees that broker may cooperate with other brokers and divide commissions in any manner satisfactory to them.
　This offer shall be deemed revoked unless accepted in writing within Ten (10) days after date hereof, and such acceptance is communicated to first party within said period. Broker is hereby given the exclusive and irrevocable right to obtain acceptance of second party within said period. Time is the essence of this contract.

Dated. _____ Jan. 15, _____ 19 78 .

A C C E P T A N C E

Second party hereby accepts the foregoing offer upon the terms and conditions stated and agrees to pay commission for services rendered, to:-

William Smith _____ of. 62 Light St. Strawberry _____ Calif. _____
　　　　Broker　　　　　　　　　　　　　　　　　　Address　　　　　　　　　　Phone No.

as follows:- 　　as agreed in the terms of a separate listing agreement.

Second party agrees that broker may act as broker for all parties here to and may accept commission therefrom, and may co-operate with other brokers and divide commissions in any manner satisfactory to them.
　Should first party be unable to convey a marketable title to his property then second party shall be released from payment of any commission, unless he elects to accept the property of first party subject thereto.

This offer is accepted providing, within THIRTY (30) days, another property is found for the undersigned in lieu of the SIX (6) unit apartment at 156 Lincoln Street.

Dated. _____ Jan. 16 _____ 19 78 .

FORM E 14　　　　　　　　　　　　　REVISED APRIL 1972

Figure 5.4 (continued)

EXCHANGE AGREEMENT

CALIFORNIA ASSOCIATION OF REALTORS STANDARD FORM

WILLIAM C. WOODS & MARTHA WOODS

first party, hereby offers to exchange the following described property, situated in the city of Strawberry

County of Monterey California:

Two houses located at 541/543 Townsend Street. (Legal: Lots 18, 19. Block 4, Upper Valley Tract)

Properties Free and Clear of any loans.

For the following described property of VICTOR ZERBO (Owner in acquisition)

second party, situated in the city of Strawberry County of Monterey California:

A SIX (6) Unit apartment property located at 156 Lincoln Street. (Legal: Lot 21, Block 14, Country Club Tract)

Subject to a Note secured by a First Trust Deed in the current amount of SIXTY THOUSAND and No/100 ($60,000.00) DOLLARS

PROPERTY IS VALUED AT ONE HUNDRED TWENTY THOUSAND and No/100 ($120,000.00) DOLLARS.

Terms and Conditions of Exchange:

1. Offer is subject to FIRST PARTY (Woods) securing a new institutional loan on the LINCOLN STREET property in the amount of EIGHTY-FIVE THOUSAND and No/100 ($85,000.00) DOLLARS, at terms acceptable to them. Loan to pay off existing loan on property, then balance to be paid to SECOND PARTY (Zerbo).
2. This offer also subject to the CONCURRENT close of escrow of the EXCHANGE between Bravo, 156 Lincoln St/Zerbo, 505 Knott Street.

The parties hereto shall execute and deliver, within Fifteen (15) days from the date this offer is accepted, all instruments, in writing, necessary to transfer title to said properties and complete and consummate this exchange. Each party shall supply Preliminary Title Reports for their respective properties. Evidences of title shall be California Land Title Association standard coverage form policies of title insurance, showing titles to be merchantable and free of all liens and encumbrances, except taxes and those liens and encumbrances as otherwise set forth herein. Each party shall pay for the policies of Title Insurance for the property to be acquired ☐ conveyed ☒ .

Figure 5.5

MULTIPLE EXCHANGES

If either party is unable to convey a marketable title, except as herein provided, within three months after acceptance hereof by second party, or if the improvements on any of the herein named properties be destroyed or materially damaged prior to transfer of title or delivery of agreement of sale, then this agreement shall be of no further effect, except as to payment of commissions and expenses incurred in connection with examination of title, unless the party acquiring the property so affected elects to accept the title the other party can convey or subject to the conditions of the improvements.

Taxes, insurance premiums (if policies be satisfactory to party acquiring the property affected thereby), rents, interest and other expenses of said properties shall be pro-rated as of the date of transfer of title or delivery of agreement of sale, unless otherwise provided herein.

Jack Jones ....of...... 23 14th St., Strawberry .....Calif.................
Broker   Address   Phone No.

Is hereby authorized to act as broker for all parties hereto and may accept commission therefrom. Should second party accept this offer, first party agrees to pay said broker commission for services rendered as follows:-

........as agreed in the terms of a separate listing agreement.....................

Should second party be unable to convey a marketable title to his property then first party shall be released from payment of any commission, unless he elects to accept the property subject thereto. First party agrees that broker may cooperate with other brokers and divide commissions in any manner satisfactory to them.

This offer shall be deemed revoked unless accepted in writing within Ten (10) days after date hereof, and such acceptance is communicated to first party within said period. Broker is hereby given the exclusive and irrevocable right to obtain acceptance of second party within said period. Time is the essence of this contract.

Dated.......... Jan. 15, ...19 78 ....

ACCEPTANCE

Second party hereby accepts the foregoing offer upon the terms and conditions stated and agrees to pay commission for services rendered, to:-

William Smith ....of 62 Light St.,Strawberry ....Calif................
Broker   Address   Phone No.

as follows:- ....as agreed in the terms of a separate listing agreement.............

Second party agrees that broker may act as broker for all parties here to and may accept commission therefrom, and may co-operate with other brokers and divide commissions in any manner satisfactory to them.

Should first party be unable to convey a marketable title to his property then second party shall be released from payment of any commission, unless he elects to accept the property of first party subject thereto.

This off is accepted providing, within THIRTY (30) days, another property is found for the undersigned in lieu of the houses on Townsend Street.

Dated..... Jan. 16 ....19 78 ....

FORM E 14   REVISED APRIL 1972

Figure 5.5 (continued)

EXCHANGE AGREEMENT

CALIFORNIA ASSOCIATION OF REALTORS STANDARD FORM

ARTHUR ABLE

first party, hereby offers to exchange the following described property, situated in, ... the city of Strawberry

.... County of .... Monterey .... , California:

An unimproved lot located at 128 15th Street. (Legal: Lot 2, Block 3, Terrace Park Tract).

Lot Free and Clear of any loans.

For the following described property of .... VICTOR ZERBO (Owner in acquisition)

.... second party, situated in

the city of Strawberry .... County of .... Monterey .... , California:

Two houses located at 541/543 Townsend Street. (Legal: Lots 18, 19. Block 4, Upper Valley Tract)

Properties free and clear of any loans.

Terms and Conditions of Exchange:

1. Offer is subject to FIRST PARTY (Able) securing a new institutional loan on each of the Townsend Street houses in the amount of TWELVE THOUSAND FIVE HUNDRED and No/100 ($12,500.00) DOLLARS, for a total amount of TWENTY-FIVE THOUSAND and No/100 ($25,000.00) DOLLARS, at terms acceptable to him. Proceeds of loan to be paid to SECOND PARTY (Zerbo).

2. This offer also subject to the CONCURRENT close of escrow of the EXCHANGE between Woods, 541/543 Townsend/Zerbo 156 Lincoln Street.

The parties hereto shall execute and deliver, within Fifteen (15) days from the date this offer is accepted, all instruments, in writing, necessary to transfer title to said properties and complete and consummate this exchange. Each party shall supply Preliminary Title Reports for their respective properties. Evidences of title shall be California Land Title Association standard coverage form policies of title insurance, showing titles to be merchantable and free of all liens and encumbrances, except taxes and those liens and encumbrances as otherwise set forth herein. Each party shall pay for the policies of Title Insurance for the property to be acquired ☐ conveyed ☒ .

Figure 5.6

If either party is unable to convey a marketable title, except as herein provided, within three months after acceptance hereof by second party, or if the improvements on any of the herein named properties be destroyed or materially damaged prior to transfer of title or delivery of agreement of sale, then this agreement shall be of no further effect, except as to payment of commissions and expenses incurred in connection with examination of title, unless the party acquiring the property so affected elects to accept the title the other party can convey or subject to the conditions of the improvements.

Taxes, insurance premiums (if policies be satisfactory to party acquiring the property affected thereby), rents, interest and other expenses of said properties shall be pro-rated as of the date of transfer of title or delivery of agreement of sale, unless otherwise provided herein.

John C. Brown   of   147 15th St., Strawberry   Calif.

Broker   Address   Phone No.

is hereby authorized to act as broker for all parties hereto and may accept commission therefrom. Should second party accept this offer, first party agrees to pay said broker commission for services rendered as follows:-

     as agreed in the terms of a separate listing agreement.

Should second party be unable to convey a marketable title to his property then first party shall be released from payment of any commission, unless he elects to accept the property subject thereto. First party agrees that broker may cooperate with other brokers and divide commissions in any manner satisfactory to them.

This offer shall be deemed revoked unless accepted in writing within **Ten (10)** days after date hereof, and such acceptance is communicated to first party within said period. Broker is hereby given the exclusive and irrevocable right to obtain acceptance of second party within said period. Time is the essence of this contract.

Dated **Jan. 15,** 19 **78**

ACCEPTANCE

Second party hereby accepts the foregoing offer upon the terms and conditions stated and agrees to pay commission for services rendered,

to- William Smith   of   62 Light Street.,Strawberry   Calif.

Broker   Address   Phone No.

as follows:-   as agreed in the terms of a separate listing agreement.

Second party agrees that broker may act as broker for all parties hereto and may accept commission therefrom, and may co-operate with other brokers and divide commissions in any manner satisfactory to them.

Should first party be unable to convey a marketable title to his property then second party shall be released from payment of any commission, unless he elects to accept the property of first party subject thereto.

Dated **Jan. 16,** 19 **78**

FORM E 14   REVISED APRIL 1972

Figure 5.6 (continued)

Each owner then paid the normal title and escrow expenses for the property he originally owned. Since each property is deeded only once, there are no duplications of charges (Remember, Zerbo was named as a participant in each agreement).

Each owner owed his broker a real estate fee or commission, based on the listing contract between them. The fees were referred to in the exchange agreements based on those contracts. Again the owner did not have duplicate expenses. He paid only one fee based on the original property that he owned. If the actual fees were written on the exchange agreements, it might have appeared that Zerbo owed more than one fee.

Each owner, except Zerbo, received no cash from the exchange. Each had to pay escrow, title and brokerage fees from their own funds.

[¶503.9]   Generating the Maximum Cash in an Exchange

NEW LOANS ON PROPERTIES. The five-way exchange for tax purposes resulted in each owner getting the type of property that he wanted. The one owner, Zerbo, who wanted a sale, received more cash than he had been asking for in his original terms. All of this cash was secured from new loans on the properties.

By writing the agreements to move Zerbo down through each property as the new loan was placed, the cash was given to him from each new loan in the transaction. Zerbo was a dealer in real estate, unable to save taxes in an exchange, so he had no more tax consequences with the cash from the exchange than he would have had with a sale.

Each of the other owners would have had a tax problem if he had received the cash, then passed it to another. When cash is received in a transaction, it is a taxable event.

[¶504]   HOW TO ADD CASH TO HELP THE EXCHANGE

Owners can add cash to balance equities in an exchange. An example:

OWNER:	A	B
Value of property:	$10,000	$30,000
Loan:	—0—	10,000
Equity:	$10,000	20,000

If A and B wish to exchange properties, it is obvious the equities do not match. A can add enough cash to balance the equity.

OWNER:	A	B
Value of property:	$10,000	$30,000
Loan:	—0—	10,000
Equity:	10,000	20,000
+ Cash	+10,000	
Total Equity & cash	$20,000	$20,000

Total equity and cash given by *A* equals the equity given and received by owner *B*.

[¶505] THE OWNER AS A LENDER—HOW TO USE THE EXCHANGE AND LOAN BACK

An example of this idea started with an exchange between two owners of properties in different cities.

Jackson had a warehouse property on the beach in a seaside resort. The warehouse was vacant. The town had changed from a shipping center to a vacation area. The new economic base was tourism.

The warehouse was approximately 25,000 square feet and was located on a pier. Jackson owned it free and clear of loans and valued the property at $500,000.

Jackson lived in a city, Centerville, 300 miles away and was active in the wholesale jewelry business.

The second owner, Sanders, was a builder/developer. He had recently completed an apartment complex in Centerville and was looking for new challenges. The new apartment complex was valued at $1,200,000 and had a $700,000 existing loan. Since Sanders' equity was $500,000, it matched the value of Jackson beachfront warehouse.

Jackson's broker initiated an offer of the warehouse property for the apartment complex. It was an excellent exchange for Jackson. His benefits were many:

1. His equity would be moved geographically to his home city.

2. His basis in the warehouse property would be stepped up by $700,000 to give him more depreciation for tax shelter.

3. He moved his equity from a dead position, with no income, to an active investment with a spendable income.

4. Any capital gains on the old property would not be taxed as the transaction would be tax-deferred.

Sanders' received the offer from his broker and they took a trip to the seaside town. After a short inspection of the building and the area, he was convinced that he wanted to continue the negotiation. The town swarmed with tourists and the warehouse was perfectly located to convert to shops, restaurants, etc. to cater to the visitors.

Sanders received an enthusiastic response from the city planners in the seaside town. The city was anxious to expand the tourist economy and was willing to cooperate with permits and zoning changes, to convert the eyesore warehouse to a commercial complex.

Sanders accepted the offer, subject to:

1. His ability to secure a new loan of $400,000 on the warehouse property to finance the conversion; the loan to be funded within 60 days of the acceptance of the offer.

2. Receiving permits and rezoning on the warehouse property from the city and approval of his conversion plans within 30 days.

An escrow was opened and Sanders and his broker began to work on removing the contingencies. The rezoning and permits were quickly gotten from the city, and the contingencies quickly removed. The problem developed with the financing of the property.

Money was "tight" nationwide at this time and few loans were being made on commercial property. The local lenders had some money for loans, but had reserved most of it for financing single-family homes in their community.

In addition, Sanders had less than a perfect financial statement at this time. Since he was realizing no cash out of the apartment complex, he had less cash than the banker felt he should have to make the $400,000 loan. In addition he was not well known to the local lenders.

The speculative nature of the venture that Sanders had planned was also reason for lenders to shy from the loan.

After trying for weeks, Sanders and his broker had exhausted all leads and had been turned down by all the local banks. It appeared that the transaction would be canceled by the failure to clear the financing contingency.

Sanders broker reported the problem to Jackson and Jackson's broker. Jackson had been waiting impatiently to close the escrow and move his equity into the new apartments. The tax benefits of the new property would save him a great deal of money on his next income tax payment.

Jackson's answer was, "How much does he need and how soon can we close the escrow?" The jeweler had a large cash flow from his business and was always ready to invest in a good, sound enterprise.

He had looked favorably on Sanders' plans for development of the warehouse from the start. Jackson felt that he might have done it himself if he was not so busy and so far away.

Jackson became the lender, put up the $400,000 and now had a mortgage on the property that he had previously owned.

With the loan contingency removed, the escrow closed.

[¶506]   EIGHTEEN-POINT CHECKLIST FOR DRAFTING EXCHANGE AGREEMENTS

☐ Parties: The full names and addresses of all interested parties should be clearly set forth. Also their interest in the property should be clearly expressed (for example, John H. Jones and Mary S. Jones, husband and wife, as joint tenants; John Fennell and Joseph Fennell, each as to an undivided one-half interest).

☐ Properties: A complete legal description of each of the properties which are the subject of the exchange should be set forth. The description should include the actual legal description and the address of each of the properties.

☐ Encumbrances: After the legal description of each of the properties has been set forth, the property should further be described with reference to encumbrances of every kind against it. The terms, conditions, and balances of loans of record should be specified in complete detail. Since each property should be considered as encumbered insofar as tax liens are concerned, all tax liens should be recited. All covenants, conditions, restrictions, reservations, rights, rights-of-way, and easements of record to which each property is subject should be fully recited. In addition, if there is a ground lease, the terms of that lease should be recited.

☐ Terms and Conditions: How the exchange is to be accomplished should be stated specifically and in detail. There should be a complete and accurate statement of how the exchange is to be accomplished showing what specific acts each of the parties must perform. The idea here is to present what amounts to a clear blueprint for setting up the escrow instructions. If all the terms and conditions of the exchange are satisfied before going into escrow, you have, in effect, a complete exchange. While values for each of the properties need not be stated, how the equities are to be equalized should be set forth. Thus, it should be stated that the first party or the second party, as the case may be, is to deposit in escrow the amount of cash required to balance these equities, if that is the arrangement that the parties agree to. If equities are to be balanced by receipt of a first or second mortgage or trust deed, the amount and terms of the mortgage or trust deed should be spelled out. Whether or not there is to be approval of rental statements should be clearly stated.

Other terms and conditions should also be spelled out. For example, in the case of apartment rental properties, provisions for refinancing any of the properties should be clearly set forth. How and when the refinancing is to be accomplished should be spelled out. If the exchange is made dependent on the occurrence of certain contingencies, these contingencies should be set forth. How and when the contingencies are to be eliminated should be specifically stated.

☐ Blank Spaces: Don't leave any blank spaces in your form. For example, dates and the number of days within which specified acts must be performed should be carefully filled in.

☐ Title: The title reports and title insurance policies that the parties are required to supply, the nature of the title the parties are required to establish should all be clearly set forth. The parties' duty to pay for title insurance policies for the properties acquired or conveyed should be specifically spelled out.

☐ Brokers: The broker's (or brokers') name, address, and telephone number should be set forth. Complete information with respect to all the brokers involved should be given so as to identify, without question, every broker.

☐ Exclusive Right: Where the parties so agree, the form should set forth the broker's exclusive and irrevocable right to obtain acceptance of the offer to exchange from the second party within the period during which the second party can accept the offer. This, in effect, gives the broker an exclusive right to negotiate with respect to the first party's property. How much time after the signing of an exchange agreement will be required to obtain acceptance depends on many factors. Each broker will have to judge for himself how much time he will need, keeping in mind that in arranging any exchange one of the key factors is sufficient time.

☐ Commissions: State exactly, in dollars and cents, the amount of commissions and how that amount is to be paid. Detailed instructions for payment may be required where you have a multiple exchange. The statement may be that a commission shall be paid "as set forth in a commission agreement signed this date." Each of the individual brokers involved should enter into a commission agreement with his principal.

But if there are no complicated or lengthy commission agreements, the actual amount of commission each broker is to receive, in dollars and cents, should be set forth in the exchange agreement.

☐ Revocation of Offer: The form should set forth that the offer to make the exchange shall be deemed revoked unless it is accepted in writing within a specified time and such acceptance is communicated to the offeror within that time.

☐ Defects of Title: Provisions should be made that if either party cannot convey title as agreed within a specified time, the agreement shall be of no further effect except as to payment of commissions, etc., unless the opposite party elects to accept the title the other party can convey.

☐ Destruction of Improvements: A similar provisions should be included applicable where improvements on one of the properties are destroyed or materially damaged.

☐ Proration of Expenses: A provision should be included calling for the proration of taxes, insurance premiums, rents, etc.

☐ Signatures and Authorization: The party (or parties) making the offer to exchange should sign his (or their) full name (or names) at the conclusion of the instrument.

Some exchangors recommend that where the form requires a date, the principal write the date in his own handwriting.

In the case of a corporation, the authorized signatures for the consummation of an exchange by the corporation should be indicated and, in addition, the seal of the corporation should be affixed to the exchange agreement. A copy of the resolutions of the minutes authorizing the exchange should also be made a part of the exchange agreement.

☐ Acceptance: The acceptance form should clearly state that the second party (the offeree) accepts the offer on the terms and conditions set forth therein and agrees to pay commissions to the broker for the services rendered. The broker's name, address, and phone number should be given so that there is no question as to his identity.

☐ Commissions: The terms and conditions of the broker's right to commissions should be stated. The amount should be set forth. If there is a separate commission agent, the acceptance form should so state.

☐ Signatures: The second party or parties should sign the acceptance form at its conclusion. It is recommended that the date be handwritten by one of them.

☐ Binding Contract: An exchange agreement, when properly executed and signed by both parties to the exchange, is a valid and binding legal document. With this document the escrow officer can actually set up the required escrow. Each of the parties to the exchange must specifically perform his function as described in the exchange agreement.

[¶507]   AGREEMENT FOR EXCHANGE OF PROPERTIES
CONTEMPLATING SALE BY THIRD PARTY

This agreement, entered into this _____ day of _____, 19 __, between ABC Corporation, a corporation organized and doing business under the laws of the State of _____, hereinafter referred to as "Owner," and XYZ Corporation, a corporation organized and doing business under the laws of the State of _____, hereinafter referred to as "Optionee,"

<u>Witnesseth:</u>

Whereas Owner is the owner in fee of certain real property (give description), hereinafter referred to as "Subject Property." And whereas, for purposes of this Agreement, Subject Property is divided into two parcels, hereinafter referred to as Parcel A, comprising 200 acres, and Parcel B, comprising 250 acres (give description).

And whereas Owner desires to exchange Parcels A and B of Subject Property for other property of like kind and having these transactions qualify as exchanges under §1031 of the Internal Revenue Code of 1954 (and under state revenue laws), now, therefore, the parties mutually agree as follows:

(1) In consideration of $_____ paid by Optionee to Owner, the receipt of which is hereby acknowledged, Owner hereby grants to Optionee the sole and exclusive option to acquire Parcel A of Subject Property. This option shall automatically terminate and be of no further force and effect at _____ p.m. on the _____ day of _____, 19__. If Optionee has not duly exercised this option to acquire Parcel A of Subject Property as herein provided, the $_____ paid to Owner by Optionee as consideration for this option shall be retained by and be the exclusive property of Owner without any liability to Optionee, and this Agreement shall automatically terminate in its entirety and be of no further force and effect.

(II)   The option as to Parcel A of Subject Property shall be executed by Optionee delivering written notice of exercise addressed to Owner not before the _____ day of _____, 19__. and not later than _____ p.m. on the _____ day of _____, 19__., at the place herein provided in this agreement for notices to be sent. Such written notice shall be considered to have been delivered after personal delivery to Owner at the address to which notices are provided to be sent in this agreement or within 24 hours after deposit in any branch of the Post Office in the State of _____, addressed as provided in this agreement, registered or certified mail, return receipt requested, with postage prepaid in full.

(III) On the timely exercise of the option as provided above, Owner shall thereafter have until the _____ day of _____, 19__, to exchange Parcel A of Subject Property for other property of like kind provided, however, that such exchange be consummated on or before the _____ of _____, 19__.

On Owner's entering into an exchange of Parcel A for other property, Owner will cause the person or persons who will become the owner or owners of Parcel A to agree in writing to sell Parcel A to Optionee according to the following terms and provisions:

(1) In the event that Parcel A is not exchanged by Owner in a consummated transaction within the time provided above, said Parcel A shall be sold by Owner to Optionee as follows:

(2) Optionee shall acquire Parcel A from Owner or from such other person or persons who then own Parcel A, for the price and on the terms as set forth herein. On or before _____ business days after Optionee has duly exercised the option herein granted, Owner shall enter into an escrow at KLM Title Company, City of _____, State of _____, or cause the person or persons with whom Owner has entered into an exchange for Parcel A to enter therein, with Optionee, for the sale of Parcel A. The escrow shall provide for closing not later than the _____ day of _____, 19__. The value and purchase price of Parcel A shall be $_____, which shall be paid in cash at the close of escrow, and Optionee shall not be entitled to any credit for the sum of $_____ already paid under the terms of paragraph I of this Agreement.

(3) The parties agree to execute escrow instructions as an accommodation for assisting the escrow holder in consummating the escrow transaction. If no escrow instructions are executed, the terms of this Agreement shall be considered to be instructions to the escrow holder.

(4) The escrow shall be governed by the following provisions:

(a) Parcel A shall be conveyed to Optionee free and clear of encumbrances, except any lien or liens for real property taxes and assessments not then delinquent, and any lien or charge suffered or created by Optionee on Parcel A. The title shall be subject only to restrictions, reservations, easements, and right-of-way of record as of the date this Agreement is executed but no others. Title shall also be subject to any future bonds and assessments placed of record after the date hereof.

(b) All real property taxes and assessments for the then current fiscal year shall be prorated to the close of escrow.

(c) The seller and purchaser under the escrow shall pay the customary charges of KLM Title Company for its services and delivery of a standard coverage title insurance policy. In particular, seller shall pay for the standard title insurance policy. Seller and purchaser shall each pay one-half of the escrow fee. Purchaser shall pay for the recordation of documents. Any unusual charges shall be at the expense of the party causing such expense.

(IV) If Optionee exercises the option set forth in Paragraph I of this Agreement and acquires Parcel A of Subject Property according to all of the applicable conditions thereto, Optionee shall have the exclusive right and option to acquire Parcel B of Subject Property on the terms and conditions hereinafter set forth. The option to acquire Parcel B shall automatically terminate and be of no further force and effect on the Optionee's failure to perform any condition hereinabove specified in this Agreement within the time limitation provided therefor, or on the Optionee's failure to exercise such option as hereinafter provided, and, in such event the $_____ paid by Optionee to Owner under Paragraph I hereof as consideration for this option shall be retained by Owner and be its exclusive property.

(V) Optionee shall exercise the option as to Parcel B of Subject Property by delivering to Owner at the address to which notices herein are provided to be sent, a written notice of exercise of option as hereinafter provided in paragraph VI. Said written notice, shall be considered to have been delivered after personal delivery to Owner at the address to which notices are provided to be sent or within 24 hours after deposit in any branch of the Post Office in State of _____, addressed as herein provided, registered or certified mail, return receipt requested, and postage fully prepaid.

(VI) The written notice of exercise of the option to acquire Parcel B of Subject Property shall be made in the manner described in paragraph V but shall be effective only if given during one of the periods of time set forth below. The value and purchase price of Parcel B shall be adjusted upward depending on the date the option is exercised. The applicable value and purchase price of Parcel B per gross acre is hereinafter set forth opposite the respective periods of time for exercise of such option, as follows:

Period of Time	Value Per Gross Acre
(1) 16 day of June 19— to 30 day of June 19—	$_____
(2) 16 day of Sept. 19— to 30 day of Sept. 19—	$_____
(3) 16 day of Dec. 19— to 31 day of Dec. 19—	$_____
(4) 16 day of March 19— to 31 day of March 19—	$_____
(5) 16 day of June 19— to 30 day of June 19—	$_____
(6) 16 day of Sept. 19— to 30 day of Sept. 19—	$_____

(VII) On timely exercise of the option as hereinabove provided, Owner shall thereafter have _____ days within which to exchange Parcel B of Subject Property for other property of like kind provided, however, that such exchange will be consummated on or before _____ days from the date the option is exercised. On Owner's entering into an exchange of Parcel B for other property, Owner will cause the person or persons who will become the owner or owners of Parcel B to agree in writing to sell Parcel B to Optionee according to the following terms and provisions.

(1) In the event that Parcel B is not exchanged by Owner in a consummated transaction within the time provided above, it shall be sold by Owner to Optionee as follows:

(2) Optionee shall acquire Parcel B from Owner or from such other person or persons who then own Parcel B for the price and on the terms set forth herein. On or before _____ days from the date the option is exercised, Owner shall enter into an escrow at KLM Company at its then existing office in _____ County, State of _____, or cause the person or persons with whom Owner has entered into an exchange for Parcel B to enter therein, with Optionee for the sale of all of Parcel B. Said escrow shall provide for closing by not later than _____ days from the date the option to acquire Parcel B is exercised. The purchase price shall be paid in cash at the close of escrow but Optionee shall be entitled to credit for the sum of $_____ already paid as option money under the terms of paragraph I of this Agreement.

(3) The escrow shall be governed by the following provisions:

(a) Parcel B shall be conveyed to Optionee free and clear of encumbrances, except any lien or liens for real property taxes and assessments not then delinquent, and any lien or charge suffered or created on Parcel B by Optionee. The title shall be subject only to restrictions, reservations, easements, and rights-of-way of record at the date of execution of this Agreement, but no others. Title shall also be subject to any future bonds and assessments placed on record after the date hereof.

(b) All real property taxes and assessments for the then current fiscal year shall be prorated to the close of escrow.

(c) The seller and purchaser under such escrow shall pay the customary charges of KLM Title Company for its services and delivery of a standard coverage title insurance policy. In particular, seller shall pay for the standard title insurance policy. Seller and purchaser shall each pay one-half of the escrow fee. Purchaser shall pay for the recordation of documents. Any unusual charges shall be at the expense of the party causing such expense to occur.

(VIII) As an alternative to the manner of exchanging Parcels A and B of Subject Property as set forth above in paragraphs III and VII of this Agreement, Optionee agrees to cooperate fully with Owner and to purchase other lands which Owner may wish to receive in exchange for Parcels A or B, or both. Optionee shall be put to no additional cost or expense because of the exchange transactions. The closing dates and other provisions of this Agreement shall remain unchanged.

(IX) Owner hereby grants to Optionee a nonexclusive license to go onto Subject Property from time to time during the option period referred to in paragraph I hereof, for the sole and exclusive purpose of allowing Optionee to conduct engineering, soil, and other tests thereon. Optionee shall indemnify and hold Owner harmless from any and all damage caused by Optionee or its agents to the land, crops, and the cattle grazing thereon. Optionee shall be responsible for any hazards created by reason of its conduct on Subject Property. After performing its tests and engineering work, Optionee shall restore the land substantially to the same condition that existed before Optionee's conduct thereon. Before Optionee goes onto said land, Optionee shall direct a notice to Owner so stating its intention in order to enable Owner to post such notices of nonresponsibility as Owner may wish. Owner's failure to post notices of nonresponsibility shall not be deemed to be a failure on its part to mitigate damages, if any, caused by Optionee through its conduct on such land. Optionee shall indemnify and hold Owner harmless from any and all materialmen's, mechanics', laborers' and other liens arising out of its activity on Subject Property. Said license to go onto Subject Property shall be only for the limited purpose of performing engineering, soil tests, and other tests by Optionee, and such license shall automatically terminate and be of no further force and effect after the option period referred to in paragraph I hereof expires, or when said tests have been completed, whichever occurs first. After that time, Optionee shall not have the right to possession of any portion of Subject Property until Optionee acquires fee title to Subject Property.

(X) Neither this agreement nor any right or interest thereunder shall be assigned by Optionee without Owner's prior written consent. Optionee may, without first obtaining Owner's consent, assign Optionee's entire rights under this Agreement to a corporation in which Optionee owns at least 50% of the voting stock, or to a joint venture in which Optionee owns at least a 50% interest in the profits therefrom. But Optionee shall notwithstanding any such assignment remain liable hereunder.

(XI) Notice which either party may be required under this Agreement to give or which either party is permitted or may desire to give to the other party or to the escrow holder shall be in writing. Notice may be given by personal delivery or by mailing it by certified or registered mail, return receipt requested, to the party to whom the notice is directed at said party's address as follows or at such other address as may be hereafter designated by the parties:

Address of Owner:

_____

_____

Address of Optionee:

_____

_____

Address of Escrow Holder (Title Co.):

_____

_____

Notice given by mail shall be considered as given on the day after the day on which it is deposited in the mail, properly addressed as provided above with postage thereon prepaid in full, if mailed in the County of _____. If mailed elsewhere, notice shall be considered as given on the second day after mailing.

In witness whereof this Agreement has been executed at City of _____, County of _____, State of _____, by the parties hereto as of the day and year first above written.

CHAPTER 6

R.E.O. Marketing

[¶600]   **BANKS AND SAVINGS AND LOANS
MAKE MISTAKES TOO!**

Foreclosure! Sold for taxes! Taken back by the bank!

Bad situations. These phrases have an impact on anyone who hears them. Most people immediately form a mental picture of some sort of situation. A heartless banker portrayed in a play, movie or T.V. drama. The Okies in "The Grapes of Wrath." The mental picture usually will be of the property owner—at the end of his rope, losing his property.

It happens. Every day, everywhere in the country, property does go back to lenders through foreclosure. People have financial problems. They go broke and file bankruptcy. They move away and abandon property. Some of them have to be evicted. Others make it easy and deed the property to the lender "in lieu of foreclosure."

In many of these cases, the property loan was the biggest contributor to the problems of the owner. He may have gotten the loan when he shouldn't have. In this type of situation—a small percentage—the lender started the inevitable foreclosure when the loan was granted.

Most have other problems, usually unforeseen. Medical problems, business reverses, failures of marriages are big contributors. The list of reasons can include almost any problem, financial or otherwise, that one can imagine.

The result is the same. The lending institution or an individual who forecloses now has the property. It must now be marketed.

[¶601]   **R.E.O. OR O.R.E.
(OR WHATEVER IT IS CALLED)**

Many Savings and Loans call their foreclosed properties their "Real Estate Owned" (R.E.O.). Often, commercial banks call them their

106

"Owned Real Estate" (O.R.E.). These seem to be the most used names for the foreclosed properties that these lending institutions have—and wish that they did not.

In addition to these names, there are probably hundreds of others used for these properties in individual lending institutions throughout the United States.

We will use *R.E.O.* in this chapter as the designation for the property owned by the lender "involuntarily" by foreclosure.

[¶602] FORECLOSURE IS NOT USUALLY PROFITABLE FOR ANYONE

When a property owner is in financial trouble and all else fails, he often sells his real estate rather than lose it. For a quick sale, he may offer it at, or reduce it to, a bargain price. We may see his or his broker's ad in the paper—"Distress Sale—Make Offer." Many of these properties are sold quickly for cash at bargain prices before a foreclosure. This type of advertising will certainly attract lookers and bargain hunters.

To the seller, it seems logical that getting something—anything out of a property through a sale may be better than losing it completely.

Therefore, many properties that are in the lender's R.E.O. portfolio are the ones that couldn't be sold. The owner didn't have enough equity above the loan to make a sale offering attractive to a buyer.

HERE'S AN EXAMPLE:

A buyer purchases a house for $45,000 in a California city. He makes a down payment of $4,500—10 percent. He applies for, and gets, a new 80 percent loan on the house. The lender puts up $36,000. The seller agrees to "carry back" a second loan of $4,500.

So, our buyer has only an equity of $4,500 in a $45,000 home. He owes two loans, one to the Savings and Loan for $36,000 and one to the previous owner for $4,500. If everything goes well, he can make out.

When the previous owner had placed the home on the market at $45,000 he had lived there several years. His loan was paid down to only $19,000. When he sold, he received $17,000 cash from the new loan ($36,000 less 19,000 = $17,000) plus the $4,500 down payment. This gave him total cash at the sale of $21,000. In order to sell, he also carried back the second loan of $4,500.

The buyer's financial trouble started a few months later. He was laid off. He fell behind in both loans. In a short time it was obvious—he was going to lose the house.

During the few months of occupancy and the period time that a foreclosure takes, the house and grounds were abused. The buyer knew he was losing the property and didn't care, and part of the time it was abandoned. Quickly, windows were broken and doors were hanging. A partially dismantled car was in the driveway.

The home could not be sold by lowering the price. The owner's equity had disappeared with the vandals.

The previous seller had moved to another state. When he checked the property, he was appalled by the condition. Since no payments had been made for months, the interest on the first loan had increased the balance above $36,000. The seller weighed the costs of refurbishing—and the selling costs of another sale. It could easily amount to more than his second loan. Since he had received $21,500 in cash from the original sale, he decided not to foreclose.

So, in due time, the Savings and Loan acquired a new property for the R.E.O. portfolio. When the first trust deed, held by the lender foreclosed, the second loan was "wiped out." The holder of the second loan lost his $4,500.

The original loan from the Savings and Loan was $36,000. Six months had passed without any payments of interest. At 9 percent, this was an interest loss of $1,620. If the property was sold "as is" for a price of $40,000, the costs could easily eat up the difference. The lender could see his position as follows:

Interest Loss	$ 1,620
Original Loan	36,000
Selling Commission (6% of $40,000)	2,400
Misc. Expenses, Title—Recording	700
etc.	$40,720

These figures are typical. Very few lenders have ever made any money on a foreclosed property.

In addition to the break-even or loss figure at the foreclosure, every day that the property is owned costs more money. Since the loan originally made on the property is not bringing in any interest, that amount of loss continues to mount each day.

[¶603]   CONVENTIONAL MARKETING PLAN FOR FORECLOSED PROPERTY

Large lending institutions have a department to handle their foreclosed property. Smaller companies may assign the marketing of the R.E.O.'s to an officer as an additional assignment.

The marketing usually consists of advertising by the lender in newspapers and circulating lists of the properties to real estate brokers. The lending institution usually will not list the property with a real estate firm on an exclusive basis. As shown in our example, the real estate commission might put the account into a much larger loss. The hope is that the lender can sell it and save that substantial amount.

Since the lenders have some experience in disposing of real estate, they usually have better luck selling property without a broker than does the general public. However, a "slow" real estate market—caused by local conditions or by a mild national recession, can put the conventional marketing plan into a disaster. Of course, during this type of economic slump, the foreclosures multiply.

Suddenly, the R.E.O. portfolios bulge. Millions of dollars of the lenders' assets are tied up in property. There is no cash return to the banks on any of these millions.

[¶604]   WHO MIGHT HAVE R.E.O. PROPERTIES

We have been referring to Banks and Savings and Loans. Here is a partial list of lenders or insurors who might have R.E.O.s.

1. Savings and Loans (Historically the largest R.E.O. owner. A high ratio of loan to value and loans on homes and small apartments contribute to high numbers.) On the other side of the coin, these properties are easiest to dispose of.
2. Banks. (Banks may soon be largest source of R.E.O. property in the country because of loans to R.E.I.T. customers.)
3. Real estate Investment Trusts (R.E.I.T.)
4. Insurance Companies.
5. Federal Housing Administration.
6. Veterans Administration.
7. Bonding Companies.
8. Mortgage Guarantee Insurance Corp. and other private mortgage Insurors.
9. Private 2nd Trust Deed or Mortgage lenders.
10. Private Mortgage Companies.
11. Small Business Administration (Real Estate received back with a business.)
12. General Services Administration.
13. Credit Unions.
14. Bank Trust Departments. (Usually different from a R.E.O. Department.)
15. Union Pension Funds.

[¶605]   **BENEFITS OF EXCHANGES**
                         FOR R.E.O. PROPERTY

While the public usually will buy property for cash directly from a lending institution, brokers usually think cash *and* exchange. Of the exchange offers that lenders may receive, most will be submitted by brokers. Often these will be for the brokers' own investment portfolios—or for sophisticated clients.

The benefits that one can get from an exchange with a lender with R.E.O. property are:

1. There is a great amount of property of all classes. It has been estimated that banks have *Eight Billion* in delinquent loans from R.E.I.T.s alone.
2. The broker usually gets a cash commission.
3. Since the lender is in the "money" business, there is built-in financing available in *any* market.
4. The broker's commission is usually a full commission without a "split" with another broker. He works directly with the bank's R.E.O. representative.
5. The lender can solve other problems for both the broker and the broker's clients. He can make loans on other properties in addition to the problems that are solved for him.
6. The lender will be cooperative in most beneficial transactions, allowing time or any other assistance in arranging tax deferred exchanges.

[¶605.1]   Benefits to the Lender

1. The lender may reduce his R.E.O. file. Millions of dollars of dead equity are transformed into interest-earning notes. The lender is back in business on these equities.
2. The loans are often with a "strong" investor—probably a better-secured loan than the original loan.
3. Through the exchange, the lender may get opportunities to make loans on other good properties.
4. Through association with an aggressive knowledgeable exchangor, the lender may avoid some foreclosures. By referring his delinquent owners to the exchangor, the problems may be solved for the debtor without the problems and expense of foreclosure.

[¶605.2]   Examples of Benefit Exchange of R.E.O. Property

Example #1

Lester Smith had listed his land for sale with a broker, Helen Stokes.

During the interview with the owner, Helen had found that Smith had a very low cost basis in the land. He had paid only $2,000 for the three-acre parcel ten years before. The property was now valued at approximately $100,000.

Since the original purchase, the adjacent street had been transformed into a major boulevard, as the city grew in that direction. The estimated value was based on comparable sales of nearby property.

Smith agreed to list the property with Helen's firm for $110,000.

When the listing was started, Helen discussed Smith's tax problem with him. He would have a taxable gain of $108,000 on a $110,000 sale, at long-term rates, of course. Lester was aware of this problem.

However, Smith felt that the money was tied up in a property that was doing him little good. His motivation was to free up his investment capital for other investments. He was not a developer and could not personally use the property.

The three-acre parcel was zoned for Roadside Commercial, such as motels or service stations. Lester wanted to invest in residential income property as he preferred that type of investment.

After Helen Stokes explained the possible benefits of a tax-deferred exchange, Smith became enthusiastic about the possibility.

Soon, Helen located an excellent apartment property priced at $450,000. Lester's equity of $110,000 would make a perfect down payment. After showing the property, she and Smith prepared an offer of exchange of the $110,000 parcel for the apartment property, subject to the sale of the acreage for the apartment owner.

The offer was considered by the apartment owner, but was refused. The seller of the apartment had another offer—all in cash—for $435,000. He chose to accept the offer of a little less, rather than close on the three-acre parcel. He was afraid of waiting for a sale on the smaller parcel.

In the meantime, Helen had been advertising the roadside parcel. A few weeks after the failed exchange, a representative from a major oil company approached the broker. The parcel looked good to them and was under consideration as a site for a service station. An offer would probably come when their study was completed. The sale would be for all cash.

Now, with a buyer imminent, the broker was unable to locate a suitable apartment property for Lester Smith. Checking all of the properties that had been for sale, she found that none were now available. It appeared that a wait for the best property might be the best idea. The oil company was a perfect user for Lester's acreage. Smith suggested that it might be best to accept the sale and pay the tax.

It appeared that a sale at $110,000 would give him the gain of $108,000 resulting in a tax for Smith of about $27,000. This would leave him with approximately $83,000 as a down payment on his new investment.

Helen made the following proposal to Smith. She knew of a number of houses at various prices that were owned by a bank after foreclosure. She thought that they could exchange the three-acre parcel for houses valued at a total of $110,000 in an equity for equity exchange.

Here's how it would work. With a list of 20 houses of the bank's R.E.O. listings, they would inspect all of them. When they found the best, valued at around a total of $110,000, they would make an offer of exchange.

After they inspected the houses, the broker prepared an exchange agreement, offering Smith's three-acre parcel for the four houses that they had chosen. The houses were valued at $25,000, $32,500, $25,000 and $27,500, for a total of $110,000.

When Helen Stokes presented the offer to the bank's officer, she showed him the file of corespondence with the oil company. The bank, after a meeting of several officers and the branch manager, accepted the offer, (1) subject to the sale of the three-acre parcel at terms acceptable to the bank and, (2) a time limit of sixty (60) days on the entire transaction.

Helen Stokes opened the escrow. It was a simple transaction, calling for an equity for equity exchange. Smith's lot of three acres valued at $110,000 for four houses valued at the same amount. The real estate on each side of the transaction was free and clear of any loans.

Helen notified the oil company of the steps that had been taken. Within a few days, the oil company contacted Helen with an offer to purchase the roadside site for $110,000.

Thirty days later, the exchange and subsequent purchase of the three acres closed escrow. The bank and Lester Smith exchanged properties as agreed. The bank then sold the roadside parcel to the oil company for cash.

Smith received the four houses. The bank received the three-acre parcel, then sold it for $110,000 cash. The oil company had purchased the land that they had wanted, but not from the original owner.

Following the close of the transactions a few days later, Helen Stokes and Smith, her client, again contacted the bank. Since Lester now owned the four houses free and clear of any loans, he applied for new 80 percent loans on the properties. Since Smith's financial statement was excellent, the loans were granted. A few days after he received $88,000 cash in new loans on the four houses.

The broker took over management of the four houses for Smith. The properties were rented for a figure that paid the monthly payments and expenses. Smith received no spendable income, but the houses did not cost him anything to own, a break-even investment.

Three months later, Helen Stokes found the perfect investment property that Smith was seeking. The apartment was for sale for $440,000. Smith purchased it, using his $88,000 cash as 20 percent down. Since this transaction was a purchase, Smith had a cost basis in the property for the full amount of his purchase price of $440,000.

Recapping the transactions, here are the benefits that *Smith* realized:

1. He made a tax-deferred exchange from the highway frontage property to the four houses.
2. After the close of escrow, he applied for loans of $88,000 on his new properties. This was a tax-free event. Borrowing money on property already owned is not taxable.
3. He had $5,000 more cash than he would have had if he had sold the property. The loans brought $88,000 while he probably would have had only $83,000 after taxes on a sale. He also had $22,000 equity in houses.
4. Smith had the benefit of cash to negotiate with, rather than equity. His bargaining would be stronger.
5. Smith's original adjusted cost basis of $2,000 had been transferred to *four* properties instead of just *one*. It was his intent to hold these properties for some time as investments. In later years, if he chose to sell them, he had the benefit of choosing *when* he wanted to be taxed on his gain. He could have the flexibility to spread his capital gains tax over *four* different tax years.
6. The four houses also gave Smith the flexibility to exchange "up" into other properties, separately or as a group.
7. Smith now had five different properties, the houses and the apartment building giving him the benefit of debt reduction. The tenants in all five properties were reducing the mortgages each month with little cost to Smith.

Benefits to the *bank*.

1. Moved $110,000 worth of R.E.O. houses in an exchange for the lot.
2. Immediately cashed out the lot for $110,000.
3. Acquired a new, good customer—Smith.
4. Made four good loans on four houses to an owner with a strong financial statement, at current interest rates.

Benefits to the *oil company*.

1. Acquired a new business site immediately at fair market value.

Benefits to *Helen Stokes,* broker.

1. Solved her client's problem of disposing of his highway lot. Collected her fee of $6,600 from Lester Smith.
2. Collected a full commission of another $6,600 from the bank for disposing of their R.E.O. houses.

3. Collected a third commission of another $13,200 in a split of the commission of $26,400 on the sale of the apartment sold to Smith. (Other half of commission was paid to the broker representing the seller.)
4. Acquired five properties for management.
5. Probably will continue to handle Lester Smith's future real estate transactions. May, also, be hired by the bank for handling other problem properties for them.

Example #2

Jackson has land near the edge of growing town. It might be ready for development in two to three years if the town continues its growth in that direction.

The land has been appraised at $50,000.

Jackson needs some cash. He does not want to sell the land because of future growth in value, but the local lenders have a policy of not making loans on unimproved properties.

Jackson offers an exchange of his land for two houses valued at $50,000—both R.E.O. properties at a Savings and Loan. The Savings and Loan refuses the offer, preferring to keep the houses rather than have the land.

Jackson then offers to buy back the land for $55,000 with a $25,000 down payment, immediately after the exchange.

The Savings and Loan accepts.

While the exchange is in escrow, Jackson places loans of $20,000 on each house through his bank. At the close of escrow on the exchange, he receives the two houses—now with a loan on each. So, he has a $10,000 equity in the two houses, plus $40,000 in cash from the two loans. He then pays $25,000 cash down on the land, the Savings and Loan carrying back a $30,000 first loan on the land. This leaves $15,000 cash for Jackson to use now.

Benefits to *Jackson:*

1. He acquired $15,000 in needed cash now.
2. He still owns his land, now with a $30,000 loan on it.
3. He acquired $10,000 equity in two houses.
4. Jackson owns three properties—if land is ready for development in two years, he may be able to sell the houses to pay off much of the loan.

Benefits to the *Lender:*

1. Rid themselves of $50,000 in R.E.O. properties.
2. Sold land for immediate $5,000 profit. Acquired for $50,000 in the exchange and sold for $55,000 on terms.
3. Has a well-secured loan for $30,000 drawing interest for the company.

Example #3

A bank had a large motel as an R.E.O. property. This property was valued at $800,000. The original owner was underfinanced and made a wrong guess about the traffic count on the new highway. He went broke.

After the foreclosure, the bank sold the motel. The down payment had been small and the bank had carried back a large first mortgage. Again, they had been forced to take back the property.

Broker Green was knowledgeable about motel operations. Several years earlier, he had built, operated and then sold several motels.

Recently, Green had been operating a general real estate brokerage firm and had also been building a few small tracts of houses.

When Green received a printed notice from the bank regarding the motel, offered at $800,000, he looked into it.

After an investigation that took a few days, Green was ready to make an offer to the bank. He made the following proposal:

Green offered to exchange $800,000 worth of notes secured by mortgages on houses that he had built during the past few years. In a number of cases, Green had carried back some of the financing for the buyers.

It would be an equity-for-equity exchange. $800,000 in paper in exchange for the $800,000 motel. But Green was not through. He had another condition. The exchange would be contingent upon the bank giving Green a new $500,000 loan on the motel.

After examining the payment records and the security offered by Green (the houses as security for the notes totaling $800,000), the bank accepted the offer with Green's conditions.

Here are the benefits to the *bank*

1. It acquired $800,000 worth of good notes secured by houses. Most of the notes were "seasoned" and were well secured. Foreclosure on any of these seemed very remote.
2. It made a good loan of $500,000 to a strong motel operator. Since Green had a $300,000 equity "above" the note, the lender felt that the loan was well secured.
3. It got rid of an enormous problem, probably for good, transferred the R.E.O. equity into interest-producing notes.

And the benefits to *Green*

1. Green "spent" $800,000 worth of notes for full face value. He did not have to discount the notes as he might have had to do if he had sold them for cash.

2. He acquired a good motel property with only a 60 percent loan on it ($500,000 loan vs. $800,000 value).

3. He had $500,000 cash from a new loan to do whatever he wanted.

[¶606]   **WHO SHOULD BE CONTACTED
                          FOR R.E.O. PROPERTY**

1. BANKS AND SAVINGS AND LOANS

Larger banks and Savings and Loans have departments set up to handle foreclosed property. Smaller institutions may put an officer or branch manager in charge of an occasional property in this category.

Larger organizations may have a Senior Vice-President in charge. Officers may range down to an assistant treasurer or a department manager.

Small banks may refer the property package back to the branch manager who O.K.'d the original loan. (As a punishment?)

Some of these managers of R.E.O. portfolios are efficient and organized. As in other corporations, some individuals are totally incompetent. Since the lender is *not* in the real estate business, care should be exercised. The department handling the property may know very little about it—perhaps no one there has even seen or inspected it.

Contact the regional branch offices of larger banks. They will be able to refer an inquiry to the right individual or department. The same for Savings and Loans. With smaller and local banks and Savings and Loans—start with the local manager for directions. He may be the one.

2. REAL ESTATE INVESTMENT TRUSTS

The president of the trust may be the one who has to make the final decision. A vice-president in charge of property may be in direct charge, but often is property-management oriented. He will probably have to bring most decisions to the president or the Board of Directors. Write or make direct inquiry.

3. INSURANCE COMPANIES

Branch managers in major cities may handle foreclosed property for that area. They can refer you to the right man.

4. F.H.A. and V.A.

Mailing lists are distributed by both the Federal Housing Administration and Veteran's Administration. In addition, both often place ads in the newspapers. Most solicitations are for cash bids. While good loans are available on these properties—it is usually a cash-only market.

5. PRIVATE MORTGAGE INSURORS AND BONDING COM-
PANIES

Inquire. It may be difficult to locate the responsible persons.

6. PRIVATE SECOND LENDERS AND PRIVATE MORTGAGE
COMPANIES

Inquire. They may have their own marketing plans.

7. GENERAL SERVICES ADMINISTRATION AND SMALL
BUSINESS ADMINISTRATION

Mailing lists of surplus government land, Army bases, etc. S.B.A.
may have real estate that was used with a business. Usually a cash-only
market, but may have incredible terms.

8. BANK HOLDING CO.

Locate through the bank R.E.O. department or the bank trust department.

9. BANK TRUST DEPARTMENT

Usually separate from regular R.E.O. department. This will be a
cash-only market usually. However, they might be creative if you will take
some R.E.O. properties also.

[¶606.1]   Problems With R.E.O. Departments

Since lenders are constantly guarding their images, it is often difficult
to find the man in charge of foreclosed property. When he is located, he
may not be able to make any decisions on an unusual-type offer.

An exchange offer may have to be referred to a committee used to
evaluating cash decisions only. If the maker of the offer is not present to
explain the benefits, the committee will probably fail to understand the
offer.

Further, two committees may be involved. The first may rule on the
transaction—the second (and separate) committee may evaluate the transaction again to approve or disapprove any loan that is requested as a part of
the transaction. The offer could be accepted, then the loan turned down by
the second committee.

[¶607]   LENDER ATTITUDES

Attitudes vary greatly. Remember that individuals in a corporation
are not dealing with their own money, so a safe route—doing nothing—

might be the way to preserve a job, even get a promotion.

To clear an R.E.O. portfolio:

One lender may be eager and anxious, (Let's try to make a deal.) Another may be willing to hold the property and hope that inflation will solve all the problems next year.

The aggressive lender may give a real estate broker an exclusive listing on large amounts of property. But, that broker must have a track record of solving previous problems for them.

Before working on R.E.O. property, a broker might wish to interview the department manager to ascertain:

1. Are they anxious to move the properties? Now?
2. The attitude on loans. Will the company carry back loans? Will they make "loans to facilitate?"
3. Whether they will exchange. Have they closed exchanges on R.E.O.s in the past?
4. Who makes the decisions? Is there a committee? Is there more than one committee?
5. What is the lender's listing policy? If no exclusive listing, why not?
6. What is the fee schedule?
7. Will they consider loaning on another property, if we can move an R.E.O.?
8. Can any other entity make a loan if the lender will not? Is there a pension plan that might make a loan? An employee syndicate? Any other?

[¶608]   OTHER R.E.O. TYPE TRANSACTIONS

There are unique things about most R.E.O. properties:

1. The property is usually free and clear of loans.
2. The owner is willing to make loans to qualified individuals, or is willing to "carry back" financing on agreeable terms (in order to solve his problem).
3. The owner usually doesn't really need money.
4. The owner is more interested in getting the equity converted into interest-bearing secured notes than in selling for cash.

There are many other real estate parcels, improved and unimproved, that have most of or all of the same four unique things about them.

The owners of these "R.E.O. type" properties are often older people—perhaps retired. They have accumulated various types of investments in real estate, stocks, bonds, gold and any others that we might think of. During their working years, their investing years, the accent has been on accumulation.

When nearing retirement, or after retirement, the investor now wants the following benefits:

1. Income (regular monthly income from stocks, bonds, mortgages at highest interest rate possible).
2. Care-free investments—he no longer wants to cope with direct management, tenants and similar problems.
3. Safety and security. At this time of life, chance taking has to be over. No time is left to go out, start over and make it all over again.

These benefits wanted by these individuals resemble the safe investments that are also wanted by lending institutions. This owner and the lenders own similar types of property and are looking for similar benefits. Therefore, some of the R.E.O. type exchanges that are made with lenders can also be made with individuals.

Older owners who have retirement income, may be receiving non-taxable or low-tax pensions and Social Security. An exchange that is taxable to them may not be too devastating. The taxable gain may be the only taxable income for the year. Since it will be at long-term rates (usually) and a low tax bracket, it may not hurt much.

For example:

Mr. and Mrs. Jordan just passed retirement age. Each had a small retirement income from a pension plan in addition to Social Security benefits. They had a small, steady income.

At retirement, they had purchased a condominium unit in Florida and were moving from their home in a northern state.

The Jordans had sold their home and had deferred income taxes on the gain because of the purchase of the new residence (condo). However, an investment property that they had owned for years had not sold so quickly.

The investment property was an eight-unit apartment. It had been listed for sale at $200,000. The Jordans owed only $50,000 on a first loan on the property, at 6 percent interest. The payments on the loan were at $500 a month.

The plan was to sell the apartment and invest the proceeds, after tax, in a secure stock or bond for income. They were looking for a safe, management-free investment.

After a few months, the apartment property had not sold. The Jordans were reluctant to move and leave the apartment with someone else to manage. It was holding up their move to the Sun Belt.

Since their broker knew their circumstances, he attempted to find a "user" with a small down payment—hoping that the Jordans would carry back part of the equity in a carry back loan.

Finally an offer was received. An exchange, with no money down. The Jordan's broker brought the following offer:

1. A free-and-clear house valued at $40,000 as "down" on the eight-unit apartment.
2. The Jordans were to carry back an all-inclusive note secured by a deed of trust for the balance of $160,000 at 9 percent interest. The payments were to be at $1,600 per month including the interest, with the total balance due and payable in ten years.

The provisions of an all-inclusive or wrap-around trust deed in (2) call for the original borrower to remain responsible for the "underlying" financing. He must make the payments on the original loan out of the amount received from the *wrap-around*.

In this case, the Jordans would receive $1,600 per month on the $160,000 all-inclusive loan. Out of this, they would have to pay $500 monthly on the original $50,000 1st loan on the property. Although the income was adequate, they rejected the offer for the following reasons:

1. They received no cash. Although they didn't need much cash, there wasn't any in the offer. There was none for the $12,000 commission that was owed to the broker and the other small expenses of the transaction.
2. They would still own a local property. It was the local house valued at $40,000. They still didn't want to own even one rental when they moved to Florida.

The broker returned the following day with the following proposal. The commission due to him would be used to purchase the home for him (the broker) as an investment. He would apply for a new loan of $28,000 on the residence property, the proceeds to be paid to the Jordans.

He then showed the Jordans the benefits of the original exchange offer with his additional offer to purchase.

1. The Jordans would own no property in the northern state and could move to Florida.
2. They would have $28,000 cash from the financing of the house received in trade.
3. The commission on the sale of the apartment would be paid in full as the broker would be given $12,000 equity in the house ($40,000 value less $28,000 new loan = $12,000).
4. The Jordans would have a net income of $1,100 a month from the note on the apartment property. ($1,600 less $500 paid on the old loan = $1,100.)
5. Since the old loan of $50,000 would be paid off in approximately 11 years, and the new "wrap around" would run for 15 years, the monthly income would increase to the full $1,600 for the last four years of the loan.

6. The effective interest on the note received was higher than face value. Since the Jordans were receiving 9 percent interest on the whole $160,000, they were receiving 3 percent interest on the $50,000 that was owed to the bank (that loan was at 6 percent). During the first year they would receive $14,400 interest, approximately ($160,000 × 9% = $14,400.) They would be paying $3,000 interest on the original loan ($50,000 × 6% = $3,000.) The difference was the actual interest received by them. ($14,400 less $3,000 = $11,400). Since their actual equity in the loan was only $110,000 ($160,000 less the $50,000 original loan), their yield was 10.36 percent interest. ($11,400 yield ÷ $110,000 equity = 10.36%.)

7. Finally they had the benefit of an installment sale. The down payment was $40,000—only 20 percent of the total value of the apartment. The gain on the sale of the apartments would be spread out over their retirement years—when their taxable income was at its lowest.

With the new offer from the broker, three of the problems were eliminated—(1) cash in hand, (2) broker paid off, and (3) local property moved. With all of the other benefits explained, the Jordans quickly accepted the offers.

All exchanges must benefit everyone in the transaction. Here are the benefits to the other party in this exchange:

The other party was just as motivated as the Jordans. He had owned a house for several years and had used it as a rental. It had originally been purchased for $22,000. His accumulated depreciation was $4,500 so his adjusted cost basis was $17,500.

The house was now appraised at $40,000. This owner's gain would have been $22,500, if he had sold the house ($40,000 less $17,500 basis = $22,500).

When this owner listed his house, it was for exchange up into a larger suitable income property—but only on a tax deferred basis. After the exchange, the owner's new position was:

1. He owned a $200,000 eight-unit apartment.
2. His adjusted cost basis was $177,500. (Old basis + new loan less old loan.) He could re-allocate and start a new depreciation.
3. He was in a better leveraged position.
4. He had deferred all capital gains tax on the gain.

[¶609]   ANOTHER EXAMPLE OF R.E.O. TYPE EXCHANGE

Mrs. Jones had recently been widowed.

She and her husband had purchased a larger home a few months before. Since the first smaller home had not yet been sold, they had not moved into the new home when Mr. Jones died suddenly.

Now that he was gone, the cottage that she lived in was large enough and Mrs. Jones wanted to stay in it. She listed the other house for sale. The price was $50,000, the same as the purchase a few months earlier. The Jones had paid cash, so there was no mortgage on the property.

Mr. Jones had been well insured so Mrs. Jones did not need a large amount of cash. With the help of an investment advisor, she had invested most of the insurance money in safe, secured investments.

The financial advisor also advised that Mrs. Jones carry back the loan on the house being sold. The interest on this investment would bring her 9 or 10 percent, a very good return.

The terms of her listing with a Realty firm were: Price $50,000, with $10,000 as down payment. The owner was to carry back a first loan of $40,000 with payments of $400 per month, including 10 percent interest, with the entire balance due in ten years.

At these terms, a great deal of the monthly payment, at least for the first few years, would be interest. For instance, the first payment of $400 would include $333.33 of interest and only $66.67 of principal. This was a much higher interest than she would have received from investing the $40,000 in a bank or Savings and Loan.

Mrs. Jones didn't actually need the $10,000 down payment. She could have sold the home for nothing down. The entire $50,000 could have been represented in a note secured by the home. However, her financial advisor recommended the down payment of $10,000 for two reasons:

1. It was conventional. Buyers expected to pay a down payment.
2. For security reasons. The house, security for Mrs. Jones' loan, would probably be better cared for if the new owner had a good-sized equity in cash in it. Foreclosures go up, percentage-wise, the lower the down payment.

At this particular time, homes in the area were in supply. After two months of exposure to the sale market, no offer to purchase had been received. Mrs. Jones considered renting the home.

At the same time, in the same town, a developer named Carter was also having problems. Carter had recently acquired a commercial building site to build on. He had paid $100,000 cash for the property. It had seemed like a good idea at the time; he got an excellent buy. Now, he wished he had some of that cash back.

For business reasons, Carter now needed some cash. The lenders in the area would lend on the commercial lot, but the interest rates and "points" on an unimproved lot were high—far too high.

Carter would have jumped at a loan, if he could get the kind of rates being quoted on houses, 9 percent, about 2 percent lower than the commercial loan.

Carter's broker suggested the following offer. Try to acquire the Jones house by offering:

1. $10,000 cash as the listing called for.
2. A note for $40,000. However, instead of the home as security, the note would be secured by a trust deed on the commercial building site worth $100,000.

Carter stated that he needed cash. He didn't have the $10,000 cash for the down payment. The broker explained the following results for both owners:

For Carter:

1. By securing the loan on the shopping center site that he already owned, he would own the home free and clear of any loan.
2. Carter could apply for a new loan on the house for $40,000 while the exchange was in escrow. (The broker had investigated and found that the loan was available.)
3. No tax consequences for Carter. He was buying a property with a note and refinancing a property. Neither was a taxable event.
4. His down payment of $10,000 would come out of the loan.

For Mrs. Jones:

1. The offer would result in terms almost as advertised—$10,000 in down payment.
2. $40,000 in a note secured by a $100,000 property rather than a $50,000 one. (Terms were 10 percent interest only—her advisor strongly recommended this transaction.)
3. This was a no-tax transaction. It would have been taxable an unlike exchange, but Mrs. Jones had *no* gain. Basis was $50,000 in the house.

The offer was accepted. When the transaction closed, here is how each ended up.

For Mrs. Jones:

1. She had $10,000 in cash.
2. She had a $40,000 note at 10% secured by a $100,000 property. Should she have to foreclose, the property would be very valuable. This gave real security to the note.

For Carter:

1. He had cash. He applied for a new loan of $40,000 on the house. At the close of escrow he paid $10,000 to Mrs. Jones and kept $30,000 for himself.

2. $10,000 equity in a house. He now owned the $50,000 house subject to the $40,000 loan.
3. He still owned his commercial building site, worth $100,000, but now with a $40,000 1st loan against it.

Carter had secured $30,000 cash that he needed badly. So he acquired that cash plus the $10,000 equity in the house for creating a $40,000 note against another property. This was an excellent exchange for him.

Mrs. Jones received the same terms that she had asked for.

These exchange transactions were completed by individuals with other individuals—neither of them a lending institution. Each had some of the ingredients found in the typical R.E.O. situation with a lender.

The real estate exchange is possible only when some of the motivations of the owners are known. The less known about the people, the narrower the terms in the transaction. The more we know about the people and what they might do, the more likely we are to make a beneficial transaction for both.

CHAPTER 7

The Role of the Exchange Broker

[¶700]   SALES—BROKERS VS. OWNERS

Look at random through the real estate columns in the classified sections of the newspaper. In many places, ads start, "FOR SALE BY OWNER," then describe the property offered. In some places, the ads from owners are nearly as numerous as the ads placed by professional real estate companies.

These properties offered by owners sell too. At least, some do. Sometimes the buyer and seller get together, negotiate the terms and get the property transferred. Usually, however, the owner gives up after a while and lists with a broker.

There are a number of reasons why an owner might have trouble selling his own property. Some of them are:

1. Often he has only vague information about even simple things that might be asked. Square footage of house or lot, school districts, zoning might not even be known.
2. The owner has little or no information on availability of new loans. Since a buyer may not have this information either, no terms are quoted—only a price.
3. The owner has no ability to find out if the prospective buyer can qualify for any loan. He has no knowledge of the criteria for "qualifying" a potential buyer.
4. The owner is emotionally involved in the property. Simple comments about the property from a prospective buyer often cause an emotional confrontation, particularly if the comments are about deficiencies in the property.
5. Since the owner is not usually adept at any selling techniques, a willing buyer may not even be recognized.
6. The buyer and seller have difficulty with even simple negotiations. Any attempt at changing terms on either side results in either an argument or a stalemate.

Any sales transactions made between the owner and a buyer are often off-balance in benefits to one side or the other. Examples:

1. A desperate seller in trouble offers a sale at bargain prices.
2. A buyer uses a large cash down payment to dictate a lower selling price.
3. The seller outwits the buyer by hiding some pertinent details about the property.

A few owner-to-owner sales are negotiated at fair terms to both sides. In relation to the number of sales that are negotiated by real estate brokers, the percentage is quite small. The real estate professional brings to the transaction all of the factors needed by the buyer and seller to close. He or she will:

1. Complete the "homework" on the property. The professional will be able to answer most questions about the property, the area, zoning, schools, etc., instantly. When a more complicated, unusual problem arises, he knows how to quickly research and get the answer.
2. Before starting the marketing, the broker is aware of available financing for this class of property and can quickly "qualify" a potential buyer as to his ability to secure such financing.
3. The property is only inventory to the broker. He will market it professionally—showing the property as it is. Any questions about any deficiencies are quickly and truthfully answered, and are often items of final negotiation rather than sales "killers."
4. The broker will have up-to-date examples of comparable sales or other appraisal factors to show the value of the property.
5. The professional has been trained in "closing" techniques to assist the buyer to make the offer on the property when he has made up his mind to buy.
6. The "third person" negotiator status of the broker solves the negotiation problem. Offers and counter offers, sometimes up to a dozen different areas of the terms are smoothly worked out between the buyer and the seller.

[¶701]   BROKERS VS. OWNERS IN
NEGOTIATING EXCHANGES

When we examined the real estate columns in the classified section, there was occasionally the ad headed, "FOR EXCHANGE BY OWNER." These are rare.

Even rarer are the actual completed exchanges of real estate by owners. In interviewing dozens of escrow officers and title company executives, and asking about owner-negotiated exchanges, the answer usually was, ''I can't remember ever seeing an exchange between two owners.'' One escrow officer remembered one owner-to-owner exchange in ten years.

Another escrow company manager remarked that owner-to-owner sales were in a ratio of about one to twenty-five to broker-controlled sales. His estimate of owner-to-owner exchanges ''must be no more than one in a thousand.''

Since most exchanges are handled between the owners by brokers, what are the reasons for the high failure rate without the broker?

[¶702]   THE THIRD-PARTY INFLUENCE

Throughout history, negotiations on all levels seem to work better if there is a disinterested third party operating between the adversaries. For instance, a marriage counselor can often solve the problems between a husband and wife. On the national level, third-party negotiators, like Kissinger in the Middle East, can handle negotiations between adversaries who haven't enough common ground to even communicate.

Having an ''in between'' negotiator in a real estate exchange seems to be absolutely necessary. The broker is able to remind each owner why he is trying to exchange the property and the benefits he is seeking.

Most owners either can't or won't list all of the benefits that they have in property, and can't relate benefits to value in an exchange. When owners negotiate, the price of each property becomes the thing that each negotiates or fights over. Each may have only a vague idea of the value of his own property and less of the other's offering.

It has been said that there are three prices or values for each property offered in the marketplace:

1. The value placed on the property by the present owner.
2. The value placed on the property by the potential new owner.
3. The real value of the property.

If this is true, then there are six prices or values to consider when two properties are being traded. No wonder owner-to-owner exchanges fail. If it was possible to get a three-way exchange started between three owners, the opinions of value would be multiplied.

In earlier chapters, it was shown that exchanges can be made if the owners have enough facts to understand the benefits that each will get from the exchange. No exchange can really work unless there are benefits for each owner in the transaction. It is the function of the broker or brokers in the exchange to:

1. Negotiate the best possible transaction that will give benefits for his client.
2. Communicate constantly with the client to be sure that there is an understanding of the benefits originally sought and the progress toward the solution.
3. When the negotiations are completed, take care to handle details to close the transaction.

[¶703]   THE BROKER GETS IT IN WRITING

In interviews with escrow officers, stories have been told of the results of negotiations for the sale of real estate directly between buyer and seller. Since escrow instructions supersede and summarize previous agreements, the terms entered on these are the final terms of transfers.

Often, buyers and sellers enter a title company or escrow office with nothing in writing. They have agreed on a selling price and the general terms of a sale of real estate. They attempt to work out the final terms in the first meeting with the escrow officer. A thorough escrow officer must question them at length to find out the many small details and charges and how the buyer and seller want them handled. It is not unusual for the "sale" to fall through at this point. There were just too many unresolved details between them.

Since so few exchanges are ever attempted between owners in the first place, no escrow officer interviewed could recall an instance of the negotiations between the owners.

Because of legal and practical reasons, real estate brokers use written documents, signed by the parties involved, to negotiate sales or exchanges. Negotiations are handled on a point-by-point basis in writing, so both parties to the transaction have a complete written record.

Here is an example of some simple negotiations between a buyer and a seller in a purchase/sale transaction.

1. Jones offers a house for sale through a listing with a broker. His asking price is $40,000. The house is free and clear of loans.
2. The broker brings a written offer from a potential buyer. The offer is for a price of $35,000 with a $5,000 down payment. The seller is to carry back a $30,000 loan at $300 monthly including 8 percent interest.
3. The seller will not accept. His counter-offer: $38,500 as the price with a $5,000 down payment. Buyer to get a new bank loan for $33,500. This will give the seller all cash.

4. The buyer counters with new terms: $38,500 price with $5,000 down is agreeable. However, he will get a $30,000 loan. Seller to carry back a second loan of $3,500.
5. The seller accepts these terms.

The broker has helped the buyer and seller to negotiate these terms. Each time a change was made between buyer and seller, the change was made in writing and signed. When he presented this change to the other party, the reasons behind the counter in terms were also presented. For instance in #4 above, the buyer had made a preliminary check with his bank and found that a loan of $30,000 was all that the bank would allow.

With his understanding, low-key, third-party influence, the broker is able to hold down emotional confrontations between the principals in the transaction. Without this influence and control, and the constant insistence on all negotiations in writing, buyer and seller seldom get beyond the first tentative verbal offer.

[¶704]   NEGOTIATION USING THE
EXCHANGE AGREEMENT FORM

Negotiating an exchange is different from a sale negotiation. The sale negotiation is for price or terms, or both, on one or more pieces of property. Price is often the most important point in the offers.

In an exchange, since there are always at least two properties, the best points for negotiation are for terms.

Let's say that owners are trying to exchange two properties, both valued at $100,000.

If owner A feels that owner B's property is worth only $95,000, he might counter offer with a lower price. This might bring a reaction from Mr. B. B then simply lowers A's property to $95,000 in his next offer. Both then "stand pat." End of negotiations.

Since the owners are not exchanging cash, but equities, A's broker may have pointed out B's obvious reaction to a price change. If A honestly feels that the equities do not balance, it might be better to do one or more of the following without a change in price:

1. Ask for something as boot. (Perhaps a note or cash.)
2. Change the interest rate up or down on any notes being carried back by one or the other.
3. Change a due date on a note to get quicker use of cash.
4. Counter offer asking Mr. B to pay all title costs, escrow expenses, etc.
5. Ask B to substitute cash in the transaction for any offered notes.
6. Ask B to have the improvements in his offering painted before the close of escrow.

7. Require repairs to any problems in Mr. B's offering during the escrow.

There are many other possibilities to use in a negotiation. If attention can be focused on trading off terms rather than prices, agreements seem to be easier to work out. Some brokers deliberately place terms into the original offer that might be items that can be easily negotiated away in a counter offer.

For instance, in the previous example, Mr. A's broker might ask B to add a note for $10,000 as "boot" in the exchange. If B counter offers at $5,000, then A may have gotten exactly what he wanted. Again, Mr. B might have counter offered to cancel the entire note—but might be ready to accept a compromise in another area of the terms.

The following is an example of a negotiation between two owners in an exchange.

Mr. Able was exchanging a free-and-clear lot valued at $30,000 for a four-unit apartment owned by a builder and developer, Mr. Baker.

Mr. Able was trying to make a tax-deferred exchange up into the income property. Mr. Baker only wanted to move out of the new four-plex that he had just completed. Baker wanted to sell, but was willing to take a lot for part of the consideration.

In the original offer (see Figure 7.1), Able offers his $30,000 lot in exchange for the four-plex. Able offers both cash and a note as "boot" to even up the equities. (The cash is from a new loan to be placed on the acquired property.)

The note that Able offers is "soft" in two ways. It is only at 7 percent and it has a long due date—five years.

Baker will not accept the terms on the note. His counter offer is for 10 percent interest and a due date in only two years (Figure 7.2).

Able counters again with the Seven Percent interest note. This time, however, he agrees to pay off the note in two years. In addition, he changes the terms from INTEREST ONLY to $100.00 per month including interest (Figure 7.3).

Baker now accepts. He will trade the terms of a shorter due date and the larger monthly payment for the low interest note.

Neither owner changed prices on either property in the exchange. All negotiations were in the terms of the second note.

EXCHANGE AGREEMENT

CALIFORNIA ASSOCIATION OF REALTORS STANDARD FORM

MR. ARTHUR C. ABLE

2424 Bonnie Place, Strawberry, Calif.

first party, hereby offers to exchange the following described property, situated in _____ the city of Strawberry

_____ County of _____ Monterey _____ California:

An R-1 zoned 50' X 100' lot located at 1915 Victor St. (Lot 2, Block 25, Tract 124, Strawberry). Free and clear of loans. VALUED AT THIRTY THOUSAND and No/100 ($30,000.00) DOLLARS.

Subject to current property taxes, covenants, conditions, reservations, restrictions, and rights of way of record.

For the following described property of _____ MR. BARTON C. BAKER,

137 Main St. Strawberry, Calif.

the city of Strawberry _____ County of _____ Monterey _____, California:

A four unit apartment located at 2319 Lorna St. (Lot 16, Block 23, Tract 1934, Strawberry). VALUED AT ONE HUNDRED FIFTY THOUSAND and No/100 ($150,000.00) DOLLARS. Subject to a construction loan of EIGHTY THOUSAND and No/100 ($80,000.00) DOLLARS.

Also subject to current property taxes, covenants, conditions, reservations, restrictions, and rights of way of record.

Terms and Conditions of Exchange:

1. FIRST PARTY (ABLE) to transfer lot at 1915 VICTOR ST to SECOND PARTY (BAKER) free and clear of any loans.

2. Subject to FIRST PARTY (ABLE) securing new institutional loan secured by a first trust deed on the LORNA St. property. Loan to be in the amount of ONE HUNDRED TWELVE THOUSAND FIVE HUNDRED and No/100 ($112,500.00) DOLLARS, terms acceptable to FIRST PARTY. Loan to pay off existing loan on the property, then balance paid to SECOND PARTY (BAKER).

3. FIRST PARTY (ABLE) to execute and SECOND PARTY (BAKER) to carry back a note secured by second trust deed on the LORNA St. property in the amount of SEVEN THOUSAND FIVE HUNDRED and No/100 ($7,500.00) DOLLARS, payable monthly at INTEREST ONLY at SEVEN (7%) PERCENT ANNUAL INTEREST, with the full balance due and payable FIVE (5) YEARS from the date of the close of this escrow.

The parties hereto shall execute and deliver, within Thirty (30) days from the date this offer is accepted, all instruments, in writing, necessary to transfer title to said properties and complete and consummate this exchange. Each party shall supply Preliminary Title Reports for their respective properties. Evidences of title shall be California Land Title Association standard coverage form policies of title insurance, showing titles to be merchantable and free of all liens and encumbrances, except taxes and those liens and encumbrances as otherwise set forth herein. Each party shall pay for the policies of Title Insurance for the property to be acquired ☐ conveyed ☒ .

Figure 7.1

If either party is unable to convey a marketable title, except as herein provided, within three months after acceptance hereof by second party, or if the improvements on any of the herein named properties be destroyed or materially damaged prior to transfer of title or delivery of agreement of sale, then this agreement shall be of no further effect, except as to payment of commissions and expenses incurred in connection with examination of title, unless the party acquiring the property so affected elects to accept the title the other party can convey or subject to the conditions of the improvements.

Taxes, insurance premiums (if policies be satisfactory to party acquiring the property affected thereby), rents, interest and other expenses of said properties shall be pro-rated as of the date of transfer of title or delivery of agreement of sale, unless otherwise provided herein.

Prof. Real Estate Co. __of__157 15th St. Strawberry,_____Calif.__ (408) 649-1111
_____
            Broker   Address   Phone No.
is hereby authorized to act as broker for all parties hereto and may accept commission therefrom. Should second party accept this offer, first party agrees to pay said broker commission for services rendered as follows:-
Six (6%) Percent of value of offered property.
_____

_____
Should second party be unable to convey a marketable title to his property then first party shall be released from payment of any commission, unless he elects to accept the property subject thereto. First party agrees that broker may cooperate with other brokers and divide commissions in any manner satisfactory to them.
This offer shall be deemed revoked unless accepted in writing within____Five (5)__days after date hereof, and such acceptance is communicated to first party within said period. Broker is hereby given the exclusive and irrevocable right to obtain acceptance of second party within said period. Time is the essence of this contract.

_____
_____
                                                    _____Arthur C. Able_____
                                                    _____

Dated____March 3,_____19 79____.

A C C E P T A N C E

Second party hereby accepts the foregoing offer upon the terms and conditions stated and agrees to pay commission for services rendered, to:-
Jones Real Estate _____of____116 Short St. Strawberry_____Calif.__ (408) 555-1212
_____
            Broker   Address   Phone No.
as follows:-_____Six (6%) Percent of valued of offered property.
_____
Second party agrees that broker may act as broker for all parties here to and may accept commission therefrom, and may co-operate with other brokers and divide commissions in any manner satisfactory to them.
Should first party be unable to convey a marketable title to his property then second party shall be released from payment of any commission, unless he elects to accept the property of first party subject thereto.
_____This offer accepted subject to the attached counter offer dated March 5, 1979____
_____
                                                    _____Burton C. Behn_____
                                                    _____

Dated____March 5,_____19 79____.

Figure 7.1 (continued)

EXCHANGE COUNTER OFFER

Dated: _MARCH 5, 1979_

The offer to exchange the real property known as _1915 Victor St,_
_Strawberry_____ for real property known as ____
2319 Lorna, Strawberry

Dated _March 3, 1979_____, is not accepted in its present form, but
the following counter offer is hereby submitted:

4. Paragraph #3 is cancelled.

5. FIRST PARTY (ABLE) to execute and SECOND PARTY (BAKER) to carry back a note
___ _secured by a second trust deed on the LORNA ST. property in the amount of_
___ _SEVEN THOUSAND FIVE HUNDRED and No/100 ($7,500.00) DOLLARS, payable monthly_
___ _at INTEREST ONLY At TEN (10%) PERCENT ANNUAL INTEREST, with the full balance_
___ _due and payable TWO (2) YEARS from the date of the close of this escrow._

OTHER TERMS: All other terms remain the same.
RIGHT TO ACCEPT OTHER OFFERS: _Second Party_____ reserves the right to
accept any other offer prior to _First Party_____ acceptance of this
counter offer and _Second Party_____ 's agent being so notified in
writing.
EXPIRATION: This counter offer shall expire unless a copy hereof
with _Mr. Able's_____ written acceptance is delivered to _Mr. Baker_ 's
agent within _Three (3)_____ days from above date.

X__Baylor C. Baker_____

X_____

. . . .

Dated:_____ March 6, 1979_____

The undersigned accepts the above exchange counter offer. SUBJECT TO
COUNTER-OFFER FORM ATTACHED.   X__Arthur C. Able_____

X_____

Figure 7.2

133

EXCHANGE COUNTER OFFER

Dated: <u>March 6, 1979</u>

The offer to exchange the real property known as <u>1915 Victor St.</u>
<u>Strawberry</u>   for real property known as <u>   </u>
<u>2319 Lorna, Strawberry</u>
Dated <u>   March 3, 1979   </u>, is not accepted in its present form, but
the following counter offer is hereby submitted:

6. <u>Paragraph #5 is cancelled.</u>
7. <u>FIRST PARTY (ABLE) to execute and SECOND PARTY (BAKER) to carry back a note</u>
   <u>secured by a second trust deed on the LORNA ST. property in the amount of</u>
   <u>SEVEN THOUSAND FIVE HUNDRED and No/100 ($7,500.00) DOLLARS, payable at</u>
   <u>ONE HUNDRED AND No/100 ($100.00) DOLLARS monthly including SEVEN (7%) annual</u>
   <u>interest, with the full balance due and payable TWO (2) YEARS from the date</u>
   <u>of the close of this escrow.</u>

OTHER TERMS: All other terms remain the same.
RIGHT TO ACCEPT OTHER OFFERS: <u> FIRST PARTY </u> reserves the right to
accept any other offer prior to <u>SECOND PARTY</u> acceptance of this
counter offer and <u>FIRST PARTY</u> 's agent being so notified in
writing.
EXPIRATION: This counter offer shall expire unless a copy hereof
with <u>Mr. Baker's</u> written acceptance is delivered to <u>Mr. Able</u> 's
agent within <u>Three (3)</u> days from above date.

X <u>   Arthur C. Able   </u>
X <u>   </u>

....

Dated: <u>   March 7, 1979   </u>
The undersigned accepts the above exchange counter offer.

X <u>   Borton C. Baker   </u>
X <u>   </u>

Figure 7.3

[¶705]   DEFINING THE PROBLEM WITH THE OWNER

Few owners of real estate start out employing a broker to exchange their property. When a contact is made, usually the owner is inquiring about a possible sale. The few that do start with an idea of exchanging have probably been sent by their attorney or accountant.

A thorough interview is necessary whenever an owner contacts a broker for any reason. Too often, the owner lists his property, sells it, and then brings up the subject of an exchange. A broker can easily say, ''When you sell this property, there will probably be a large gain. What are you going to do with the money?'' This could save a lot of problems later, if asked near the start of any interview with a new client.

About 25 percent of the time, the answer to that question is, ''We are going to purchase another property.''

When this is the answer, the broker now has an opportunity to do a real service for the owner. By arranging an exchange, he can go far beyond the service usually available in a real estate office. And, of course, whenever an exchange is completed, two or more owners have closed a satisfactory transaction.

Many times, when the original contact is made, the owner may be looking for information. He may have made money or may have a large gain in a property. He really may be trying to work with the broker as a consultant, more than as an agent.

''Now that this apartment has this large increase in value, should I sell it?'' is a typical question. Or, ''Do you think that these properties will continue to increase in value?'' Another opener might be, ''I think that I can't sell—my taxes would be too much. What can I do?''

A broker's first impulse might be to suggest something. Many things are available. An owner can sell. He can exchange. He can buy more property. He can refinance and retire. He can do nothing. Any one of the many options available might be right, depending on many factors.

Here are a few questions that might be asked of an owner. When the answers are known, maybe a better evaluation could be given.

1. What is the adjusted cost basis of the property?
2. Was it purchased? Inherited? Received in an exchange?
3. How long have you owned it?
4. Who shares the ownership with you?
5. How do these other owners feel about the property?
6. Have you discussed the property with your accountant? With your attorney?

7. What other property do you own?
8. Do you have other investments? What?
9. If you incurred a large taxable gain, how would it affect your taxes this year? How about next year?
10. Do you understand how a tax-deferred exchange works?
11. Do you know the rules of an installment sale?
12. What is your age? Spouse's age?
13. What are the ages of your children?
14. Do you have a formal estate-planning program?
15. Are you employed or self-employed?
16. What is your business entity? Sole proprietor? Partnership? Corporation?
17. What do *you* feel is the best avenue to pursue with this property?
18. Do you need cash?

Each of these questions can be easily brought into the interview. No need to make the discussion seem like an interrogation. The answers lead to a full, usually enjoyable conversation that allows both the broker and owner to learn more about the ownership.

Many of these questions may have never been considered by the owner. Just answering them will often help him to understand his situation and assist him in making decisions.

Since most owners have never considered an exchange—often never heard of it, the possibility and benefits may have to be explained in detail. The depth of the detail depends again on the client and his needs.

[¶706]   REAL ESTATE CONSULTING

This leads to consultation. Before any kind of an unusual transaction can be undertaken, the owner should understand it. If the owner feels that he wants to exchange his property, it would help to have examples of how it might work to show to him. The more familiar he is with the ideas and concepts, the easier the ultimate transaction should be.

To give any owner a thorough understanding of the possibilities and results of an exchange can be quite time-consuming. Most brokers will charge an hourly consulting fee for this service.

Care should be taken to define in a written agreement just what will be covered in the consultation. Further, when the consultation is completed, a separate contract or listing should be entered into for the property exchange transaction.

[¶707] SETTING GOALS OF BENEFITS THAT THE OWNER IS SEEKING

After the owner has consulted with the broker, he has been introduced to the concept of the "benefits" of the property. To best assist an owner to evaluate what the property is currently doing for him or "to" him, it helps to have all owners list the current benefits of the property.

A list of benefits of a property owned now might be: (Broker questions in parenthesis.)

1. Pride of ownership.
2. Income. (How much?) $2,000 per year.
3. Depreciation. (How much?) $1,500 per year.
4. Appreciation, hopefully.

Later during the interview, the broker and owners might set a new list of goals hoped for in an exchange. (For example, a list in order of preference.)

1. Income. (How much?) $5,000 annually.
2. Depreciation. (How much?) $7,500 annually.
3. A better-leveraged position.
4. A large-enough property to support professional property management.
5. Pride of ownership. A well-built building in a good neighborhood.

With a definite set of goals, defined in advance, both the owner and broker will now be able to recognize the right property when it is found. There will be other things that might be of concern, such as present physical condition of buildings, age, condition of roof, location. These will certainly be evaluated in any decision, when a property is being examined. However, if the property is in an average acceptable condition, then the previously set financial goals are important. *Without these goals set in advance, owners and brokers may never find the right property.* They manage to find a little something wrong with each offering—hoping that the next one will be the one that is perfect.

Both the owner and broker must have a clearly defined objective before the search is started. Unless they know exactly where they are going, it is impossible to recognize the destination.

When the broker has these objectives, he can "zero-in" on the size, value, type of neighborhood, etc. For instance, when one of the benefits sought is cash flow, then an extremely highly leveraged property is out. He may improve the leverage position, but will certainly shop for a property where the client will have a good-sized equity.

If overflow tax shelter is the requirement, the search would be different. Now, the objective would be the highest leverage position. Other considerations might be negotiated terms for interest only loans and possibly leased land under the investment property.

[¶708] HOW BROKERS HANDLE FEES IN COOPERATIVE TRANSACTIONS

The real estate industry has long been known for a most cooperative attitude among brokers. Most Realtors belong to some sort of multiple listing service that is used to furnish all of the members with information on listed properties. Any broker or salesperson who has this information has the right to work on the listing to try to sell it.

Brokers who work mostly in exchanges cooperate with other brokers also. The methods of marketing will be covered in a later chapter.

Properties listed for exchange are listed on an "exclusive" basis like most sale listings (see Figure 7.4). One difference may be in the fees. Although many listings are taken for a percentage commission, as sale listings, most are listed for exchange for a flat fee. The exchange broker is more apt to list the property for a fee of $1,000, $5,000, $10,000 rather than that 6 percent, 7 percent or 10 percent. The fee may have no relation to the value of the property figured in a percentage. The broker sets the fee on the basis of difficulty of the problem. Thus, one property valued at $500,000 might have a fee for an exchange of $20,000 while another of the same value might have a fee of $50,000. The difference could be that the first property might be a readily salable commercial property that would be easy to handle in any transaction. The other might be unimproved land located in the California coastal zone. (Coastal zone land is nearly impossible to do anything with. The law provides for a commission to decide on use, development, etc.)

In a sale, the fee or commission paid is usually split in some predetermined percentage between the listing and selling agents. If the commission was 6 percent, often the split will be 50/50. However, it can be 60/40, 65/35 or any other possible combination. Agents may negotiate the commission split prior to each transaction or may have an agreement between their offices. An agreement will cover all business transacted between the two offices on all sales.

EXCLUSIVE EMPLOYMENT OF BROKER TO EXCHANGE, SELL, LEASE OR OPTION

CALIFORNIA ASSOCIATION OF REALTORS® STANDARD FORM

1. The undersigned,_____
(PRINCIPAL), hereby grants to_____
a licensed real estate broker, hereinafter called "agent," the EXCLUSIVE AND IRREVOCABLE RIGHT commencing on_____
_____, 19_____and terminating at midnight on_____, 19_____to advise, offer, solicit, and negotiate for
the disposition of the Principal's right, title, and interest, through sale, lease, option or exchange on terms acceptable to Principal of
the real and personal property described as follows:_____

_____
_____
_____
_____
_____
_____
_____

SUBJECT TO:_____
_____
_____
_____

2. Agent is hereby authorized to accept and hold on my behalf a deposit from any offeror pending Principal's acceptance. No offer shall be submitted to Principal unless signed by the individual offeror or his authorized agent.

3. I warrant that I am the owner of or can obtain and deliver marketable title to the property described above. Evidence of title to the real property shall be in the form of a California Land Title Association Standard Coverage Policy of Title Insurance to be paid for by_____ .

4. Agent may ☐ may not ☐ place a for sale or exchange sign on the property.

5. Compensation to Agent: I hereby agree to pay Agent a fee of $_____upon any agreement for or transfer of title, during the term hereof or any extension thereof by Agent, or through any other person, or by me, or if said property is withdrawn from exchange, sale, lease or option without the consent of Agent, or made unmarketable by my voluntary act during the term hereof or any extension thereof.

(a) If within_____days after expiration hereof, or any extension thereof, Principal enters into an agreement with anyone with whom Agent has had negotiations prior to final expiration, provided I have received notice in writing thereof before or upon expiration of this agreement or any extension thereof.

6. If action be instituted to enforce this agreement, the prevailing party shall receive reasonable attorney's fees as fixed by the Court.

7. Agent may represent all parties and collect compensation or commission from them provided there is full disclosure to all principals of such Agency. Agent may cooperate with sub-agents and may divide with other agents such compensation or commission in any manner acceptable to them.

8. Other Provisions:
_____
_____

9. I acknowledge that I have read and understand this Agreement, and that I have received a copy hereof.

DATED:_____ , 19_____   _____ , California

_____   _____
OWNER   OWNER

_____
ADDRESS   CITY   STATE   PHONE
10. In consideration of the above, Agent agrees to use diligence in the performance of his obligations.

_____
AGENT   ADDRESS   CITY   STATE

By _____
PHONE   FORM EX-11   DATE   (Rev. 4-76)

NO REPRESENTATION IS MADE AS TO THE LEGAL VALIDITY OF ANY PROVISION HEREOF IN ANY SPECIFIC TRANSACTION. IF YOU DESIRE LEGAL ADVICE, CONSULT YOUR ATTORNEY.

Figure 7.4

[¶709]   EXCHANGE COMMISSION SPLITS

Exchange fees are handled very much like sales fees. Since each property and owner may have a fee, the procedures may differ in some respects.

[¶709.1]   Pool and Splits

This may be used more than any other way between cooperating brokers in exchanges. Simply, all fees are pooled, then split equally between contributing brokers. For instance, if broker Black and broker Brown successfully negotiate an exchange between their clients, each earns a fee based on his listing contract. Say, Brown's listing calls for a fee of $5,000 and Black's listing for $6,000. The total fees would be $11,000 and each broker would receive half of the total, $5,500.

In a multiple exchange, there might be a number of brokers and owners. Here's an example of a four-way exchange.

Broker	Client	Fee
Black	A.	$3,000
Brown	B.	1,800
Jones	C.	4,100
Smith	D.	3,700
	Total	$12,600

Using a POOL AND SPLIT formula, each broker would get $3,150. ($12,600 ÷ 4 = $3,150.)

The formula that brokers use in the POOL AND SPLIT is based on the number of contributing "legs" to the exchange. A "leg" is one client's property or properties that is exchanged. Since each broker is paid in accordance with his contribution to the success of the transaction, he receives a share of the total based on the number of "legs" he contributed to the exchange.

In the previous example, suppose that broker Black represented both clients A and B. Then his share of the total fees would have been $6,300. Jones and Smith would still each receive $3,150.

[¶709.2]   No Pool and Split (NPAS)

This is also used by professional exchangors. It is self explanatory. In the previous example, each broker would be paid only by his own client. Each would receive only the amount that his own listing agreement called for.

In recent years, more brokers are insisting on the NO POOL AND SPLIT. Since there are no fixed fees or fixed commissions in the real estate industry, each fee with each client is totally negotiable. The fees vary so much that sometimes the best division is no division.

[¶710]   BROKER ADVERTISING

Advertising for exchange clients is usually different from the buy/sell type of advertising. Newspapers throughout the country are full of advertisements of property *for sale*. Brokers advertise on television, radio, use brochures, direct mail and anything else that will attract a buyer's attention. (Or a seller's—the theory is that extensive advertising of listings attracts other sellers who like the job being done.)

For the most part, these ads are really based on one theme only. A description of the property—price, terms, and (hopefully) a feeling of urgency. It can be a one-line ad in the classified column or a 16-page, 4-color brochure, but it is a description of a property for sale for money.

Some advertising by any Realtor might be directed at personal image building. Brokers in the buy/sell market may do some of this, but the advertising budget is usually directed toward property descriptions.

Property-oriented advertising for the exchange broker might resemble sale advertising, sometimes. The following advertising (Figures 7.5 and 7.6) has been effective in attracting calls from prospective exchange clients. Like a sale ad, they generate an interest in property that is available while referring to exchanges.

AVAILABLE:

8 UNIT APARTMENT—Pacific Grove, $160,000.
Your home may be the down payment.

640 Acres—BIG SUR (CHOICE!), $680,000.
Excellent Terms to qualified investor.
(Try your existing trust deeds here)

Also: Various apartments and other investment
properties from $20,000 up
(For Sale or Exchange)

WE INVITE YOUR INQUIRY
375-9534

REAL ESTATE INVESTMENT COUNSELORS
706 Forest Ave.
Pacific Grove, Calif. 93950

Figure 7.5

THE REAL ESTATE COUNSELOR

EXCHANGED!

Real estate equities in the following properties have been exchanged by us to improve client's ownership positions.

DUPLEX — Pacific Grove*   FOURPLEX — Seaside*
COMMERCIAL BLDG. — Merced County
CARMEL VALLEY HOUSE
PALO ALTO ACREAGE
SIX-PLEX — SEASIDE*
NEWPORT BEACH HOUSE*

EXCHANGES IN ESCROW!

TRI-PLEX — Salinas*
FOUR-PLEX — Salinas*
27 Unit Apt. — Salinas*
37 Unit Apt. — Marina*
Houses — In Carmel, Seaside and Marina

READY FOR EXCHANGE!

7 UNIT APT. — Pacific Grove
8 Unit Apt. — Pacific Grove
8 Unit Apt. — Carmel Valley
19 Unit Apt. — Salinas
4 Acres — Marina
640 Acres — Big Sur

(*Tax Deferred Exchanges)
FULL TIME EXPERIENCED EFFORT BRINGS RESULTS!
REAL ESTATE INVESTMENT COUNSELORS
375-9534
JAMES SAYLOR — REALTOR

Figure 7.6

Another type of newspaper advertising is the real estate question and answer column (Figures 7.7 and 7.8). This must be done on a regular basis. The answers have never been specific answers for a problem but must be interesting enough to provoke interest.

One of the most interesting types of advertising for image building is the monthly newsletter. it is enormously effective. By mailing 200 to 500 a month, a broker can contact repeatedly all of the major property owners in his area. The newsletter can be mailed to bankers, trust officers, apartment owners and all of the known speculators in the broker's operating area.

Before long, the image of this broker among these property owners changes. He is no longer a peddler, but someone who can think!

THE REAL ESTATE COUNSELOR

Gentlemen:

I own a property out of state, and I have gotten to the age where I don't feel like traveling back and forth to watch over it. It is a good property, leased to a good company.

Do you think I could trade it for something around here where I don't have to travel so far?

M.M.

Dear Mr. M.M.

I see no problem in accomplishing your objective, providing you keep in mind the benefits you need when you select local property.

Yours is a situation familiar to the competent exchangor and, fortunately, one fairly easy to solve. Since it matters little where property is located when exchangors set out to solve a problem, and since owners of local property live in many out-of-state areas, exchangors are often able to solve two problems in one transaction.

One of the more common truisms in the exchange field is that one man's property location can be poison to him, but meat to another.

If you will arrange an appointment with a specialist in this field, I am certain the steps can be taken that will result in a more comfortable position for you. Please call us for an appointment!

ASK YOUR REAL ESTATE QUESTIONS!
REAL ESTATE INVESTMENT COUNSELORS, 706 Forest Ave.,
Pacific Grove, or call 375-9534.

Figure 7.7

One of the greatest things about this type of advertising is that only the recipients know about it. Other brokers in the area have no inkling of the image building that is going on.

In addition, the broker constantly gets his message over to the people on his list. They see the newsletter monthly. Most of them will miss the expensive messages of the other brokers unless they turn to the real estate columns often. Most people don't.

Of course, it might be difficult to write the letter and keep it up each

Figure 7.8

month. This need not be a problem as there are newsletter services that can provide well-written newsletters monthly, ready for mailing to your list. They can be completely personalized with the heading identifying the broker who is mailing them.

Following is a sample copy of a four-page newsletter (Figure 7.9), furnished by subscription from STRAWBERRY HILL, INC., P.O. BOX 142, PEBBLE BEACH, CALIF. 93953. This letter is designed specifically to present an image of an exchange-oriented investment firm. The company limits its use, by accepting subscriptions from only one firm in any given area.

THE **SAYLOR** REPORT

A MONTHLY INVESTMENT SERVICE FOR CLIENTS

JAMES SAYLOR
P.O. BOX 142
PEBBLE BEACH
CALIF. 93953
(408) 649-1111

INCLUDED IN THIS ISSUE:

DORMANT EQUITY....................PUTTING YOUR EQUITY TO WORK.

LEVERAGE..........................WHAT IT IS, HOW IT WORKS FOR YOU
                                 IN A REAL ESTATE INVESTMENT.

RECREATIONAL LAND.................IF YOU INVEST IN A MOUNTAIN OR
                                 DESERT LAND, WHAT IS THE INTENT.

DORMANT EQUITY - WHY NOT PUT IT TO WORK

The following is an interesting situation regarding equity: The professional man owns the real estate where his office is located. He has owned it many years, and wants to remain in business at that location. His loan on the property has been reduced to a very low figure and has only a small interest deduction on the loan. His depreciation deduction is low because it is based on his original cost.

In short, Mr. Professional owns a large equity in his building and it is doing nothing for him - taxwise.

He might be interested in making some changes so that his investment can do him some good on his tax form, instead of just providing a roof over his business.

It's possible that he might:

1. Turn his dormant equity into a cash producer.

2. Save income taxes by increasing his depreciation and interest deductions - - without increasing his costs.

3. Keep his original property as a business address for as long as he wants.

4. Avoid the payment of any capital gains taxes while he is accomplishing all of the above.

He can accomplish all of these things! For example, here is a recent transaction in which these results were achieved:

Mr. Professional had an equity of $50,000 in his own office building. His Real Estate Investment Broker found a 30 unit apartment property which required a $50,000 down payment. The Investment Broker also knew another investor who would like to own a leased commercial building.

The Investment Broker arranged a tax-deferred exchange of the office building as a "down" on the 30 unit apartment building. Mr. Professional had to "take on" a

---

Figure 7.9

DORMANT EQUITY - CONTINUED

larger loan (the second property was valued at $375,000), but the income from the apartment more than paid all the expenses. Even after professional management, Mr. Professional had a nice spendable income from the property.

The owner of the apartment traded "down" into the office building, and "sold" it immediately to the investor that the broker had standing by. The investor bought the office building only on the condition that Mr. Professional lease it back, giving him a tenant for the property.

The results of the transaction were:

The apartment owner had a cash sale.

The third party investor had a fine management free office building.

Mr. Professional has made an excellent investment move. He has acquired a 30 unit apartment property giving him additional income, sheltered by the acquired property's higher depreciation schedule. He still has the use of the office building and since he is now a lessee, all expenses he pays are fully deductible. The rent on his office is paid by the spendable income from the apartments.

Since he made the transaction - Mr. Professional pays far less income tax. The new property gives him what he really needed more than anything - TAX SHELTER.

LEVERAGE - WHAT IT IS, HOW IT WORKS FOR YOU IN A REAL ESTATE INVESTMENT

A customer recently came into the office, elated about his apartment property that was nearly free and clear of loans. His ambition was to own the apartment free and clear so that "all of that income" could be his alone. He was counting the months until the property was paid off.

As an exercise, I plotted the following as an illustration to him of a purchase of two properties, both with $100,000 cash down payment. One of these (A) was bought outright for the $100,000 and the other (B) was purchased with a 25% equity position (25% down).

Transactions	A	B
1. Purchase price	$100,000	$400,000
2. Equity (Down Payment)	100,000	100,000
3. Mortgage	-0-	300,000
4. Net Rental Income (after normal expenses)	8,000	32,000
5. Mortgage payment (8%, Interest only)	-0-	24,000
6. Cash Flow	8,000	8,000

Assumptions: Tax Bracket of Buyer - 50%
            Depreciation: 5% per year on 80% of Purchase Price (20% is allocated to land and is not depreciable).

Result:

2

Figure 7.9 (continued)

		A	B
7.	Cash Flow	8,000	8,000
8.	First year's annual depreciation allowance	-4,000	-16,000
9.	"Tax Free" Cash flow	4,000	8,000
10.	Taxable Cash flow	4,000	-0-
11.	Tax on taxable cash flow (50% Bracket)	-2,000	-0-
12.	Net after-tax cash flow	6,000	8,000
13.	Overflow depreciation X 50%	-0-	4,000
14.	Total after-tax cash return	6,000	12,000

Our customer with his property that he had owned for a long time was actually in a worse position than Mr "A" in the illustration. He had far less depreciation than Mr. "A" did because his schedule of depreciation was based on a low purchase price years ago, not on today's value.

After our customer saw the example above, he realized that leverage was important in an investment - it provides depreciation based on the total purchase price and gives today's needed tax shelter. We have since exchanged that near free and clear property up into a larger property that gives our customer a position that is nearer to Mr. B's.

RECREATIONAL LAND - IF YOU INVEST IN A MOUNTAIN OR DESERT TRACT, WHAT IS YOUR INTENT.

During the past ten years, there has been a great interest in land as an investment to hold for the big gain. There have been some huge gains in land investments over the years, but wherever the gains can be large, the risks can also be large.

There has been a cycle of ownership in land as follows:

1. User
2. Investor (speculator)
3. Developer
4. User (new use)

Take rural acreage and you will often see the land being used for its highest and best use as grazing for cattle or possibly as row crop land. The property is now in the hands of a "user."

When this "user" property is near a highway, city, or town, an investor may see it as an investment for the future based on a different use. When he buys it, the price paid is often higher than the value of the property under its present use.

Now that the land is in the hands of an investor, the gamble and wait has now started. If the investor has guessed right and the "path of progress" stays in the right direction and all of the other factors work out for him - then in a few months or years, he is ready for his profit. During his wait, he can often continue to lease out the property for its highest and best use (grazing).

When zoning changes are made and the property is ready for development, either the investor becomes the third part of the cycle, a developer, or he sells to one.

3

RECREATIONAL LAND - CONTINUED

The developer then builds apartments, houses, commercial or industrial, whatever is the new highest and best use of the property.

When developed, the property returns to "user" property again under its new use. It may be owned by a home owner or it may again be owned by an investor. The new investor will be actually be a "user" however as he will be investing in the property to collect rents rather than holding in a passive position as the land investor did.

This explanation may sound quite simple and elementary. It is. However, many parcels of "Recreational Land" might not have been sold, IF the buyer had been aware of this concept!

Look at the many thousands of people that have purchased property (lots) in mountain and desert subdivisions. There was a blurring of the classification of the land in someone's mind. Was it an "investment?" Was it "user" property?

The only answer we can come up with is another question - "To Whom?"

The developer and subdivider of the property sold it as "user" property, and clearly advertised it as such. He usually had provision for a builder and the lots had streets, utilities and everything that is necessary for a "user" property.

The biggest problem was: Most of the buyers of this "user" property were not users, but considered themselves investors. Each bought his lot with the idea of re-selling at a profit! When each waited for all the others to build on the lots, then the vacant subdivision went down in value and the new "investor" lost on his land investment.

If these buyers had classified the investment in advance as a "user" property, then they might have made the purchase of a real investment someplace else!

Since the only benefit in investment in land is appreciation (maybe), I only recommend the purchase to those experienced in this type of speculation. Our recommendations usually are the conservative apartments, business, and commercial property. All of the benefits of cash flow, loan reduction and depreciation are measurable in advance - before the investment is made. If there is any future appreciation, it is an extra benefit.

NEXT MONTH

TAX DEFERRED EXCHANGES.. DOLLARS AND CENTS EXAMPLES OF EXCHANGES VS. SELLING AND RE-INVESTING.

GROUP INVESTMENTS....... SHOULD YOU SYNDICATE?

THE REAL ESTATE INVESTMENT COUNSELOR...... A BROKER'S BROKER

Figure 7.9 (continued)

CHAPTER 8

The Real Estate Investment Counselor

[¶800] **WORKING WITH PEOPLE
RATHER THAN PROPERTY**

During this century, there have come into the business world, specialists who advise others in investments. Most often, when any remark is made about an Investment Counselor, people immediately think about Stocks and Bonds Advisors and Brokers.

There are, and have been for many years, Real Estate Investment Counselors. These specialists must be "people" and tax experts much as the stocks and bonds investment advisors. Just as there is a wrong stock market investment for a certain person or group of persons, there is the wrong (and right) real estate investment.

Income property specialists may advertise various properties of all sizes for sale. Since most are real-estate, rather than people-oriented, great care is put into preparing information regarding the property. Price, terms, expenses, cash return dominate the advertising. Since the brokers are agents for the seller, anyone who wishes to buy the property, can qualify for a loan and pay the down payment becomes a buyer. This is correct. The agent's job is to sell the property.

The Real Estate Investment Counselor often separates himself from the usual broker's interests, collection of fees or commissions as an agent for a sale. He offers an independent real estate service as a counselor and is retained on a fee or hourly basis.

Counselors are hired by individuals and business firms to analyze real estate as an investment vehicle for them. Their job is to take all possible factors into consideration and report all of the benefits that an investment might have for the person, family or firm. Of course, since most people and firms hiring the counselor already own real estate, exchanges are often included in the reported benefits and recommendations.

To give a simple example, take two individuals, each with $100,000 to invest as an initial investment. Neither owns any investment real estate.

INVESTOR #1. A 35-year-old doctor and his wife. They have two small children. He has been in practice for seven years and earns $75,000 a year. They have been accumulating cars, a house, club memberships and other personal things. Since they are paying income tax in the high brackets, his accountant advised a real estate investment. The accountant recommended that they see a Real Estate Investment Counselor.

INVESTOR #2. This lady's attorney called for an appointment for her. She is a widow, 45 years old, with a teenage daughter. Her husband recently died. She is not working, has only a small income each month. The attorney advised her to contact the Real Estate Investment Counselor regarding an investment in real estate. The $100,000 is the settlement from an insurance policy.

Even with this small amount of information, it is obvious that each should invest in different kinds of real property. After interviews, the counselor might initially work up a preliminary list of benefits needed by each investor—and the degree of risk.

INVESTOR #1—the doctor and his wife.

1. Since they are paying high income taxes, tax shelter from depreciation is important. (This may indicate a highly leveraged, low-down-payment investment property.)
2. They seem to need little or no cash flow from the investment. (Again, high leverage seems to fit.)
3. Has high income, is young and well insured, so can take risks. They can go into a high-risk, high-return situation. (Using a high-risk investment, if they lose they can easily recoup.)
4. Both are very busy. Doctor is deeply involved in practice and his wife in community affairs. Both will be unable to personally manage the property. They need a near care-free investment.

INVESTOR #2—the widow with little income.

1. First and obvious, tax shelter is not important. She has little income and pays very little income tax.
2. Has no skills to make further investment of money. Needs as close to a no-risk situation as possible.
3. Needs cash flow from the investment for living expenses. Because her daughter is a teenager, opportunity to be at home for next few years could be an important benefit.
4. Needs something to occupy her time, but needs flexible hours.

The Counselor might recommend that the doctor and his wife invest in a highly leveraged apartment property. It might be 100 units or more and be

$750,000 to $1,000,000 in value. It would give them little or no cash flow. The overflow depreciation could help them to reduce current income taxes and thereby increase their spendable income. The size of the property would assure them that it could easily adapt to professional property management. Since it would be fully managed, a well chosen property need never be a bother to either the doctor or his wife after their original inspections of the property.

The widow, with the same amount of initial cash, might get a recommendation to invest in a small apartment, as small as a four-plex.

For safety, she should own it free and clear of loans or with only a small mortgage. A property of $100,000 to $125,000 would seem to be the right range. She would be able to live in one unit with her daughter and rent out the other three. This would give her a comfortable place to live and a nice, steady income. There would be savings for her from doing some or all of the work around the property herself. This type of property would solve her problem of income, a place to live and an investment. She would be home daily after school hours when her daughter was home.

Later, when the daughter was grown, the four-plex would give her the flexibility to do many things. She could sell the property, exchange it for something that would give a different set of benefits or borrow on it. The free-and-clear improved property would act as a savings account also. It would nearly always be a quick source of ready cash, through a real estate loan.

[¶801]   BACKGROUND—REAL ESTATE INVESTMENT COUNSELOR

The Counselor's education to qualify him to advise people should include a good knowledge of valuation and appraisal of all classes of real estate. He should certainly be well trained in the regular practice and principles of real estate. He should have a good working knowledge of estate matters and taxation, and the workings of the stock market. He should be an expert in real estate economics and particularly the financing of real estate. Finally, he needs a thorough knowledge of income tax aspects.

According to Webster's dictionary, a COUNSELOR is defined as: "One who Counsels; an advisor."

COUNSEL is defined: "Interchange of opinions; mutual advising; deliberation together; consultation. The examination of consequences, exercise of deliberate judgement. To give advice or instruct."

Many of these definitions have to do with acting reciprocally, *mutual* advising, *consultation, deliberation together,* an *interchange* of opinions, and the *examination* of *consequences.*

These are a good description of the steps taken by a Real Estate Investment Counselor when introduced to a new client. Before any advice or counsel can be given, there must be quite a long interchange of ideas between client and counselor. They must deliberate together, and consult, before they arrive at a mutual understanding of the benefits (consequences) that the client should have.

[¶802]   COUNSELING HELPS THE OWNER REALIZE HIS PRESENT POSITION

If the Counselor is faced with a couple who presently own property, and wish to improve their position, the opening remark might come from the husband. "We have a 20-unit apartment property and wish to exchange up into a large property and a better position. What is the best way to start?"

The answer from an income property specialist might start with information about various larger properties in the area. Since he is property-oriented and always collects fees contingent upon the transfer of ownership of real estate, this is logical. Before the apartment owner knows it, he will be out looking at some other property.

The Counselor usually will answer differently. Since his job is to *deliberate* with his clients for an *interchange* of opinions for an *examination* of *counsequences* (benefits), his answer might be,

"What do you mean by a better position?" or,

"How long have you owned your property?" or,

"Tell me about your 20-unit apartment." or,

"Why did you acquire the 20-unit apartment?"

As we said before, an exchange broker or a Real Estate Investment Counselor needs to know the current position before setting out to find a new destination. He or she easily turns the meeting into an interview that will result in information, both personal and about property, coming to the Counselor.

Many Counselors keep a tape recorder on the desk between themselves and the clients. At the start of the meeting, it can be turned on with the remark, "I'll record the interview, so that I won't have to take notes. Should we decide to work together, I can go back and have enough information to start a file on your property." Few clients ever object.

Since it is proper to discuss the current position first, much personal information must also come out while the property is discussed. Personal income, savings, insurance, family situation are all pertinent facts to consider before applying for new loans. The exact value of the current property must be ascertained so that all know what is to be offered in exchange for the new property.

Seldom do the owners bring any information regarding actual income or operating expenses about their own property or their own financial position. When the first interview is concluded, another meeting can be arranged, with the clients agreeing to bring back the necessary information regarding their own property.

The information requested for a second meeting might be:

1. Plat map of the property.
2. Map of surrounding area.
3. Copies of current tax bills.
4. Photographs of buildings and improvements.
5. Statement of income and expenses (from income tax statement).

This is "bare bones" information. Only the start of what is needed to build up a file on a property. Since these owners own an income property, the following form (Figure 8.1) is given them to fill in the total information about the property, before the next meeting. This form requires the owner to sign *Warranting* that the figures are the exact income and expense figures for the apartment.

After this first meeting, the Counselor now will try to put down on paper whatever information that he now knows about these people.

Following is a form that some Counselors use to organize the information received in interviews with clients or potential clients. This is the Confidential Counseling Information Form (Figure 8.2).

Note: this form is not designed to be used as a questionnaire in a question-and-answer session, filled out in front of the owner. Nor is it handed to a client to fill out. Its use is to assist the Counselor organize his own thinking and put down in some order the information he received from the interviews. Usually the information is written down immediately after the meeting. If a tape recorder is used, it can be done later with total recall.

STATEMENT OF INCOME & EXPENSES
Apartment

Name of Resident Manager _____

Phone of Resident Manager _____

NAME OF OWNERS: _____ NAME OF PROPERTY: _____

ADDRESS OF PROPERTY: _____ CITY: _____ STATE: _____ ZIP: _____

TYPE OF PROPERTY: _____ AGE OF PROPERTY: _____

Is Professional Management Available? _____

Name: _____ Phone: _____

Address: _____ City: _____

State: _____ Zip: _____

INCOME FROM:

(1) LEASES: $ _____

(2) MO. TO MO. $ _____

DEPOSITS: $ _____

INCOME	19 ___	19 ___	EXPENSES 19 ___ 19 ___				19 ___ 19 ___	
	$			$	$		$	$
Jan.	_____	_____	Taxes R.E.	____	____	Custodial	____	____
Feb.	_____	_____	Taxes P.P.	____	____	Telephone	____	____
March	_____	_____	Ins. Fire	____	____	Furn. Repl.	____	____
April	_____	_____	Ins. Liab.	____	____	Advertising	____	____
May	_____	_____	Util. Gas–Elec.	____	____	Fees & Lic.	____	____
June	_____	_____	Water	____	____	Pest Control	____	____
July	_____	_____	Rubbish	____	____	Legal	____	____
Aug.	_____	_____	Yard Care	____	____	Accounting	____	____
Sept.	_____	_____	Pool Care	____	____	Wk. Comp.	____	____
Oct.	_____	_____	Elevator	____	____	MGT (on site)	____	____
Nov.	_____	_____	Maintenance	____	____	MGT (prof.)	____	____
Dec.	_____	_____	T.V. Cable	____	____	Lot Sweeping	____	____
TOTALS	$ _____	$ _____	Supplies	____	____	Snow Removal	____	____
	Average Vacancy: _____		Misc.	____	____	Misc.	____	____
	Vacancy this date: _____		GRAND TOTAL: $ _____				$ _____	

Condition of Personal and Real Property: (i.e., Carpets, Drapes, Washer & Dryer, Painting, etc.):

☐ Excellent ☐ Good ☐ Fair ☐ Needs Upgrading Estimate Cost $ _____

Loan service as of _____ 19 ___ : Capital Improvements: _____

1st: $ _____	(Nature: _____).	___ Years.	___ % Interest.	Monthly pmt: $ _____ .	Tot. yrly. pmt.$ _____
2nd: $ _____	(Nature: _____).	___ Years.	___ % Interest.	Monthly pmt: $ _____ .	Tot. yrly. pmt.$ _____
3rd: $ _____	(Nature: _____).	___ Years.	___ % Interest.	Monthly pmt: $ _____ .	Tot. yrly. pmt.$ _____
4th: $ _____	(Nature: _____).	___ Years.	___ % Interest.	Monthly pmt: $ _____ .	Tot. yrly. pmt.$ _____

TRUST FUND: $ _____

Remarks: _____

Tax Bill Breakdown:

_____ Land

_____ Improvements

_____ Personal Property

_____ TOTAL

The income and expenses listed above are warranted to be the actual figures for the _____ month period ended 19 ___ . The undersigned understands that in reliance on the above listed figures, commitments and obligations may be made by one or more persons which would not have been made but for reliance on these figures.

Date: _____ 19 ___ Name: _____ Name: _____

(Signed by property owners representing correct information)

Mailing Address: _____ City: _____ State: _____ Zip: _____

Owner's Phone Number: _____ Broker: _____

EXCHANGE COUNSELOR FORMS
P. O. Box 5834
San Jose, CA. 95150

Form 5

Figure 8.1

CONFIDENTIAL COUNSELING INFORMATION

1. Date: _____

2. Owner's Name: _____ Age: _____ Phone: _____

3. Home Address: _____ How long? _____

4. Occupation: _____ Phone: _____
   Business Address: _____

5. Family Status: _____ Married   Spouse's Name: _____ Age: _____
   _____ Widow(er) Number of Children: _____
   _____ Divorced   Name _____ Age _____ Sex _____ Location _____
   _____ Single   Name _____ Age _____ Sex _____ Location _____
                    Name _____ Age _____ Sex _____ Location _____
                    Name _____ Age _____ Sex _____ Location _____

6. Type of Property Owned: _____

7. Property Location: _____
   City _____ County _____ State _____

8. How is Title to Property Vested? _____

9. When was the Property acquired and how?
   Purchased _____ (Price Paid $_____); Gift _____; Exchange _____; Inheritance _____; Other _____

10. What is the present tax basis of the property? _____

11. How long has the property been for sale or on the market? _____

11a. Previously listed? _____

12. Are vehicles offered readily saleable? _____

13. Is this to be a tax-deferred exchange? _____

13a. Is there a potential "forgiveness of mortgage" problem? _____

14. Is client classified as a "DEALER"? _____

15. Client's opinion of their problem and/or reason for disposing of property. (See Item 35)
    _____

16. What do they wish to accomplish? _____

17. What can vehicle do for new owner? (Potential, refinance possibilities, etc.) _____
    _____

18. What are their needs? M-Money _____   How much? $ _____
                           A-Appreciation _____   What do they expect? _____
                           I-Income _____   How much? $ _____
                           D-Depreciation _____   How much? $ _____
                           Other- Future needs and why needed: Explain _____
    _____

19. Is there a critical time element or urgency of any type? If so, explain: _____

20. Client's readiness to act: Desperate _____; Highly Motivated _____; Shows Interest _____

21. Are title holders in accord to make decision? _____ Do they seem flexible to deal with? _____

22. Is client oriented to other areas? _____ Explain geographical limitations, if any, and why: _____

Figure 8.2

23. What price range will they consider? $_____ Can add cash. How much? $_____
    How soon? _____ Source of cash. _____
    Needs cash. How much? $_____ Why? _____

24. Do they have cash for expenses? (Fees, title insurance, escrow, etc.) _____

25. Do they have other property that can be added? ____ Describe type and approximate equity (including
    stocks and property other than real estate): _____

26. Attitude towards accepting personal property such as: Contracts ____ ; Paper ____ ; Live Stock ____ ;
    Machinery ____ ; Trailers ____ ; Boats ____ ; Cars ____ ; Trucks ____ ; Equipment ____ ; Airplanes ____ .

27. Client's attitude toward assuming or making higher loan. _____

28. Discuss initiating offers in client's behalf with weasel clauses.

29. Discuss client's business background including previous experiences as an operator (motel, cafe, etc.)

29a. Will they manage? _____ Are they a user? _____ Lease back: _____

30. What is client's present approximate annual income (sources and totals)? _____

30a. Is Financial Statement and/or I.R.S. Statements available on request? _____

31. Attorney _____ Tax Counselor _____

32. Is there any third party influence? _____

33. Can objective be reached with present vehicle? _____

34. Special interests (fishing, hunting, flying, electronics, etc.)? _____

35. BROKER'S OPINION OF OBJECTIVE AND POSSIBLE SOLUTIONS: _____

36. Remind client of why he doesn't want the property.

37. Present price $_____ ; Total encumbrances $_____ ; Equity $_____
    (See Check List Work Sheet – Form 15 for details)

38. Referred by whom: _____
    Fee Basis: $_____ How payable? _____

RECORD OF CONTACTS AND COUNSELING MEETINGS

Date	Approximate Time and Type of Contact

© Exchange Counselor
The Pony Express
P. O. Box 5906
San Jose, CA 95┃

If you haven't contacted your client in the last two weeks – CALL HIM UP!

Form 3

Figure 8.2 (continued)

**[¶803]   HOW TO FILL OUT THE CONFIDENTIAL
COUNSELING INFORMATION FORM**

Lines 1-4.

Client identification. Address and occupation. Occupation might be important—objective may be to change type of investment. Skills learned in present or previous occupation of either husband or wife might be important. Occupations or skills might suggest a type of investment property that might otherwise be overlooked.

Line 5.

Family status—ages of children. Might reflect a need for cash or the timing for a later need. Three children nearing college age could require decisions regarding cash flow in immediate future. Small children would not present this problem, but could contribute others.

Line 6.

In this case, the type of property owned is a 20-unit apartment. Type of current property should be carefully checked and defined. The owner may have a good vehicle to use for exchange, but present property may not be at all feasible for the objective he has in mind. *Example:* An apartment property can easily be exchanged up into a larger one—but open range land would be difficult to handle in the same objective.

Line 7.

Location. Much the same reason as #6. Location and type of property are the type of currency we are using to "buy" the next property.

Line 8.

Vesting of ownership. Who really owns it? Perhaps only the husband. Perhaps only the wife. How about the distant cousin who also might be in title? We can make no exchange, sale, or do anything unless all of the owners are in accord.

Line 9.

Property acquired and how? Gives an insight into type of previous transactions. Was a Counselor used? Was a broker consulted? What is the reason for the original investment?

Line 10.

Basis. Does the owner know his basis? Is a tax-deferred exchange really necessary? Is there any gain or loss if sold for dollars?

Line 11.

Has this owner tried to sell or exchange this property himself? Has he used a broker? Why didn't it sell or exchange? Were there any offers? How much—what were the terms?

Line 12.

If exchanged, a sell-out of the property may be necessary for the new owner. How long will a sale take? A month—six months? Is the property salable at all? Has any comparable property sold during the past year?

Lines 13, 13a.

Does this owner have a potential tax problem? Will the desired property be one that can be acquired in a tax-deferred transaction or will transaction be taxable? Can an installment sale and repurchase of second property give a better set of new benefits?

Line 14.

Is owner a developer or builder? Is this property classified in his hands as inventory held for sale or is it investment property? If inventory, is it problem property that must be exchanged?

Line 15.

Does this owner have a definite goal in mind? Is the exchange feasible? Do all owners have the same idea or goal for the future?

Line 16.

Again, do both owners really want the same objectives? Will one be forced into more work than the other with the new property? Have they discussed that problem? Does either seem reluctant to make a decision? Does either just seem to be going along?

Line 17.

To exchange this property, there must be benefits for the party going in to title. Does property represent cash (through new loans)? How about cash flow? Tax Shelter? Who might be a logical user for this property? For this type of property? Did owner leave any benefits available for a new owner or has he left nothing? Is he planning a refinance or other move of any kind before moving out of property?

Line 18.

Be specific. How much do they expect? Is it possible? Is it probable? Can current equity purchase property with these benefits? Are what they want and what they will accept nearly the same?

Line 19.

Are all loans up to date? Are any loans or taxes in arrears? What are the due dates on the loans? Are there any balloon payments due within the next two years?

Line 20, 21.

Do they seem anxious to make the move? Are they cooperative about furnishing information? Has the depreciation run out on this property? (if improved.) Are they paying income tax on the cash flow from rents? Do all owners seem ready to move? Does anyone seem disinterested about the whole thing?

Line 22.

If benefits owner seeks were not available in local property, how far might he go in a geographical exchange? Is it possible within those limits? How wide an area must be considered? Have they faced this possibility previously?

Line 23.

An increase in depreciation benefits means an upward exchange in value. Is this understood? Do they understand benefits of leverage? Is any cash to be added already in hand? Who has it? Is it committed? How soon available? Is it sure? If needed, how much? Is it possible to get from present property? Does cash need to be tax-free? Why?

Line 24.

Do they know the amount of extra cash needed? Do they expect to pay broker, counselor in cash? Does broker have to negotiate cash from transaction to get his fee?

Line 25.

What are the "can add" properties? Under what conditions will these be added? Why? Why are they not included in the original offering? Is anyone else in title to other property? Who?

Line 26.

What is this owner's attitude toward "boot?" Will he accept any personal property to equalize the transaction? Why not?

Line 27.

Do owners lose sleep over owing money? How much loan will bother them? What does security mean to them? What is comfort zone for each in a mortgage? What monthly payments would be comfortable if cash flow didn't cover? What interest rates seem within the comfort zone?

Line 28.

Offering this owner's property out in offers signed by the broker on owner's behalf is a technique that saves much time. Care is taken to put contingencies for inspection, etc. into offer. Broker has a contract with owner to represent him in an exchange to seek out a type of property. Since many offers are made to get a response from the other owner to see if he will cooperate, time is saved if broker can sign original offer on behalf of owner.

Lines 29, 29a.

Many types of properties might give the owner the benefits he is seeking. Has he experience in any type field related to real estate that might give him an opportunity? Motels, restaurants, laundromats, various other business opportunities might come up as a possibility for a profitable exchange.

Lines 30, 30a.

What is current cash flow? Can he feed a property with negative cash flow? Is some of his source of funds questionable? Can it be cut off without his permission? How much tax is being paid now? Is the tax situation the primary motive for a transaction?

Line 31.

Who are the legal and tax advisors? Are they conservative? Do they have to be consulted before any move or will we wait till final approval? Shall we consult with them now to take them into the original planning?

Line 32.

Often there is a relative or friend who gives the final O.K. on all financial planning of some people. If there is one here, let's get his input now—not when time is critical. Does the third-party influence have real knowledge? What is his occupation?

Line 33.

When we exchange a property for another, often we must dispose of original property after the exchange. Is this feasible? Does this property have enough equity to make the down payment on the one we are seeking?

Line 34.

More background on owner's ability to handle various businesses or opportunities that might come up.

Line 35.

This might be the BOTTOM LINE. After interviews, Counselor may have an opinion of the feasibility of the entire situation regarding people, property and objectives. Can the objective be reached? Are the owners anywhere near the real world? Can we suggest another course that might be a better way for them to go? If the objective has been broken down to just a set of benefits, can we relate these benefits to several different possible solutions?

Line 36.

After several interviews, various possibilities may have been introduced. At this point, review the original motivation and objective with owner. Is this still the way to go? He may assume the Counselor knows his objectives have been changed.

Line 37.

What is the value of the currency we are to use in the purchase of the new benefits for this owner?

Line 38.

If this client was referred by a friend or previous client, do *they* have an opinion of the client's objective? Perhaps a call thanking them for a referral will elicit some response. A third-party opinion regarding motivation might be interesting.

The fee basis for this client will be discussed in an early meeting. Hourly, weekly, monthly rates are possible. Retainer or billing? Is fee to be paid in cash? Note? Other?

By the time the Counselor has enough information from interviews to fill out this form and create a property-and-owner profile, the owner also has a great deal of new information. Most of the owner's new information is from himself. By answering questions about himself and his property, his objectives and his experience, he has a much better picture of what he might do. His original objective may still be what he wants, but he probably has widened his horizons. Instead of focusing on a particular property or type of property, he may have grasped the concept of searching for benefits.

At this point, many owners realize the value of their own estate and what it really might do for them.

[¶804] USING THE CONFIDENTIAL COUNSELING INFORMATION FORM

The most important use of this form is not to put information on it, but to guide the Counselor into the areas that must be covered. It helps to remind him of the possibilities that are open to everyone.

John and Mary Smith, the owners of the 20-unit apartment who came to the Counselor, were interested in a tax-deferred exchange. After the initial interview, the Counselor asked for further information regarding the property that they now owned. Another appointment was made.

During the next appointment, a lengthy interview, there was a discus-

CONFIDENTIAL COUNSELING INFORMATION

1. Date: __7/16__

2. Owner's Name: __JOHN SMITH/MARY SMITH__ Age: __38/33__ Phone: _____

3. Home Address: __1233 FLOWER ST.__ How long? __7 YEARS__

4. Occupation: __TELEPHONE CO./SUPERVISOR-INSTALLERS__ __14 YEARS__ Phone: _____
   Business Address: __GRAND AVE/OFFICE__

5. Family Status: __✓__ Married ~~Spouse's Name:~~ __WIFE WORKED AS BOOKKEEPER AT BANK__ Age: __BEFORE MARRIAGE__
   ____ Widow(er) Number of Children: _____
   ____ Divorced Name __BECKY__ Age __14__ Sex __F__ Location __HOME__
   ____ Single Name __JOHN__ Age __11__ Sex __M__ Location __"__
   Name __BILLY__ Age __8__ Sex __M__ Location __"__
   Name _____ Age ____ Sex ____ Location _____

6. Type of Property Owned: __20 UNIT FURNISHED APTS.__

7. Property Location: __1200 CASE ST.__
   City __CITY__ County __MONTEREY__ State __CALIF.__

8. How is Title to Property Vested? __JOHN/MARY - COMMUNITY PROP.__

9. When was the Property acquired and how? __4 YRS. AGO TRADED UP 4-PLEX__
   Purchased ____ (Price Paid $ __280,000__); Gift ____ ; Exchange __X__ ; Inheritance ____ ; Other ____
   __EX. VALUE__

10. What is the present tax basis of the property? __LOW - $180,000__

11. How long has the property been for sale or on the market? __NOT__

11a. Previously listed? __NO - SAYS NOT__

12. Are vehicles offered readily saleable? __SHOULD BE- APPEAR O.K.__

13. Is this to be a tax-deferred exchange? __YES - WANTS TO AVOID TAX IF POSSIBLE__

13a. Is there a potential "forgiveness of mortgage" problem? __NO - BASIS OVER MORT.__

14. Is client classified as a "DEALER"? __NO - LITTLE ACTIVITY - ESTATE PLANNING__

15. Client's opinion of their problem and/or reason for disposing of property. (See Item 35)
    __HAVE KNOWN PYRAMIDING + WANT TO CONTINUE (WIFE HAS MGD, LITTLE RELUCTANTL__

16. What do they wish to accomplish? __SAY UPWARD MOVE/LARGER BLDG./WIFE?__

17. What can vehicle do for new owner? (Potential, refinance possibilities, etc.) _____
    __RE FI - TAX SHELTER- GOOD CASH FLOW__

18. What are their needs? M-Money __✓__ How much? $ __3,000 ANNUAL-__
    A-Appreciation __✓__ What do they expect? __MAX -__
    I-Income ____ How much? $ __SEE MONEY__
    D-Depreciation __✓__ How much? $ __COVER BLDG. + SOME INC.__
    Other- Future needs and why needed: Explain __WANTS AT LEAST__
    __SAME INCOME AS PRESENT - DEPENDS ON IT__

19. Is there a critical time element or urgency of any type? If so, explain: __SAYS NO -__
    __NO DUE DATES__

20. Client's readiness to act: Desperate ____ ; Highly Motivated __X__ _(HUSBAND)_ ; Shows Interest __X (WIFE)__

21. Are title holders in accord to make decision? __?__ Do they seem flexible to deal with? _____

22. Is client oriented to other areas? __YES__ Explain geographical limitations, if any, and why: _____
    __BOTH WERE RAISED IN SMALL TOWN - MISS IT! MARY!!__

Figure 8.3

23. What price range will they consider? $ _5-600,000_ Can add cash? _No_ How much? $ _—0—_
    How soon? _No_ Source of cash. _____
    Needs cash. How much? $ _—0—_ Why? _HAS SMALL SAVINGS / INSURANCE_

24. Do they have cash for expenses? (Fees, title insurance, escrow, etc.) _OK_

25. Do they have other property that can be added? _?_ Describe type and approximate equity (including stocks and property other than real estate): _HAVE $20,000 EQUITY IN HOUSE. NOT HAPPY WITH NEIGHBORHOOD — MIGHT MOVE_

26. Attitude towards accepting personal property such as: Contracts _OK_ ; Paper _OK_ ; Live Stock _—_ ; Machinery _—_; Trailers _—_ ; Boats _YES_; Cars _—_ ; Trucks _—_ ; Equipment _—_ ; Airplanes _YES_.

27. Client's attitude toward assuming or making higher loan. _OK — UNDERSTAND PYRAMIDING_

28. Discuss initiating offers in client's behalf with weasel clauses. _MADE PREVIOUS EXCHANGE_

29. Discuss client's business background including previous experiences as an operator (motel) cafe, etc.). _JOHN'S DAD OWNS MOTEL / SAN DIEGO_

29a. Will they manage? _YES_ Are they a user? _MOTEL_ Lease back: _?_ _MAYBE_ (_WIFE RELUCTANT TO MANAGE ALONE_)

30. What is client's present approximate annual income (sources and totals)? _25,000 (SAL. + INC. PROP)_

30a. Is Financial Statement and/or I.R.S. Statements available on request? _OK, IF NEEDED_

31. Attorney _JACK B._ Tax Counselor _TOM A._

32. Is there any third party influence? _NONE APPARENT_

33. Can objective be reached with present vehicle? _$ 200,000 EQUITY_

34. Special interests (fishing)(hunting)(flying) electronics, etc.)? _JOHN / MARY! OUTDOOR TYPES_

35. BROKER'S OPINION OF OBJECTIVE AND POSSIBLE SOLUTIONS: _BOTH UNHAPPY WITH JOHN'S JOB — BOTH MIGHT WANT INDEPENDENCE._

36. Remind client of why he doesn't want the property.

37. Present price $ _360,000_ ; Total encumbrances $ _160,000_ ; Equity $ _200,000_
    (See Check List Work Sheet – Form 15 for details)

38. Referred by whom: _Vic. G._
    Fee Basis: $ _60.00 HOUR_ How payable? _BILLING_

RECORD OF CONTACTS AND COUNSELING MEETINGS

Date	Approximate Time and Type of Contact
7/16	3:00 PM INITIAL INTERVIEW – PROP.
7/19	10:00 AM PROP. ANALYSIS – EMPLOY. INSURANCE – FAMILY
7/20	10:00 AM TAX POSITION – SAVINGS – HOBBIES MOST PROP. MGT. FALLS ON MARY – NOT HAPPY w/ TENANT PROBLEMS

© Exchange Counselor Forms
The Pony Express 1973
P. O. Box 5906
San Jose, CA 95150

Form 3

Figure 8.3 (continued)

sion about the property presently owned. This led into the owner's current tax position. More data became necessary.

In subsequent meetings many possibilities were discussed with the Smiths; the tax-deferred exchange into a larger apartment property and others.

The Confidential Counseling Information Form, after the Counselor had completed several interviews (and with all the lines filled in), is illustrated in Figure 8.3.

The Counselor and the Smiths found out many things during the interviews. At the end of the final interview, the Counselor made the following observations.

1. The Smiths had started on an estate planning program through pyramiding apartment properties several years ago. Financially, it had worked, but the owners had found that they did not work well with the problems of the month-to-month rentals. Mrs. Smith felt that too much of the problems of management and cleanup were left to her while Mr. Smith kept his job. She had handled everything efficiently, but felt that he should be more involved with day-to-day operations.
2. Each of the Smiths had been raised in a small community. Neither was happy with the city in which they had to live—near his work and their apartment property.
3. John was unhappy with his job.
4. John had no idea until the meetings with the Counselor that Mary had the problems with management that she wanted him to share. She had no idea that his work was a problem to him.

The following were the benefits that might be available if the Smiths exchanged for a larger apartment as they originally wanted.

1. A tax-deferred exchange. They could improve cash flow and other cash benefits without a tax liability.
2. They would have a larger property that would shelter more of John's income from his job.
3. It would continue their previous estate building plan.
4. There would be possible relief from tenant problems. The new property might be large enough for professional management.
5. A larger property usually will operate more efficiently than a smaller one.

The Counselor also mentioned an exchange for another type of investment and the possible benefits.

INVESTMENT: Motel in resort area. Ski resort. Apartments at beach or mountains. The possible benefits:

1. Husband and wife could work together.
2. Family could get out of the city.

3. Smith children could be raised in a rural area.
4. John could quit his pressure job. (Under some conditions, he might transfer retirement plan funds from his previous job. The new investment would have to be a corporation and have a pension plan started. An attorney could be consulted.)
5. Since both would be totally self-employed, each would be enjoying the direct benefits of his (and her) own efforts.
6. Mrs. Smith would have someone to share her responsibility.
7. Current equity in the 20 units plus the equity in a home would handle a down payment (exchange).

The Smiths were quick to pick the second alternative. They admitted that they were never happy in the apartment business, but it did make them money. It was also making them miserable.

The possibility of living in a small community and working in their own business seemed like a dream. even a motel with tenants was different from apartments, and John would be there to handle things.

The Counselor referred the Smiths to an exchange broker. A few months later, a successful exchange was closed, moving the Smiths into a mountain resort. It was a combination motel-restaurant at the entrance to a national park. It had all of the benefits they were looking for.

[¶805]   THE EXCHANGOR-COUNSELOR

The previous example showed a Real Estate Investment Counselor who did not work in other fields of real estate. When the actual goals of his clients were set, he referred them to the specialist who might help them.

Most exchange brokers use some techniques of the Real Estate Investment Counselor. Since exchanges are so often for benefits rather than money, any client can usually be helped with a few questions regarding motivations and goals.

An actual training course in Real Estate Counseling is available throughout the United States several times each year. It is sponsored by local real estate boards and is given by the Chatham Educational Corporation, 517 W. Glenoaks Blvd., Glendale, California 91202.

This training course is probably the single most valuable course that is available to anyone in organized real estate. Whether involved in selling, exchanging or any other field of real estate, brokers and salespersons can only profit from really assisting clients to establish their objectives and the benefits sought.

CHAPTER **9**

Marketing Property

[¶900]   **THE EXCHANGE MEETING OR
          MARKETING SESSION**

After sufficient "interview" time with his client, the broker is ready to begin his search for an exchange. Perhaps property offered seems to be unsalable in the normal sale marketplace under the present ownership. Many interviewing hours have been spent exploring possibilities of solutions that an exchange might bring. In some cases, the owner is just looking for action and the opportunities in the exchange arena.

The broker has by this time explored the client's current income tax situation with him. He knows if the exchange must be tax-free—or whether it can be taxable or partially taxable. He knows his client's work experience, experience in business and hobbies.

He knows about the client's immediate family and their needs, and often has asked about other relatives.

Some or all of these facts might assist in helping to find the right property, business opportunity or investment property that might be an exchange opportunity best for his client.

Of course, the owner's current income, occupation, retirement date and income sources can also be very important when the broker starts using his judgment into which possible properties he should start offers for the client.

Following are two forms used as a guide by many brokers, (Figures 9.1 and 9.2). Usually they are not used as an "interview form" while discussing possibilities with a client, but as a place to "add up" what the broker knows and needs to know about his customer that might help with a solution.

𝔓ersonal 𝔇ata

Name		Age	Address						Date / /
			Children's	M	M	M	M	M	
Wife's Name		Age	Age	F	F	F	F	F	TOTAL
Occupation	Yrs.	Business Address			Phone - Bus.			Home	

LINE No.	NET WORTH									
		(1) CURRENT YEAR NET	(2) 1 YEAR AGO		(3) GAIN OR LOSS		(4) 2 YEARS AGO		(5) GAIN OR LOSS	
1	Cash in Banks									1
2	Savings Scd. IC6 L5									2
3	Stock Scd. IIC6 L13									3
4	Other Scd. IIIC6 L21									4
5										5
6	Real Estate Scd. IVC8 L32									6
7										7
8	Total Net Worth									8
9	ANNUAL INCOME & EXPENSE									9
		(1)	(2)		(3)		(4)			
10	Gainful Occupation Husband Gross		$							10
11	Gainful Occupation Wife Gross									11
12	Total Gainful Occupation				$					12
13	Interest Schedule IC9 L5	%	$							13
14	Dividends " IIC9 L13	%								14
15	Other " IIIC9 L21	%								15
16		%								16
17	Real Estate " IVC11 L32	%								17
18	Total Investment Income	100 %			$					18
19	Capital Gains									19
20	Total Income (Spendable)						$			20
21	Less Expense									21
22	Income Tax Federal $ (1) State $ (2)		$							22
23	Food	$								23
24	Clothing									24
25	Medical									25
26	Utilities									26
27	Miscellaneous		$							27
28	Personal Property Tax (Home - etc.)									28
29	Insurance									29
30	Personal Installment Payments P & I									30
31	Other									31
32	Total Annual Expense						$			32
33	Balance Available for Investment						$			33

34	INCOME TAX ALLOCATION			INVESTMENT ALLOCATION				34
35	Federal Income Tax L22(1)	$		ITEM	AMOUNT		TAX	35
36	Gainful Occupation L12	$		Interest %	$		$	36
37	Less Exemp. & Deduc.			Dividends %				37
38	Tot. & Tax on Some	$		Other %				38
39	Inc. Tax on Invest. (L 35 - L 38)			Real Estate %				39
40				Total 100 %	$		$	40
41								41

Addendum A

The statements and figures presented herein, while not guaranteed, are secured from sources we believe authoritative.

PREPARED BY_____

Figure 9.1

CONFIDENTIAL COUNSELING INFORMATION

1. Date: _____

2. Owner's Name: _____ Age: _____ Phone: _____

3. Home Address: _____ How long? _____

4. Occupation: _____ Phone: _____
    Business Address: _____

5. Family Status: ____ Married   Spouse's Name: _____ Age: _____
                    ____ Widow(er) Number of Children: ____
                    ____ Divorced   Name _____ Age ____ Sex ____ Location _____
                    ____ Single   Name _____ Age ____ Sex ____ Location _____
                                    Name _____ Age ____ Sex ____ Location _____
                                    Name _____ Age ____ Sex ____ Location _____

6. Type of Property Owned: _____

7. Property Location: _____
    City _____ County _____ State _____

8. How is Title to Property Vested? _____

9. When was the Property acquired and how? _____
    Purchased ____ (Price Paid $_____); Gift ____; Exchange ____; Inheritance ____; Other ____

10. What is the present tax basis of the property? _____

11. How long has the property been for sale or on the market? _____

11a. Previously listed? _____

12. Are vehicles offered readily saleable? _____

13. Is this to be a tax-deferred exchange? _____

13a. Is there a potential "forgiveness of mortgage" problem? _____

14. Is client classified as a "DEALER"? _____

15. Client's opinion of their problem and/or reason for disposing of property. (See Item 35)
    _____

16. What do they wish to accomplish? _____

17. What can vehicle do for new owner? (Potential, refinance possibilities, etc.) _____
    _____

18. What are their needs? M–Money _____   How much? $ _____
                           A–Appreciation _____ What do they expect? _____
                           I–Income _____   How much? $ _____
                           D–Depreciation _____   How much? $ _____
                           Other– Future needs and why needed: Explain _____
    _____

19. Is there a critical time element or urgency of any type? If so, explain: _____
    _____

20. Client's readiness to act: Desperate ____; Highly Motivated ____; Shows Interest ____

21. Are title holders in accord to make decision? ____ Do they seem flexible to deal with? _____

22. Is client oriented to other areas? ____ Explain geographical limitations, if any, and why: _____
    _____

Figure 9.2

23. What price range will they consider? $_____ Can add cash. How much? $_____
    How soon?_____ Source of cash._____
    Needs cash. How much? $_____ Why?_____

24. Do they have cash for expenses? (Fees, title insurance, escrow, etc.)_____

25. Do they have other property that can be added? ____ Describe type and approximate equity (including stocks and property other than real estate):_____

26. Attitude towards accepting personal property such as: Contracts ____; Paper ____; Live Stock ____;
    Machinery ____; Trailers ____; Boats ____; Cars ____; Trucks ____; Equipment ____; Airplanes ____.

27. Client's attitude toward assuming or making higher loan._____

28. Discuss initiating offers in client's behalf with weasel clauses.

29. Discuss client's business background including previous experiences as an operator (motel, cafe, etc.).

29a. Will they manage? _____ Are they a user? _____ Lease back:_____

30. What is client's present approximate annual income (sources and totals)?_____

30a. Is Financial Statement and/or I.R.S. Statements available on request?_____

31. Attorney_____ Tax Counselor_____

32. Is there any third party influence?_____

33. Can objective be reached with present vehicle?_____

34. Special interests (fishing, hunting, flying, electronics, etc.)?_____

35. BROKER'S OPINION OF OBJECTIVE AND POSSIBLE SOLUTIONS:_____

36. Remind client of why he doesn't want the property.

37. Present price $_____; Total encumbrances $_____; Equity $_____
    (See Check List Work Sheet - Form 15 for details)

38. Referred by whom:_____
    Fee Basis: $_____ How payable?_____

RECORD OF CONTACTS AND COUNSELING MEETINGS

Date	Approximate Time and Type of Contact

If you haven't contacted your client in the last two weeks – CALL HIM UP!

© Exchange Counselor Forms
The Pony Express 1973
P. O. Box 5906
San Jose, CA 95150

Form 3

Figure 9.2 (continued)

[¶901]   SEARCHING FOR AN EXCHANGE OPPORTUNITY

The broker's search for a solution starts in his own office by reviewing other listed properties. He analyzes these properties and visualizes the effect of the ownership of that property if owned by the new client. He may have two owners doing business with his office who might improve each other's position with a two-way exchange.

He may find that one owner's property may serve as an opportunity for the other, but not the reverse.

Since the properties represented in any one real estate office would be limited, only a few opportunities or solutions are found here. The next stop is to contact other exchange specialists for assistance in "putting together" the exchange.

[¶902]   AN OVERVIEW OF THE
MARKETING SESSION

It is obvious that meeting with a broker or brokers from another office would expand the choice of exchange situations that could be offered to a client. Brokers could meet over lunch or in each other's offices to discuss their clients' real estate holdings and the new positions that were being sought for them.

In years past, fewer real estate brokers were oriented toward exchanges. Exchange specialists might have to travel 50 or 100 miles to meet for a few hours with other brokers in this specialty.

These brokers quickly became aware of the opportunities that might become available to them if they got together and "matched" as many client problems as possible at one meeting.

The Marketing Session or Exchange Meeting was born. A broker in one area sent notices to other exchangors in adjoining areas that he was hosting a marketing session on a certain date. The meetings were originally held in the host's office, but as the groups became larger, moved to hotel meeting rooms. Later, the hotels picked often were near freeway or expressway interchanges or at airports, to assist brokers coming from a distance.

[¶903]   MULTIPLYING THE POSSIBLE SOLUTIONS

If a broker represents three clients needing exchanges, the possibility of an exchange between the three is remote. There is just too great a variety of types of real estate that might be owned. However, if 30 or more brokers meet together, each representing three clients, then the possibilities are good for many possible solutions for each client.

When 90 or 100 exchange properties are presented as possibilities to an individual client's property package, there may be as many as ten ways to solve his problem or enhance his position.

Note: this is in no way related to the Multiple Listing Service that Boards of Realtors use for the sale of their properties. Normally, multiple listings are placed in the market place looking for one solution only—a cash sale. Usually, no other possibility is considered.

[¶904]   PRESENT DAY MARKETING SESSIONS

Marketing sessions for exchange are now usually by invitation only. As real estate practitioners get known as being knowledgeable on taxes, counseling and multiple-exchange techniques, they are invited to attend. As more people attend the meetings, the procedures of the meetings have become quite formalized to handle as much business as possible in a limited time.

Marketing sessions are held locally, regionally and on a national basis.

[¶904.1]   The Local Meeting

A small group of brokers may meet weekly or monthly at a breakfast or luncheon meeting to discuss clients and client properties. As the group grows to 20 or more and attracts interest from brokers in neighboring communities, the meetings may become more formal and organized. The meeting is then moved to a conference room or hotel.

The business done by this group is related to smaller or less valuable properties and most exchanges are local. The owners seldom exchange for a property any distance away.

[¶904.2]   The Regional or Statewide Meeting

Brokers from several local groups may form an exchange group that has members from a larger geographical area. The area may be several counties of a State or may cover a whole State.

While the local groups allow any broker in the community who is interested to attend, the regional group usually is formed by more aggressive "doers" in the business. Therefore, the membership in this organization may be by invitation only. The invited members often are the better-known members of local groups who have earned a reputation for completing transactions.

Since the participants are coming from a wide area, this is the meeting that will be held at an airport hotel or near a main freeway. These meetings are usually held monthly or bi-monthly.

The properties offered are, for the most part, more valuable, larger properties. The owners may be more sophisticated and are less area-bound. An owner may exchange an apartment complex in his city for a shopping center in a nearby State. The shopping center owner may be exchanging up into a third property clear across the country.

[¶904.3]   The National Meeting

For several years, a national marketing meeting has been held once a year in Las Vegas, Nevada. Brokers from all over the country attend the meeting which lasts several days. Often 300 to 400 brokers attend.

The properties and clients represented are looking for solutions and opportunities on a national basis. When an owner has a multi-million dollar shopping center for exchange, he must be free of most geographic restrictions in order to find an exchange into a property that will suit him financially and taxwise.

The larger the property in value or the more difficult the client's problem with his property, the larger the geographic area that must be considered.

[¶905]   HOW THE MEETINGS WORK

When a group of brokers meet for a marketing meeting, the prime object is to communicate. Each participant wants all of the other attending brokers to understand fully the situation of his client and the exchange property or situation sought. In turn, he also wants to understand fully the same about all other's owners and clients. The property he represents has to be both a "purchase" equity and a "solution" to some one else's problem.

[¶906]   THE PRESENTATION

It has been found that the "stand-up" presentation does the best job at the meeting. (See Figures 9.3 and 9.4 for layout.) Each participant is given a short allotted time—maybe 10 or 15 minutes, at the podium. During his time, the others give him and his client their complete attention. Everyone

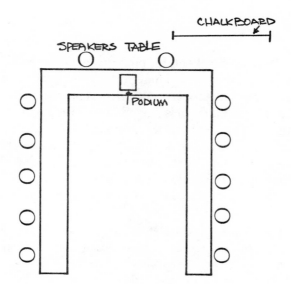

Figure 9.3

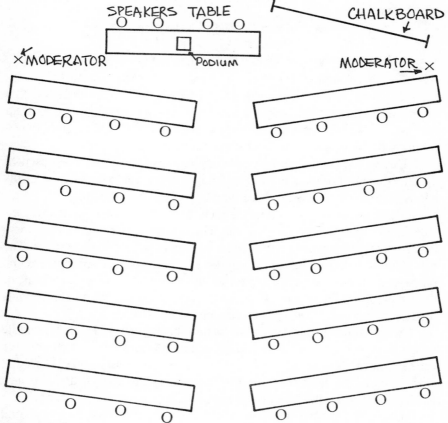

Figure 9.4

173

strives to understand the client, his property and what will be best for him.

Just before the presenting broker steps to the podium, a sheet giving a partial discription of the property and client is passed. Usually on a 8½" x 11" paper, a copy of the form is passed to all. (See Figure 9.5.) They then can focus attention on a written description of the property while listening to the broker elaborate on the client and his need for an exchange.

This description or "package" as it is called, also includes a short outline of the owner and some of his objectives.

When at the podium, the broker's presentation is usually in the following order:

1. A short discussion on the client and his background. This will usually include age, business background or occupation, personal situations such as marital, children. Personal problems that might be caused by current tax situation and anything else that the brokers may need to assist them in making a decision on the best property for this owner to exchange into.
2. Further information about the property not shown in the short description on the "package."
3. The problems the client has had with the property—what the property will do for a new owner.
4. The ideal objective the broker is seeking for his client.

The discussion of the client may include his motivation for an exchange, his desires, outside influences in his life and any other factors that might be important. The property that he is seeking may be less important than what it will do for him—income or a job may be needed more than a property that will give "pride of ownership."

Depending, then, on the wants and needs of the owners represented by the offering brokers, the presenter may have the raw material in his hands for several two-way, three-way or four-way exchanges.

Then the next presentation starts. The next broker passes out his "package" and goes to the podium. The last presenter and all the others now focus all their attention to the new person at the center of the room. The new property being presented may be another possible solution for the property previously described to the group or might be a solution for one of the other offers. It might fill out a three-way exchange. Everyone gets ready to "write-in" if they can see a possible exchange.

When three or four presentations have been given, a 10- or 15-minute break is called for coffee and quick meetings between participants for further information to assist in getting a long-form formal offer started.

Usually the next three or four presenters are named and the new moderators for the next group are appointed before the break starts.

Using this format, the meeting will continue for a day, two or several

ABC REALTY
157 FIFTEENTH STREET
PACIFIC GROVE, CA. 93950

Price: $70,000.00
Loans: 22,000.00
Equity: 48,000.00

HAVE: A duplex just off a major street in Pacific Grove, Calif. This is a two story building with one apartment on each floor. Two single garages. Rents: $325.00 each unit. This year's taxes $1,560.00

ADDRESS: 201 Bonnie Place

PRICE: $70,000.00

LOANS: $22,000.00 Purchase money first T.D. $300.00 Month Inc. 8% Int. till paid.

EQUITY: $48,000.00

WHY DOES NOT WANT: Owner has owned for six years. His equity has increased with increase in value of properties in this community. At this time, analysis shows that equity is not doing job for him. Wishes to exchange equity in a tax-deferred exchange into a better leverage position.

SUGGESTED SOLUTIONS: Wants to stay in residential income property. Suggest we try exchange into 8 or more units. Also submit leased commercial or other possible solutions as owner may show interest.

REMARKS: Apartments are equipped with built-in ranges, dishwashers, & refrigerators. Each has an excellent ocean view. Both tenants have been here for years.

OWNERS: Mr. & Mrs. T. C. Gilbert

FEE: $4,200.00

BROKER: V. C. Saylor
ABC Realty
157 Fifteenth St.
Pacific Grove, Ca. 93950
(408) 649-1111

This information is from sources deemed reliable, but is not guaranteed by agent. Package is subject to price change, correction, error, omission, prior sale and withdrawal.

Figure 9.5

days depending on the number of participants at the marketing session. Before it is over, most of the brokers will have many written proposals—both written "out" and received from others. The possibilities for each participant will be many and varied.

[¶907]   THE MODERATORS

One or two moderators are appointed from the ranks of the attending brokers. They are usually successful, experienced brokers who have attended exchange meetings for years. It is their job to question the broker at the podium to bring out important facts that might be overlooked.

When the presenter has given a description of the property package that is for exchange, the moderators will ask a few questions that have occurred to them during the presentation. The answers may fully clarify points that have raised a question in the minds of the other brokers in the room.

The following are a list of typical moderator questions:

1. Can you easily define the client's problem?
2. Can your client define what he thinks the problem is?
3. How many personal interviews have you had with all of the owners in title?
4. What is the client's short range objective?
5. Does the client have long range objectives? What?
6. What is the preferred property that he is seeking?
7. What do *you* see him taking?
8. What offers has he turned down? Why?
9. Is the client MONEY—oriented or is he truly looking for other benefits?
10. Have you consulted with other professionals about the client or his property? Banker, CPA, Attorney, Appraiser?
11. Have you, as a broker, completed any previous transactions with this client?
12. In previous meetings, what has the client offered into?
13. Do you feel your client is realistic?
14. Do you think *you* are realistic in thinking about the client's wants?
15. To solve the problem, would your client buy back the property?
16. Do you have primary and secondary loan commitments?
17. What can your client add in cash and other property?
18. What is really more important to him—a sale or a solution?
19. Will he create notes against current property to reach a solution?
20. Is appreciation really important?
21. Is money important to him? Monthly income or re-finance?

22. Is depreciation important? Now? Future? When?
23. Will the client manage property?
24. Has the property been listed before? Sale? Exchange? How long?
25. What are the geographic limitations for this client? Why?
26. Will he add cash to BUY his way out of the problem?
27. Will he split the property?
28. Will he go into a partnership or joint venture?
29. What skills does he have to contribute to a user property?
30. Motel management? Restaurant management? Resort management?
31. How long will it take him to react to an offer?

After this questioning, the moderators will call on brokers at the meeting who indicate that they have further questions. When the questioning is completed, everyone in the room will have a fairly clear idea of the property, tax situation of the owner and other general information about the client and property. They also have a good idea of the solution that he is seeking. In addition, they may have an idea of a possible solution that the owner has never considered.

The moderators then ask the group for solutions. At this point members of the group will write "preliminary offers" and briefly tell the group the nature of the property offered. (Of course, all offers are preliminary and all will be subject to approval of the principals involved. However, if the members of the group have interviewed well, the solutions will often go to escrow and close an exchange.)

The offers come in three parts:

1. A solution for the property.
   Who in the room has an owner with any kind of property who might be a "taker" or a "user" for the property that was presented? The owner can offer real estate, personal property or cash. Cash always remains the best medium of exchange!
2. A solution for the client.
   Who in the room has an owner with a property that might be a solution property for the client of the presenting broker? This may be a "solution" that was asked for or maybe something that a member of the group might think would be a better solution.
3. When these solutions have been related to the group, a third call is for possible "takers" for any of the other properties that have been "broadcast" as property or client solutions.

[¶908]   THE SOLUTIONS

When the first question is asked, hands are raised throughout the meeting room. Maybe five or more brokers have a possible "taker" for the presented property. Each is called on for a short description. The answers might be: "I have a client with a duplex in Los Angeles who might want the property."

Or, "I have a client with a R-1 lot in San Diego who might want to own it."

After all the takers are recorded, the second group is questioned. Now we need solutions for the client. Who has a property or another solution for him. The answers might be: "I have a client with ten apartment units in Santa Barbara that might fit his needs." "I have my own property—a strip shopping center in Anaheim that sounds like what he wants."

Each of the brokers with either a "taker" or a "solution" to the exchange writes a short memo form to the presenting broker. The form, called a Preliminary Exchange Proposal is written immediately while the thought is still fresh in the broker's mind.

A sample of the form is reproduced in Figure 9.6. It is also called, "a mini-offer."

On this form, the brokers write the outline of what an exchange idea might be. Since the form is only designed as a "memo" it does not have room for extensive terms and conditions or long legal paragraphs, only the basic thoughts. If the principals agree with the preliminary idea, a longer legal form with all of the proper paragraphs is used for the next step in the negotiations.

When the presenting broker returns to his seat at the meeting, he may be handed up to 20 "mini-offers" written on Preliminary Exchange Proposals. Attached to each will be a "package" description of the offered property and perhaps a complete homework package of the property being offered for consideration. Some will be "takers" for the presented property and others will offer "solutions" for the client to trade into.

[¶909]   ROUND TABLE PRESENTATIONS

With smaller meetings, a popular method of reaching client solutions is by use of the "Round Table" meeting. The "Round Table" consists of a few brokers and up to 15 or so sitting at a table or tables of any shape brainstorming the client's real estate portfolios and problems in a more informal way than at an exchange meeting.

A table leader is appointed to lead the discussion and keep it on track.

Each participant is again given the opportunity to present his or his client's property to the group to help find a solution.

The leader calls on all participants, one by one around the table, for

PRELIMINARY EXCHANGE PROPOSAL

F R O M

T O

Date:

Subject:

MY CLIENT: _____

    Type of Property: _____ Address: _____

             : _____ : _____

             : _____ : _____

Encumbrances: _____

YOUR CLIENT: _____

    Type of Property: _____ Address: _____

             : _____ : _____

             : _____ : _____

Encumbrances: _____

TERMS AND CONDITIONS _____

NOTE: Other data on properties outlined herein as per sheets attached and submitted herewith. Final terms and conditions, if any, to be in subsequent offer and/or escrow instructions.

This proposal is subject to prior disposition of the above properties, and shall expire on

(date) _____

Both Brokers agree to direct their immediate attention to this proposal and submit any additional data requested by either broker.

| SUBMITTING COUNSELOR | DATE | BROKER RECEIVING OFFER | DATE |

Remarks: _____

Form 1
© Exchange Counselor Forms
The Pony Express 1973
P. 0. Box 5906
San Jose, CA 95150

Approved: _____

Date: _____

Approved: _____

Date: _____

Figure 9.6

their thoughts on an exchange or possible exchange for the first property presented. Exchanges of any types of property might be proposed. At the end of the discussion of each property, the table leader calls for "takers" and "solutions" as done after the "stand-up" presentation.

For a small group of exchangors, the round table is an effective method of working on a few properties with a few participants. It would not adapt well to a very large group. However, at a very large exchange meeting, sometimes 100 to 150 brokers will break down the meeting into several Round Tables. The groups might be broken down into tables for properties up to $500,000 in equity at one table, $500,000 to $1,000,000 at another table, then over $1,000,000 in equity at another. After an hour or two, the members would move around and mix up the groups at each table.

[¶910] EXCHANGE MEETING WITH THE "OPPORTUNITY AND CATALYST SYSTEM"

The "Opportunity and Catalyst" system of exposing exchange properties can be used with either "stand-up" presentations or with smaller groups at a Round Table.

Using this system, the participants at the meeting try to "force" their thinking into exchange situations that might not otherwise occur to them. With many client properties being exposed, participants might feel overwhelmed by sheer numbers of properties. Now they can focus on one problem or opportunity and one solution, but with the ability to substitute various properties.

The following columns and headings are placed on a chalkboard:

Problem	Takers	Solutions	Catalysts

After a presentation to the group by the broker of his client's "package"—property, owner and solution sought, the following is listed on the board by the meeting moderator.

First Column: A discription of the property being presented, value of property, loans and equity. The focus of the group will be to attempt to provide properties and information that will "start" an exchange.

Second Column: When the information is down in Column #1, and questions have been asked about the client and his property, the group is asked for information on owners with properties that can be traded for the property in Column #1. All of the thought and concentration of the group should be on "users" only, no matter what the property of the "user" might be. The objective at this stage of the meeting is to list on the board as many owners and properties as possible who might want the property shown in Column #1. The brokers call out the information on their properties and it is written on the board.

Third Column: During the broker presentation, the participants heard the type of property, its use, notes or personal property, cash, that might be a solution for the first column client. This is the information on property that he might go into. Again in this column, it is not important if the broker thinks his client will accept the first column property. It is only important to *write* listed properties that might be an exchange solution for the First Column owner. In this column also, the participants at the meeting call out the information which is then written on the board.

Fourth Column: Now there may be anywhere from a few to 20 or more properties written in the first three columns. Members of the group may already see possible two- or three-way exchanges on the board. In Column #4, they now list properties and owners that might be "users" or "takers" for any property listed in Columns #2 or #3. This column lists the properties that might be the "Catalyst" to help put together the multiple exchange.

By having the information broken down in columns we have diagrammed for all participants to see "users" for properties all over the board. We have overcome any reluctance of people to make an offer on a property when the whole transaction is not obvious.

An example of a completed chalkboard at an exchange meeting is showin in Figure 9.7.

During the "opportunity and catalyst" system, the first objective is to find a "taker" for the Column #1 property, and a new property for the present owner to go into.

Happily, each time a "user" property is called out by a member of the group, the whole group hears a one-minute description of another listed property that can be moved. Since more than one owner represented by the group might want similar real estate, other exchanges might be initiated.

Again, when the "Solution" and "Catalyst" columns are filled in, the information communicated is noted by the group.

After the columns are all filled in, the moderator of the meeting will put arrows on the board showing the direction that Preliminary Exchange Proposals should be written.

Since all of the Column #2 entries were *users* who might want the Column #1 property, each broker should be writing an offer from owner in #2 to owner in #1. The meeting moderator will ask the broker representing #1 if any of the "user" properties in #2 seem to be something that owner

CATALYST METHOD OF PROBLEM SOLVING

PROBLEM	TAKERS	SOLUTIONS	CATALYSTS
CLIENT: BROWN PROPERTY: 19 UNIT APT. PRICE: $285,000 LOAN: 104,000 EQUITY: 181,000 SOLUTION: BUILDER WANTS COMM. LAND FOR DEVELOP.	1. $50,000 F/C LAND BROKER: JONES 2. 3 DUPLEXES $195,000 PRICE -117,000 LOANS 78,000 EQUITY BROKER: SMITH 3. 8 UNIT APART. $85,000 F/C BROKER: JACKSON	1. 4 ACRES COMM. ZONING - NEAR FREEWAY RAMP $200,000 F/C BROKER - SMITH 2. MOTEL SITE $100,000 VALUE 20,000 LOAN 80,000 EQUITY BROKER: DREW	1. 50 ACRES GRAZING LAND $60,000 F+C BROKER: BARNES 2. $60,000 IN PAPER (2ND T.D. SEASONED) BROKER: CARNES 3. $10,000 CITY LOT F+C (R-1) + $25,000 IN PAPER (TO BE CREATED) BROKER: WARDEN

Figure 9.7

182

#1 might want to own. If the answer is affirmative, he puts an arrow between them, with points at either end (◀————▶), indicating a possible two-way exchange. Most of the arrows will be one-way, for it is not often that a quick two-way solution pops up.

Then he moves to Column #3. Since these are "solution" properties for #1, he asks if any of the owners of the #3 properties might also be users for #1. If so, the arrow will again have two points, indicating a possible "two-way." Again, this is unusual, as it probably would have been in Column #2, rather than Column #3 if the owner was a "user." So the arrows will be one-way from Column #3 to Column #1. The broker representing the Column #1 owner now has the obligation to write the Preliminary Exchange Proposals to the brokers and owners of the properties listed in Column #3.

Finally the moderator moves to Column #4. These may be the most important. They are properties whose owners might be "users" for any real estate or personal property listed in Columns #2 & #3. These are the CATALYSTS that might solve the three- or four-way exchange. The moderator questions the #2 and #3 brokers about a possible "two-way" between their owners and the #4 owners. Arrows are drawn. The responsibility for the written preliminary offer is established by agreement. Either may initiate the offer.

It is not unusual to have two or three exchanges, both multiple and two-way, result from one "Catalyst" system exposure on the chalkboard.

After this presentation, as many brokers who are involved with the properties on the board make copies of the board. Some take a picture with an instant camera to record the information.

Checking back on many of the brokers involved with this type of exchange meeting, many exchanges are started here. It is interesting to note that often the property in Column #1, which started it all, is not involved in the exchanges. So many other ideas are generated during the meeting that result in excellent beneficial exchanges, the original property is left out.

[¶911]   AFTER THE MEETING

When the brokers from the exchange meeting return to their offices, they may have quite a stack of preliminary exchange proposals to show their client. Now the serious work begins.

As we have shown, some of the offers are proposals written by this broker for his client toward a property that is a solution. Others were received as users for this client's real estate package.

The client is interviewed about the possibility of the "solution" properties. If they appear to work, a long-form formal offer may be prepared or a physical inspection of the property may be undertaken.

The broker for each client must now try to negotiate exchanges that satisfy the desires of the client he represents. The negotiations will usually take a number of phone calls and meetings individually with the brokers and their clients, similar to any other real estate transaction.

Offers and counter offers move back and forth. Property inspections are completed. Finally, if everything works out, two or three or more offers with the last negotiations completed are accepted on all sides.

A two-way or multiple exchange is completed and is escrowed or closed by the method of the state or states where the properties are located.

In the following chapter, we will cover a four-way exchange, showing the information from the exchange meeting, the negotiations and the final agreements.

CHAPTER **10**

Negotiating the Exchange

[¶1000]   **A SAMPLE PROBLEM**

Mrs. Peters, the owner of two small apartment properties in the city of Pasadena, near Los Angeles, contacted Larry Price, a real estate broker in Northern California. She wanted to move her equity in these apartments to her new home, Monterey County in the North. She had just moved to this area, approximately 350 miles from the Los Angeles area.

When Price discussed the exchange transaction with Mrs. Peters, he found out the following during the first interview:

1. The property in the South had been purchased 27 years ago by Mrs. Peters as her own property, not in joint tenancy or community property with her husband. She had been and was still the sole owner. She was now a widow, her husband having died ten years ago.

2. Though rundown, the Pasadena properties (a duplex and a four-plex) brought in good income and had recently been appraised at $80,000.

3. Mrs. Peters had a strong feeling about the stability of real estate ownership and wanted to remain invested in property.

4. Her accountant had warned of the capital gains tax on a sale and recommended that she contact Broker Price about a tax-deferred exchange.

Price also found in his interview that Mrs. Peter's son lived nearby and would assist her in managing the new property. His opinion would be valued by Mrs. Peters. The son, Vernon Peters, was Mrs. Peter's sole heir. Price suggested that they meet again when Vernon could be with his mother.

At the next meeting, after meeting Mrs. Peter's son, Price agreed to list the Pasadena properties for exchange.

After a listing agreement was signed, Price met with Mrs. Peters and her son several times. He wanted to know various things that would help him with the exchange of the properties. He asked questions regarding:

1. The feelings of both regarding taking on new debt (the Southern California property was free and clear).
2. Their feelings on the age of buildings that they might own. Would older buildings suit them or did they need to be new?
3. Whether they wanted just a few units as Peters now owned or larger property.
4. Did they want apartments or commercial property, or did it matter?
5. Would the expenses (brokerage, escrow, etc.) be paid out of cash savings or would the money have to be generated out of the transaction?
6. Would they manage the new property themselves or would they require professional management?

After these interviews, Price determined that they wanted to see Mrs. Peters' equity exchanged up into a larger apartment property of about 10 to 20 units valued at $200,000 to $300,000. They wanted the units in good condition, but not necessarily new. Mrs. Peters had other income from securities and could use the additional tax shelter that a stepped-up basis could provide.

She also wanted to control a larger property that would someday be passed on to her son. Expenses of the transaction would be paid out of cash savings, so the entire equity from Pasadena could be utilized in the exchange.

During the same few weeks, Price was developing a homework package on the apartments. Though he felt it was not absolutely necessary, he went to Southern California to see the apartments and the surrounding areas. He always tried to personally inspect property that he had listed, unless it was too far away.

Since the property was being managed by a Pasadena broker, Price found it easy to secure copies of the individual rental agreements, inspect the apartments and meet some of the occupants. He had previously picked up copies of the deeds and other recorded legal documents at the Court House. The Peters also furnished a statement of expenses and income for the past two years.

The broker's property package was completed at about the same time that his interviews with Mrs. Peters and her son were finished. It was just five weeks since he had met them, and he was now ready to take the Pasadena properties into the exchange marketplace.

[¶1001] SEEKING A SOLUTION

The strategy that Price had developed was to find the larger apartment in Monterey County first, attending local and regional meetings in his local area. Depending, then, on what the larger apartment property owner wanted, he would then try to find a "user" for the Pasadena property. Hopefully, the user of the Pasadena units could satisfy the needs of the Northern California owner. Since this was a geographic exchange, in addition to a tax-deferred transaction, Price felt that somewhere the equity might need to be converted to a neutral vehicle that almost anyone could accept, such as trust deed notes or mortgage notes.

Price attended a local meeting in Monterey and presented Mrs. Peters' Pasadena apartments. Although the units were far away, there would be some interest in them because they were free and clear of loans. A copy of the package that Price passed out at the meeting is shown in Figure 10.1.

At the same meeting, a package for a 22-unit apartment property in Salinas, California, was also brought before the group. This was only 15 miles from the Peters' home and was easily within their geographic limits. A copy of the package for the Salinas units is also shown (Figure 10-2). The broker was Bill Smith who had worked with the owner of the units in several other transactions.

During Smith's turn at the podium, Price listened carefully. It appeared that the 22-unit would be a good property for Mrs. Peters. It was local. It was fairly new and in good condition. It was in the range of value and number of units that Price wanted for his client.

Smith gave further information regarding the size of each apartment, the income, the neighborhood. He stated that the income property was located in a workingman's neighborhood, lower middle class tenants who were seldom out of work. The vacancy factor was favorable—low. The existing loan on the property was a bank loan and was easily assumable by a new owner.

The owner of the property, Edward Carillo, was a builder and developer who had owned these apartments for several years as an investment property. Two years ago, Carillo had been injured in an accident and had not worked since. He was now recovered and felt well enough to return to work.

Smith also explained that Carillo had used most of his savings for medical and living expenses and had little in assets except the apartment property. He had listed it with the broker for sale. He planned to use the proceeds of a sale to purchase land ready for development for commercial buildings or more apartments.

When the property was listed, Smith suggested also to Carillo that they also try to exchange it directly for a property that the builder could use for development.

MONTEREY PENINSULA EXCHANGE COUNSELORS

HAVE:
Six rental units. A Duplex and a four-plex located near
one another in a good rental area of Pasadena.
Scheduled gross income of duplex $5,130.00 annually,
SGI of fourplex is $9,630.00. Current taxes $735.00 &
$1,243.00. Currently being managed by local broker.
Buildings older but in good condition.

ADDRESS:
26 Hunter Ave (Duplex) & 139 Corta St.

PRICE:
$80,000 total. $26,000 for Duplex & $54,000 for Four Unit.
(Appraisal by B.B. Cater Co.)

LOANS:
-0-

EQUITY:
$80,000

**WHY DOES
NOT WANT:**
Owner has moved to Monterey County from Southern Calif.
Wishes to make a tax-deferred exchange while moving equity
closer to her present home.

**SUGGESTED
SOLUTIONS:**
Exchange up into larger income property. Would like to
control 20 to 30 units as wants the benefits of leveraged
position in new apartment property.

REMARKS:
Owner has extremely low basis in these properties. Has
owned for 27 years and completely depreciated improvement.

OWNER:
Mrs. Mary Peters

FEE:
6%

COUNSELOR:
James R. Price
Price Realty
2600 Lighthouse Ave.
Monterey, Calif. 93940

Figure 10.1

22 UNITS SALINAS

Price: $285,000
Loans: 104,000
Equity: 181,000

HAVE: Eleven two bedroom and eleven one bedroom apartment units in a good rental area of Salinas. Located in Alisal area. Owner establishes gross rents at $40,500 annually. Complete homework package showing all income and expenses for past two years available.

ADDRESS: 433 Elysian St.

PRICE: $285,000

LOANS: $104,000 1st T.D. $1,048.00 mo. inc. 9% Int. First Salinas Savings & Loan.

EQUITY: $181,000

WHY DOES NOT WANT: Owner is a builder. Would like to acquire commercial property ready for development.

SUGGESTED SOLUTIONS: Exchange directly into commercial. Sell on installment sale or cash out. Will exchange down into readily saleable properties - houses, lots.

REMARKS: Client primarily a seller. Not concerned with tax consequences. Has had property on sale market.

OWNER: E. C. Carrillo

FEE: Six per cent

COUNSELOR: J. C. Smith
11 Romie Lane
Salinas, Calif. 93901

This information is from sources deemed reliable, but is not guaranteed by agent. Package is subject to price change, correction, error, omission, prior sale and withdrawal.

Figure 10.2

After Smith's presentation, Price prepared a Preliminary Exchange Proposal offering Mrs. Peters' Pasadena properties in for exchange for the 22 units of Mr. Carillo (Figure 10.3). Since Peters' equity was only $80,000, he proposed that Carillo carry back junior financing of $100,000 on the Salinas property. (See Price's Preliminary Exchange Agreement, Figure 10.4).

During the next break, Price explained his proposal to Smith. Smith agreed to take the mini-offer to Carillo although the Southern California properties were certainly not what Carillo wanted. Price asked that Carillo consider the exchange proposal as "taker" for the Salinas property. Both brokers could then try to find a development property to round out a three-way exchange.

The following day, Price met again with Mrs. Peters and her son. He showed them the income and expense statements on the 22-unit apartment. They agreed that it looked good "on paper."

Price thoroughly explained Carillo's situation. He proposed that Mrs. Peters sign a long-form offer, offering the Pasadena properties in for the Salinas apartments. Mrs. Peters understood that Carillo definitely would not accept her property as his final solution. Price would present the offer to Smith and try to get Carrillo to accept the offer "in lieu."

Smith had met with Carrillo and explained the mini-offer. He explained that Carrillo would be converting his equity in the apartments into two smaller properties and a $100,000 note which might give him the flexibility to find a buildable project quickly.

Since Smith and Carrillo had no offers on the apartments during the previous sixty days, Carrillo accepted the offer Price sent. (See Figure 10.5.)

Carrillo understood that Mrs. Peters was a taker for the Salinas property and was not haggling over the value or any details. He also understood that he had no obligation to close the transaction with Mrs. Peters. If the brokers were not able to find a suitable property for him during the "in lieu" period for 60 days, the offer was canceled. The exchange agreement had contingencies about another property for Carrillo that had to be met before Peters got the property.

After the exchange agreement was signed, the two owners now had the following as "owners in acquisition."

1. Mrs. Peters had the property that she wanted in a tax-deferred exchange. Her equity was transferred in a good leverage position.

2. Carrillo had the Pasadena apartments worth $80,000 which were free and clear of loans. He also had a secured note in the amount of

PRELIMINARY EXCHANGE PROPOSAL

FROM

J.R. PRICE

TO
J.C. SMITH
11 ROMIE LANE
SALINAS, CALIF.

Date: *Nov. 23, 1978*

Subject: EXCHANGE

PETERS — CARRILLO

MY CLIENT: MRS. MARY PETERS

Type of Property: 6 UNITS — Address: 26 HUNTER, PASADENA
: (2 UNIT + 4 UNIT) — : 139 CORTA "

Encumbrances: NONE — FREE + CLEAR OF LOANS

YOUR CLIENT: E. C. CARRILLO

Type of Property: 22 UNIT APARTMENT — Address: 433 ELYSIAN ST.
: — : SALINAS

Encumbrances: $104,000 1ST T.D. (FIRST SALINAS S + L)

TERMS AND CONDITIONS CARILLO TO CARRY BACK $100,000 2ND
T.D. AT TERMS TO BE NEGOTIATED.

NOTE: Other data on properties outlined herein as per sheets attached and submitted herewith. Final terms and conditions, if any, to be in subsequent offer and/or escrow instructions.

This proposal is subject to prior disposition of the above properties, and shall expire on (date) DEC. 10, 1978 .

Both Brokers agree to direct their immediate attention to this proposal and submit any additional data requested by either broker.

J. R. Price   10/23/78
SUBMITTING COUNSELOR   DATE   BROKER RECEIVING OFFER   DATE

Remarks: _____

Form 1

Exchange Counselor Forms
The Pony Express 1973
P. O. Box 5906
San Jose, CA 95150

Approved: _____ Approved: _____
Date: _____ Date: _____

Figure 10.3

EXCHANGE AGREEMENT

CALIFORNIA ASSOCIATION OF REALTORS STANDARD FORM

MRS. MARY PETERS

first party, hereby offers to exchange the following described property, situated in.......... the City of Pasadena
.... County of......... Los Angeles .... California:

1. 26 Hunter Street (2 Unit Apartment)   Valued at $26,000.00
2. 139 Corta Street (4 Unit Apartment)   Valued at $54,000.00

Both properties free and clear of Loans. Full legal description of properties to be furnished in escrow.

Properties subject to current property taxes, covenants, conditions, restrictions, reservations and rights of way of record.

For the following described property of.......... MR. E. C. CARRILLO .... second party, situated in

the City of Salinas .... County of......... Monterey .... California:

A 22 unit apartment property at 433 Elysian. (Full legal description to be furnished in escrow. Valued at $285,000.00 Subject to a Note secured by a 1st T.D. of approx. balance of $104,00 payable at $1,048.00 monthly inc. 9% int. Also subject to current property taxes, covenants, conditions, restrictions, reservations and rights of way of record.

Terms and Conditions of Exchange:

1. FIRST PARTY (PETERS) to execute and SECOND PARTY (CARILLO) to carry back a Note secured by a second trust deed on the SALINAS property in the amount of ONE HUNDRED THOUSAND AND NO/100 ($100,000.00) DOLLARS payable at interest only or more monthly at TEN (10) PERCENT annual interest for THREE (3) YEARS, then ONE THOUSAND AND NO/100 ($1,000.00) DOLLARS or more, monthly for FIVE (5) YEARS including 10% annual interest. FULL AMOUNT OF BALANCE OF LOAN TO BECOME DUE EIGHT (8) YEARS FROM CLOSE OF ESCROW.
2. Offer is subject to FIRST PARTY'S inspection and written approval of SALINAS property and financial records of SALINAS property within TWENTY (20) days of acceptance by SECOND party.

The parties hereto shall execute and deliver, within........ 60 ....days from the date this offer is accepted, all instruments, in writing, necessary to transfer title to said properties and complete and consummate this exchange. Each party shall supply Preliminary Title Reports for their respective properties. Evidences of title shall be California Land Title Association standard coverage form policies of title Insurance, showing titles to be merchantable and free of all liens and encumbrances, except taxes and those liens and encumbrances as otherwise set forth herein. Each party shall pay for the policies of Title Insurance for the property to be acquired ☐ conveyed ☒ .

Figure 10.4

If either party is unable to convey a marketable title, except as herein provided, within three months after acceptance hereof by second party, or if improvements on any of the herein named properties be destroyed or materially damaged prior to transfer of title or delivery of agreement of e, then this agreement shall be of no further effect, except as to payment of commissions and expenses incurred in connection with examination of title, less the party acquiring the property so affected elects to accept the title the other party can convey or subject to the conditions of the improvements. Taxes, insurance premiums (if policies be satisfactory to party acquiring the property affected thereby), rents, interest and other expenses of d properties shall be pro-rated as of the date of transfer of title or delivery of agreement of sale, unless otherwise provided herein.

Price Realty _____of_____ 2600 Lighthouse, Monterey _____Calif._____
Broker   Address   Phone No.
hereby authorized to act as broker for all parties hereto and may accept commission therefrom. Should second party accept this offer, first party ees to pay said broker commission for services rendered as follows:—
per separate listing agreement.

ould second party be unable to convey a marketable title to his property then first party shall be released from payment of any commission, unless elects to accept the property subject thereto. First party agrees that broker may cooperate with other brokers and divide commissions in any manner sfactory to them.
This offer shall be deemed revoked unless accepted in writing within Ten (10) days after date hereof, and such acceptance is communicated first party within said period. Broker is hereby given the exclusive and irrevocable right to obtain acceptance of second party within said period. Time is the essence of this contract.

_____Mary Peters_____

ed _____Nov 25,_____ 19 78 _____

ACCEPTANCE
Second party hereby accepts the foregoing offer upon the terms and conditions stated and agrees to pay commission for services rendered.
J. C. Smith _____of_____ 11 Romie Ln., Salinas Calif._____
Broker   Address   Phone No.
ollows:— Per terms of a separate listing agreement.

Second party agrees that broker may act as broker for all parties here to and may accept commission therefrom, and may co-operate with other kers and divide commissions in any manner satisfactory to them.
should first party be unable to convey a marketable title to his property then second party shall be released from payment of any commission, ss he elects to accept the property of first party subject thereto.
This offer accepted subject to the terms of the attached counter-offer form.

_____E. C. Carrillo_____

ed _____Nov. 29,_____ 19 78 _____

FORM E 14   REVISED APRIL 1972

Figure 10.4 (continued)

EXCHANGE COUNTER OFFER

Dated: __November 29, 1978__

The offer to exchange the real property known as _26 Hunter St. &_
139 Corta Street, Pasadena, Calif. for real property known as ____

433 Elysian St, Salinas, Calif.

Dated __Nov. 25, 1978__ , is not accepted in its present form, but
the following counter offer is hereby submitted:

Offer accepted provided that another property acceptable to the
undersigned can be found in lieu of the Pasadena properties within
Sixty (60) Days.

OTHER TERMS: All other terms remain the same.
RIGHT TO ACCEPT OTHER OFFERS: _Second Party_ reserves the right to
accept any other offer prior to _First Party's_ acceptance of this
counter offer and _Second Party_'s agent being so notified in
writing.
EXPIRATION: This counter offer shall expire unless a copy hereof
with _First Party's_ written acceptance is delivered to _Second Party_'s
agent within _Five (5)_ days from above date.

X __E C. Carrillo__

X _____

. . . .

Dated: __11/29/78__

The undersigned accepts the above exchange counter offer.

X __Mary Peters__

X __Nov. 30, 1978__

Figure 10.5

100,000 from Mrs. Peters which would be carried back on the Salinas apartments.

Both owners knew that these positions were only temporary and were *subject to* Carrillo accepting another property that Price and Smith must find for him, offering the note and Pasadena properties.

[¶1002]   SOLVING THE PROBLEM WITH A THREE-WAY EXCHANGE

Since Carrillo was now going to offer out a new package of properties and a note, the brokers prepared a new "package" to present in the exchange marketplace. They were now looking for a *third leg* of a three way exchange, so the package was headed "THIRD LEG WANTED." (See Figure 10.6.)

Since the exchange between these two parties could not close until a property that would satisfy Carrillo was found, both brokers were now actively seeking a solution.

At an exchange meeting in San Jose the following week, Smith presented the new Carrillo package to another group of brokers. At this meeting, one of the packages presented was a four-acre parcel near San Jose that was ready for development. (See Figure 10.7.) It was located by an off-ramp of a freeway that was being completed within the next year.

The owner of this property was named Palm. During his broker's time at the podium, the participants heard that Palm was of retirement age and was as much interested in an annual cash flow as he was in selling the property.

When the broker (Brown) listed this property, Palm had originally asked for an exchange into a leased commercial building with AAA tenants. During subsequent interviews, Brown had suggested an alternate investment, well-secured notes on good real estate. These would give him long-term secure income and would be much easier to locate than AAA Commercial property. Palm agreed.

At the meeting, Smith wrote a Preliminary Exchange Proposal to Brown. (See Figure 10.8.) He offered the Pasadena property and the note to Palm on behalf of Carrillo. It was mentioned that the offer was subject to the close of escrow between Peters and Carrillo. After the meeting, Smith showed Brown the paperwork on the exchange already started, so that he could communicate the situation to Palm.

When Smith returned to his office, he showed the mini-offer to Carrillo along with the information on the San Jose acreage. Carrillo was enthusiastic. Together, they went to the property and inspected it.

MONTEREY PENINSULA EXCHANGE COUNSELORS

<u>THIRD LEG WANTED</u>   PRICE: $180,000
<u>APARTMENTS AND GOOD PAPER</u>   LOANS: -0-
                                 EQUITY: 180,000

<u>HAVE</u>:	1. A $100,000 2nd T.D. note on a 22 unit apartment in Salinas. Int. only @ 10% for 3 years, then $1,000 monthly at 10% for 5 years, then all due.
	2. Duplex and Four plex in Pasadena. SGI $5,130 (Duplex) & $9,630 (4 unit) Taxes $735 & $1,243.. Older prop in good condition. (Homework package available).
<u>ADDRESS</u>:	1. Note on 433 Elysian, Salinas.
	2. 26 Hunter (2 Unit) & 139 Corta (4 Unit) Pasadena.
<u>PRICE</u>:	Note has face of $100,000 (Created in 1st Leg as Carry Back) $26,000 (Duplex) & $54,000 (4 unit) Appraisal available.
<u>LOANS</u>:	-0-
<u>EQUITY</u>:	$180,000
<u>WHY DOES NOT WANT</u>:	Owner in acquisition only. Owner is a builder. Would like to acquire commercial zoned property ready for development.
<u>SUGGESTED SOLUTIONS</u>:	Exchange directly into commercial. Will sell for cash or exchange down into readily saleable properties - houses, lots, etc.
<u>REMARKS</u>:	This client primarily a seller. Not concerned with tax consequences. Has had his own property on sale market. Currently is in first step of Multiple exchange. Note will be a purchase money note on his former property.
<u>OWNER</u>:	E. C. Carrillo
<u>FEE</u>:	See broker for Amounts.
<u>COUNSELOR</u>:	J. C. Smith James R. Price
	11 Romie Lane Price Realty
	Salinas, Ca. 93901 2600 Lighthouse Ave.
	Monterey, Ca. 93940

This information is from sources deemed reliable, but is not guaranteed by agent. Package is subject to price changes, corrections, error, ommission, prior sale and withdrawal.

Figure 10.6

JOHN C. BROWN
BROWN REALTY
SAN JOSE, CALIF.

COMMERCIAL - FREEWAY ACCESS

Price: $180,000
Loans: -0-
Equity: 180,000

HAVE: Approximately four acres land at new freeway off ramp near San Jose. Property can be used for highway commercial such as service stations, motels, etc.

ADDRESS: Highway 101 - Victor Blvd.

PRICE: $180,000

LOANS: -0-

EQUITY: $180,000

WHY DOES NOT WANT: Purchased a few years ago for investment. At that time felt that larger gain would be quickly realized on this property. Delays by the State in building freeways have hurt potential gain. Now wants to retire and get out.

SUGGESTED SOLUTIONS: Owner has little gain so basis high. Would have no tax problem in a cash sale. Needs monthly income for retirement. If sold for cash, he will purchase trust deeds for income or invest in stock.

REMARKS: Exchange for leased commercial income property is first choice. Also will consider trading for Mortgages or trust deeds on good property.

OWNER: B. T. Palm/ Virginia Palm

FEE: $12,000

COUNSELOR: John C. Brown
Brown Realty
4th & Carter St.
San Jose, Calif.

This information is from sources deemed reliable, but is not guaranteed by agent. Package is subject to price change, correction, error, omission, prior sale and withdrawal.

Figure 10.7

PRELIMINARY EXCHANGE PROPOSAL

FROM J. C. SMITH

Date: DEC. 1, 1978

TO
JOHN C. BROWN
BROWN REALTY
4TH & CARTER ST.
SAN JOSE, CALIF.

Subject: EXCHANGE

CARRILLO/PALM

MY CLIENT: E. C. CARRILLO

Type of Property: NOTE FOR $100,000   Address: SALINAS
: + DUPLEX $ 26,000   : PASADENA
: + FOUR-PLEX $ 54,000   : PASADENA

~~Encumbrances:~~
SEE ATTACHED PACKAGE FOR INFORMATION

YOUR CLIENT: B. T. PALM

Type of Property: 4-ACRE COMM.   Address: HWY. 10 / VICTOR BLVD.
:   :
:   :
:   :

Encumbrances: FREE + CLEAR

TERMS AND CONDITIONS   EQUITY FOR EQUITY EXCHANGE

NOTE: Other data on properties outlined herein as per sheets attached and submitted
herewith. Final terms and conditions, if any, to be in subsequent offer and/or escrow
instructions.

This proposal is subject to prior disposition of the above properties, and shall expire on
(date) DEC. 10, 1978

Both Brokers agree to direct their immediate attention to this proposal and submit any
additional data requested by either broker.

J. C. Smith   12/1/78
SUBMITTING COUNSELOR   DATE   BROKER RECEIVING OFFER   DATE

Remarks:

Form 1

Approved:_____   Approved:_____

Date:_____   Date:_____

Exchange Counselor Forms
The Pony Express 1973
P. O. Box 5906
San Jose, CA 95150

Figure 10.8

Carrillo immediately wanted to sign an offer to secure the four acres. Smith prepared an offer (Figure 10.9), subject to Carrillo being able to secure permits, clearances on the property within a reasonable length of time. Also, since Carrillo was offering property and a note that he didn't own yet, it was made subject to the close of escrow between Peters and himself.

When Brown, the San Jose broker, presented the offer to Palm, the property owner was reluctant to accept the two Pasadena apartment properties. He liked the note for $100,000 that would give him a good monthly income, but the Pasadena apartments were nowhere near anything that they had ever considered.

Brown and Palm drove to Salinas and looked over the 22 unit apartment that would be the security for the $100,000 note. When Palm saw this property, he was anxious to get the note as it was to be secured by an excellent property.

Now Brown suggested that Palm accept the offer "subject to exchanging the Pasadena properties for something else," within 60 days (see Figure 10.10). Palm accepted, under these conditions, since Brown seemed confident that excellent free-and-clear properties in Southern California could be converted quite easily into something acceptable by Palm.

Now the three owners were in the following positions, all as "owners in acquisition:"

1. Mrs. Peters was still in the final position where she wished to close the transaction—a tax-deferred exchange into the 22-unit apartment.

2. Carrillo had also exchanged his 22 units through the offer from Mrs. Peters into his final position, a four-acre building site where he could build a shopping center.

3. Palm had converted his non-productive equity in the four-acre parcel into a well-secured note of $100,000 on the 22 units which he wanted, plus two small apartments in Pasadena which he didn't want.

Brown and the other brokers would now offer out the Pasadena properties for Palm. He would retain the secured note for $100,000.

The brokers now prepared another "package" describing the Southern California properties to present to the marketplace for Palm. (See Figure 10.11.)

Compare the package for Palm with the original package that was prepared for Mrs. Peters. Although the same properties are represented, the

EXCHANGE AGREEMENT

CALIFORNIA ASSOCIATION OF REALTORS STANDARD FORM

.....E. C. Carrillo...
.....1820 Smithers Street, Salinas...
first party, hereby offers to exchange the following described property, situated in.......the city of Pasadena...........
....County of.................Los Angeles........................ California:
1.....26 Hunter St. (2 Unit apartment) Valued at $26,000.00...
2.....139 Corta St. (4 Unit apartment) Valued at $54,000.00...
3.....A $100,000 note secured by trust deed on a TWENTY-TWO Unit.............................
.......apartment property at 433 Elysian St., Salinas. Payable interest..............
.......only at 10% for 3 years, $1,000.00 monthly including 10% int for...............
.......five years when full amount of balance is due...
Full legal description of properties to be furnished in escrow.......................
For the following described property of...........B.T. Palm & Virginia Palm.......................................
.... second party, situated in
the City of San Jose...........................County of.........Santa Clara......................... California:
Approx. four acres located at Highway 101 / Victor Blvd. (AP #1-145-63)
Full legal description to be furnished in escrow..

Terms and Conditions of Exchange:

1.....This is an equity for equity exchange...
2.....Offer subject to FIRST PARTY'S securing clearances and zoning...............
.......for construction of commercial property from city within a period...........
.......of 90 days from acceptance of this offer by SECOND PARTY......................
3.....This offer also subject to the concurrent close of escrow between...........
.......Peters/Carrillo at Farmer's Title Co., Monterey (Escrow #10001).............

The parties hereto shall execute and deliver, within....30............days from the date this offer is accepted, all instruments, in writing, necessary to transfer title to said properties and complete and consummate this exchange. Each party shall supply Preliminary Title Reports for their respective properties. Evidences of title shall be California Land Title Association standard coverage form policies of title insurance, showing titles to be merchantable and free of all liens and encumbrances, except taxes and those liens and encumbrances as otherwise set forth herein. Each party shall pay for the policies of Title Insurance for the property to be acquired ☐ conveyed ☒ .

Figure 10.9

If either party is unable to convey a marketable title, except as herein provided, within three months after acceptance hereof by second party, or if the improvements on any of the herein named properties be destroyed or materially damaged prior to transfer of title or delivery of agreement of sale, then this agreement shall be of no further effect, except as to payment of commissions and expenses incurred in connection with examination of title, unless the party acquiring the property so affected elects to accept the title the other party can convey or subject to the conditions of the improvements.

Taxes, insurance premiums (if policies be satisfactory to party acquiring the property affected thereby), rents, interest and other expenses of said properties shall be pro-rated as of the date of transfer of title or delivery of agreement of sale, unless otherwise provided herein.

J. C. Smith   of   Salinas, Calif.   Calif.

Broker   Address   Phone No.

is hereby authorized to act as broker for all parties hereto and may accept commission therefrom. Should second party accept this offer, first party agrees to pay said broker commission for services rendered as follows:-

As per the terms of a separate listing agreement.

Should second party be unable to convey a marketable title to his property then first party shall be released from payment of any commission, unless he elects to accept the property subject thereto. First party agrees that broker may cooperate with other brokers and divide commissions in any manner satisfactory to them.

This offer shall be deemed revoked unless accepted in writing within Five (5) days after date hereof, and such acceptance is communicated to first party within said period. Broker is hereby given the exclusive and irrevocable right to obtain acceptance of second party within said period. Time is the essence of this contract.

E. C. Carullo

Dated Dec 6, 1978

ACCEPTANCE

Second party hereby accepts the foregoing offer upon the terms and conditions stated and agrees to pay commission for services rendered, to:

Brown Realty   of   San Jose, Calif.   Calif.

Broker   Address   Phone No.

as follows:- TWELVE THOUSAND and No/100 ($12,000.00) Dollars

Second party agrees that broker may act as broker for all parties here to and may accept commission therefrom, and may co-operate with other brokers and divide commissions in any manner satisfactory to them.

Should first party be unable to convey a marketable title to his property then second party shall be released from payment of any commission, unless he elects to accept the property of first party subject thereto.

This offer accepted subject to the terms of the attached counter offer.

B. P. Palm

Virginia Palm

Dated 19

For these forms address California Association of Realtors 505 Shatto Place, Los Angeles 90020. All rights reserved.
Copyright 1972 by California Association of Realtors

FORM E 14   REVISED APRIL 1972

Figure 10.9 (continued)

EXCHANGE COUNTER OFFER

Dated: December 8, 1978

The offer to exchange the real property known as (1) 26 Hunter St. &
(2) 139 Corta St,Pasadena & (3) Note described below? for real property known as ____

Four Acres located at Highway 101 / Victor Blvd. (AP #1-145-63)

Dated ____ Dec. 6, 1978 ____, is not accepted in its present form, but
the following counter offer is hereby submitted:

Offer accepted provided that another property more acceptable to

the undersigned (Second Party) can be found in lieu of the Pasadena

properties within Sixty (60) Days.

Second party will accept item #3 (Note for $100,000)

*Note for $100,000 shown as item #3 on original offer dated 12/6/78.

OTHER TERMS: All other terms remain the same.
RIGHT TO ACCEPT OTHER OFFERS: _Second Party___ reserves the right to
accept any other offer prior to First Party's __ acceptance of this
counter offer and __Second Party__'s agent being so notified in
writing.
EXPIRATION: This counter offer shall expire unless a copy hereof
with First Party's __ written acceptance is delivered to Second Party's
agent within __Three (3)__ days from above date.

X __B. T. Palm__

X __Virginia Palm__

....

Dated: _____

The undersigned accepts the above exchange counter offer.

X ___E. C. Carrillo___

X ____12/10/78____

Figure 10.10

MONTEREY PENINSULA EXCHANGE COUNSELORS

ANOTHER LEG NEEDED FOR MULTIPLE EXCH.
PASADENA APARTMENTS

PRICE: $80,000
LOANS: -0-
EQUITY: $80,000

HAVE: Six rental units. A Duplex and a four-plex located near one another in a good rental area of Pasadena. Scheduled Gross Income of duplex $5,130.00 annually, SGI of fourplex is $9.630.00. Current taxes $735.00 & $1,243.00. Currently being managed by local broker. Buildings older but in good condition.

ADDRESS: 26 Hunter Ave. (duplex) & 139 Corta St.

PRICE: $80,000 total. $26,000 for Duplex & $54,000 for Four unit. (Appraisel by B.B. Cater Co.)

LOANS: -0-

EQUITY: $80,000

WHY DOES NOT WANT: Owner in acquisition in a three way exchange. Owner wants to exchange for leased commercial income property or anything that will give him good retirement income in monthly payments.

SUGGESTED SOLUTIONS: Exchange for leased commercial - exchange for notes secured by trust deeds.

REMARKS: Owner not concerned with tax consequences. Has high basis in original property so has little gain.

OWNER: B. T. Palm / Virginia Palm

FEE: See brokers.

COUNSELOR:

James R. Price	J. C. Smith	John C. Brown
Price Realty	11 Romie Ln	Brown Realty
2600 Lighthouse Ave.	Salinas, Ca. 93901	4th & Carter St.
Monterey, Calif. 93940		San Jose, Calif.

This information is from sources deemed reliable, but is not guaranteed by agent. Package is subject to price changes, corrections, error, ommission, prior sale and withdrawal.

Figure 10.11

package is totally different, because of the personal motivations of the new owner in acquisition.

Mrs. Peters offered the properties out as a vehicle to move her equity in a tax-deferred exchange into a small geographical area in Northern California.

Since Palm could sell the Pasadena units, could accept notes, could accept any other property that made sense to him, the possible transactions on the units could be totally different from when the units were offered originally by Price for Mrs. Peters.

[¶1003]   **SOLVING THE PROBLEM WITH
                      A FOUR-WAY EXCHANGE**

Since the logical place to look for a "taker" for a Southern California property was in that area, Brown and Price went to several exchange meetings in the Los Angeles area. They each made presentations of the new Palm package at different places throughout the area.

Price attended an exchange meeting at Los Angeles Airport in one of the large hotels. There were 75 brokers attending the meeting. The free-and-clear properties received a lot of attention. Several Preliminary Exchange Proposals were received. The properties offered to Palm for the Pasadena apartments were as follows:

1. A business opportunity in South Los Angeles, valued at $35,000. A self-service laundry owned by a widow, ready to retire.
2. A three-bedroom home in Long Beach. Property valued at $75,000 with a $45,000 1st Loan. Owner: young couple—wants to own income units.
3. A created note for $20,000 on a desert lot valued at $40,000. Note to be down payment on Pasadena property. Palm to carry back first notes secured by trust deeds on each Pasadena property. Offering owner to remain in title to desert lot. He is a young, unmarried engineer, named Victor Hunt, who needs tax shelter.
4. A duplex in San Diego valued at $40,000 with a loan of $10,000. This property is owned by a middle-aged couple who want to move to the Los Angeles area. He is a school teacher who has been offered a job in school system in a Los Angeles suburb near the home of their married daughter.

Price had stated in his stand-up presentation the background of the three-way exchange that Palm was already involved in. He had hoped to receive offers that would be both a "user" for the Pasadena units and would have something that Palm could also use. For this reason, he declined the use of the "opportunity and catalyst" system of forcing exchanges. He settled on the four offers received and returned to his office.

The following day Price and Brown met with Palm to submit the offers received in Southern California. While they were meeting in Price's office, the morning mail was delivered. In the mail was a long-form offer (Figure 10.12) from a Los Angeles broker, William Potter, on behalf of his client, Victor Hunt (see Figure 10.12a). This offer was the mini-offer shown in #3 previously: the created note on the desert lot as a down payment on the Pasadena properties.

Palm reviewed the offers when the brokers explained them to him. He rejected the laundry, the house in Long Beach and the San Diego duplex. He felt that each would require more exchange negotiations and the position of each would be very much like his present position in the Pasadena apartments. The notes on the desert land and on the Pasadena units appealed to Palm. He decided to accept this offer, subject to an appraisal of the lot. If the lot really had the value as stated in the attached package, then Palm would have converted his San Jose four-acre parcel into the following:

1. A well-secured note on a 22-unit apartment in Salinas with a face value of $100,000 payable at $834.00 monthly for three years, increasing to $1,000.00 monthly for 5 years, then the total balance due in full (approximately $87,000.)
2. A note on the desert land for $20,000 payable at $200.00 monthly for ten years, then the balance of approximately $13,000 due.
3. Two notes on the duplex and the four units in Pasadena for $200.00 monthly and $400.00 monthly for ten years and the balances of $13,000 and $26,000 (approximately) due and payable.

This would give Palm an income of $1,634.00 monthly for three years, then $1,800.00 monthly for the next five years when he would receive about $87,000. For the following two years, he would receive $800.00 monthly, then at the end of ten years from the close of the original escrow, the balance of the loans in the amount of about $52,000.

The offer was accepted and the four-way exchange was completed (Figure 10.13). Each owner received the benefits he had set out to get.

PRELIMINARY EXCHANGE PROPOSAL

|||
F
R
O
M
||| BILL POTTER

||| Date:
                                             JAN. 6, 1979
||| JIM PRICE   Subject: EXCHANGE
T   MONTEREY, CALIF.
O
||| PALM / HUNT

MY CLIENT: VICTOR HUNT

    Type of Property: 5 ACRE SITE   Address: APPLE VALLEY

    Encumbrances: FREE + CLEAR OF LOANS

YOUR CLIENT: B. T. PALM

    Type of Property: 6 UNITS   Address: PASADENA

    Encumbrances: FREE + CLEAR OF LOANS

TERMS AND CONDITIONS HUNT TO CREATE A $20,000 NOTE
AGAINST HIS PROPERTY TO USE AS DOWN
ON 6 UNITS.

NOTE: Other data on properties outlined herein as per sheets attached and submitted herewith. Final terms and conditions, if any, to be in subsequent offer and/or escrow instructions.

This proposal is subject to prior disposition of the above properties, and shall expire on

(date) JAN. 17, 1979

Both Brokers agree to direct their immediate attention to this proposal and submit any additional data requested by either broker.

Bill Potter   1/6/79
SUBMITTING COUNSELOR   DATE   BROKER RECEIVING OFFER   DATE

Remarks:_____

Form 1
● Exchange Counselor Forms
The Pony Express 1973
P. O. Box 5906
San Jose, CA 95150

Approved:_____   Approved:_____

Date:_____   Date:_____

Figure 10.12

WILLIAM POTTER
POTTER   REALTY CO.
SAN BERNADINO, CALIF.

APPLE VALLEY   LAND

Price: $40,000
Loans: -0-
Equity: 40,000

HAVE: 5 acre choice building site near the Lodge at Apple Valley.
                    Prime property ready for development - Luxury residence.

ADDRESS: Lengthy - metes and bounds description. See back up
                    package for complete description on copy of deed.

PRICE: $40,000

LOANS: -0-

EQUITY: $40,000

WHY DOES   Needs tax shelter. Owner has large income, is single and
NOT WANT: is in high tax bracket. Recently divorced and has little
                    cash for investment.

SUGGESTED   Exchange for income property in the Los Angeles area.
SOLUTIONS: Property does not have to show any cash flow. Hopes to
                    own a property that breaks even or gives a small spendable.

REMARKS: Lot is in an area of homes valued at $250,000 and up.

OWNER: Victor Hunt

FEE: $2,400.00

COUNSELOR: William Potter
                    Potter Realty Co.
                    San Bernadino, Ca.

This information is from sources deemed reliable, but is not guaranteed by agent. Package is subject
to price change, correction, error, omission, prior sale and withdrawal.

Figure 10.12a

EXCHANGE AGREEMENT

CALIFORNIA ASSOCIATION OF REALTORS STANDARD FORM

Mr. Victor Hunt

Personal

first party, hereby offers to exchange the following described property, situated in

County of .... California:

A Note to be created in escrow secured by a 1st Deed of Trust on a five acre parcel in Apple Valley Ca. (AP #1-444-678). Note will be in the amount of TWENTY THOUSAND and NO/100 ($20,000.00) DOLLARS payable at TWO HUNDRED and No/100 ($200.00) DOLLARS or more monthly including TEN (10) PERCENT annual interest. (Description of parcel lengthy metes and bounds - will be furnished in escrow.) NOTE TO HAVE A DUE DATE - BALANCE DUE IN 10 YEARS.

For the following described property of............. B. T. Palm & Virginia Palm

.... second party, situated in

the city of Pasadena ....County of.....Los Angeles................................ California:

1. 26 Hunter St. (2 Unit Apartment) Valued at $26,000.00
2. 139 Corta St. (4 Unit apartment) Valued at $54,000.00
Both properties free and clear of loans. Full legal description to be furnished in escrow.

Properties subject to current property taxes, covenants, conditions, restrictions, reservations and rights of way of record.

Terms and Conditions of Exchange:

1. Offer subject to SECOND PARTY'S inspection and written approval of Preliminary Title report on Apple Valley property.
2. FIRST PARTY to execute and SECOND PARTY to carry back TWO notes on the Pasadena properties. Notes to be as follows:
   A) 26 Hunter St. $20,000.00 payable at $200.00 or more monthly inc. 10% annual interest.
   B) 139 Corta St. $40,000.00 payable at $400.00 or more monthly inc. 10% annual interest.
   BOTH NOTES DUE AND PAYABLE IN 10 YEARS.
3. This offer subject to the concurrent close of escrow of exchange between Palm/Carrillo at Farmer's Title Co., Monterey (Escrow #10019)

The parties hereto shall execute and deliver, within......30............days from the date this offer is accepted, all instruments, in writing, necessary to transfer title to said properties and complete and consummate this exchange. Each party shall supply Preliminary Title Reports for their respective properties. Evidences of title shall be California Land Title Association standard coverage form policies of title insurance, showing titles to be merchantable and free of all liens and encumbrances, except taxes and those liens and encumbrances as otherwise set forth herein. Each party shall pay for the policies of Title Insurance for the property to be acquired ☐ conveyed ☒ .

Figure 10.13

If either party is unable to convey a marketable title, except as herein provided, within three months after acceptance hereof by second party, or if the improvements on any of the herein named properties be destroyed or materially damaged prior to transfer of title or delivery of agreement of sale, then this agreement shall be of no further effect, except as to payment of commissions and expenses incurred in connection with examination of title, unless the party acquiring the property so affected elects to accept the title the other party can convey or subject to the conditions of the improvements.

Taxes, insurance premiums (if policies be satisfactory to party acquiring the property affected thereby), rents, interest and other expenses of said properties shall be pro-rated as of the date of transfer of title or delivery of agreement of sale, unless otherwise provided herein.

Potter Realty Co ......of...... San Bernadino, Calif. Calif. .... Phone No.

Broker .... Address .... Phone No.

Is hereby authorized to act as broker for all parties hereto and may accept commission therefrom. Should second party accept this offer, first party agrees to pay said broker commission for services rendered as follows:-

ONE THOUSAND TWO HUNDRED AND No/100 ($1,200.00) DOLLARS

Should second party be unable to convey a marketable title to his property then first party shall be released from payment of any commission, unless he elects to accept the property subject thereto. First party agrees that broker may cooperate with other brokers and divide commissions in any manner satisfactory to them.

This offer shall be deemed revoked unless accepted in writing within Five (5) days after date hereof, and such acceptance is communicated to first party within said period. Broker is hereby given the exclusive and irrevocable right to obtain acceptance of second party within said period. Time is the essence of this contract.

Dated Jan. 6, 19 79

ACCEPTANCE

Second party hereby accepts the foregoing offer upon the terms and conditions stated and agrees to pay commission for services rendered, to:-

Brown Realty ......of...... San Jose, Calif. Calif. .... Phone No.

Broker .... Address .... Phone No.

as follows:- As per separate listing agreement.

Second party agrees that broker may act as broker for all parties hereto and may accept commission therefrom, and may co-operate with other brokers and divide commissions in any manner satisfactory to them.

Should first party be unable to convey a marketable title to his property then second party shall be released from payment of any commission, unless he elects to accept the property of first party subject thereto.

Dated JAN. 10, 1979 19

For these forms address California Association of Realtors   FORM F 14   REVISED APRIL 1972

Figure 10.13 (continued)

[¶1004]   **THE RESULTS**

1. Mrs. Peters exchanged the Pasadena units up into a 22-unit apartment property. This was a tax-deferred exchange into the new geographic area in which she lives.
2. Carrillo had used his equity in his 22-unit property to "buy" a free and clear commercial site on which he would build.
3. Palm had exchanged his four-acre site into several notes which would give him retirement income.
4. Hunt had acquired a starter income property using only the *dormant* equity in investment land.

After the contingencies regarding the inspection of the apartments by each of the "takers," the permits and building permits for Carrillo and the appraisal of the desert land, the transaction was closed.

It is interesting to note that no one in this exchange of equity in four properties had to contact any lending institution for financing.

In accordance with the negotiations between brokers during the exchange transaction, all of the commissions and fees from each of the owners in the transaction were pooled and split equally among the four brokers. Each felt that there would have been no fees to collect without the full cooperation of all the participating brokers.

APPENDIX A

Forms Used By Brokers in Exchanges— The Tools of the Trade

THE PEOPLE FORMS

There are various forms used by Exchange Brokers that differ in some ways from the forms used by brokers who sell property exclusively. Some of these forms may be used in selling also, particularly the ones that are used to analyze an income property for investment purposes. Others pertain to the owner's "WANTS"—to his tax position. Some are used in Exchange Marketing Meetings.

Following are some of the forms used, with a brief explanation. Some have been covered in detail in previous chapters.

Form #1. Confidential Counseling Information. This was covered in detail in Chapter 8. This is used to guide a broker in his search for the property that will solve the client's problem.

Form #2. Exclusive Employment of Broker. This form is used as a contract between client and broker. Note that it calls for a cash fee (Paragraph #5) rather than a percentage commission. This form is similar to other exclusive agreement forms used in the real estate business. It is a requirement of all organized exchange groups that any property presented for exchange before a group must be listed exclusively.

Forms #3 & 4. Personal Data Sheet and Individual Tax Analysis. Both are used to gather more data regarding client's property ownership, income and tax problems. Form #4 breaks down client's income from outside sources, and his income property to show what the property is doing for him or "to" him.

Form #5. Home Buyer's Problem Analysis. Another "people"-oriented form, used primarily to "qualify" buyers for a home purchase. Certainly a help in finding the right property should the owner be in need of residential property. It helps to have an up-to-date financial statement in file with this form.

THE PROPERTY FORMS

Form #6. Checklist Work Sheet. With most of the information regarding the property that he has to offer available to him, the broker can use this form as a checklist for any further information desired. In addition, it is good to use in a personal "brainstorm" session to try to picture a possible user for the property.

Forms #7, 8, 9, & 10. Statement of Income and Expenses. Apartments, Farm, Motel and Hotel, and Ranch. The information on these forms is to be furnished by the owner of the property, or by his accountant. They provide for a complete record of income and expenses for a period of two years. In addition, there is a statement above the signature line that states as follows:

"THE INCOME AND EXPENSES LISTED ABOVE ARE WARRANTED TO BE THE ACTUAL FIGURES FOR THE _____ MONTH PERIOD ENDED _____19_____. THE UNDERSIGNED UNDERSTANDS THAT IN RELIANCE ON THE ABOVE FIGURES, COMMITMENTS AND OBLIGATIONS MAY BE MADE BY ONE OR MORE PERSONS WHICH WOULD NOT HAVE BEEN MADE BUT FOR RELIANCE ON THESE FIGURES."

When this statement is signed by the owner or accountant, it has a little more impact than some general figures tossed around as "approximate" expenses and income. The signer of the form is WARRANTING the figures.

Forms #11 & 12. Land and Lot Analysis and Note Information Statement. Forms to gather information on a lot that may be offered and a note that may be offered by client. Note again WARRANTING statement on NOTE statement.

Forms #13, 14, 15. Property Analysis, Income Property Statement (Commercial) and Comparative Investment Analysis. These forms are used to analyze income property by brokers, using information from the other People and Property forms that have been filled out. When presenting the property to another broker or to a possible buyer, these forms are used as a "recap" of the information. A copy of Form #7, signed by the owner or his accountant, will usually be attached.

Forms #16, 17, 18. These are used to present exchange property at an exchange meeting and make preliminary offers. Information shown on Form #16 will be just a bare physical description, but broker must have all other back-up forms (Forms #6 through 15) completed and ready for inspection at the meeting. Form #2, client listing form, must also be ready for inspection at meeting.

Forms #19 & 20. Exchange Agreement Form and Exchange Counter Offer Forms. These have been used in various places in the book for illustration. Remember that the Exchange Agreement Form can be used as a "sales tool" in negotiation with the other owner. A lengthy legal description on the form might confuse the other owner and "turn him off." A clearly written description of the property, what it is, and where it is might help everyone to understand better.

Form #21. Exchange Recapitulation. Used by some brokers as an assist after an exchange with several properties and several owners to assist understanding by escrow officers. Most brokers do not use this form. Since there is no such thing as an exchange between more than two owners, each couplet can easily be figured separately. (What we refer to as a multiple exchange is really just a series of pairs of owners exchanging two properties—See Chapter 5 and Chapter 10.)

The Forms are shown on the following pages.

CONFIDENTIAL COUNSELING INFORMATION

1. Date: _____

2. Owner's Name: _____ Age: _____ Phone: _____

3. Home Address: _____ How long? _____

4. Occupation: _____ Phone: _____
   Business Address: _____

5. Family Status: ____ Married   Spouse's Name: _____ Age: _____
   ____ Widow(er)   Number of Children: ____
   ____ Divorced   Name _____ Age ____ Sex ____ Location _____
   ____ Single   Name _____ Age ____ Sex ____ Location _____
                    Name _____ Age ____ Sex ____ Location _____
                    Name _____ Age ____ Sex ____ Location _____

6. Type of Property Owned: _____

7. Property Location: _____
   City _____ County _____ State _____

8. How is Title to Property Vested? _____

9. When was the Property acquired and how? _____
   Purchased ____ (Price Paid $_____); Gift ____ ; Exchange ____ ; Inheritance ____ ; Other ____

10. What is the present tax basis of the property? _____

11. How long has the property been for sale or on the market? _____

11a. Previously listed? _____

12. Are vehicles offered readily saleable? _____

13. Is this to be a tax-deferred exchange? _____

13a. Is there a potential "forgiveness of mortgage" problem? _____

14. Is client classified as a "DEALER"? _____

15. Client's opinion of their problem and/or reason for disposing of property. (See Item 35)
    _____

16. What do they wish to accomplish? _____

17. What can vehicle do for new owner? (Potential, refinance possibilities, etc.) _____
    _____

18. What are their needs?   M–Money _____   How much? $ _____
                            A–Appreciation _____   What do they expect? _____
                            I–Income _____   How much? $ _____
                            D–Depreciation _____ How much? $ _____
                            Other– Future needs and why needed: Explain _____
    _____

19. Is there a critical time element or urgency of any type? If so, explain: _____
    _____

20. Client's readiness to act: Desperate ____ ; Highly Motivated ____ ; Shows Interest ____

21. Are title holders in accord to make decision? ____ Do they seem flexible to deal with? _____

22. Is client oriented to other areas? ____ Explain geographical limitations, if any, and why: _____
    _____

Form #1

23. What price range will they consider? $_____ Can add cash. How much? $_____
How soon?_____ Source of cash._____
Needs cash. How much? $_____ Why?_____

24. Do they have cash for expenses? (Fees, title insurance, escrow, etc.)_____

25. Do they have other property that can be added? ____ Describe type and approximate equity (including stocks and property other than real estate):_____

26. Attitude towards accepting personal property such as: Contracts ____; Paper ____; Live Stock ____; Machinery ____; Trailers ____; Boats ____; Cars ____; Trucks ____; Equipment ____; Airplanes ____.

27. Client's attitude toward assuming or making higher loan._____

28. Discuss initiating offers in client's behalf with weasel clauses.

29. Discuss client's business background including previous experiences as an operator (motel, cafe, etc.).

29a. Will they manage? _____ Are they a user? _____ Lease back:_____

30. What is client's present approximate annual income (sources and totals)?_____

30a. Is Financial Statement and/or I.R.S. Statements available on request?_____

31. Attorney_____ Tax Counselor_____

32. Is there any third party influence?_____

33. Can objective be reached with present vehicle?_____

34. Special interests (fishing, hunting, flying, electronics, etc.)?_____

35. BROKER'S OPINION OF OBJECTIVE AND POSSIBLE SOLUTIONS:_____

36. Remind client of why he doesn't want the property.

37. Present price $_____; Total encumbrances $_____; Equity $_____
(See Check List Work Sheet – Form 15 for details)

38. Referred by whom:_____
Fee Basis: $_____ How payable?_____

RECORD OF CONTACTS AND COUNSELING MEETINGS

Date	Approximate Time and Type of Contact

If you haven't contacted your client in the last two weeks – CALL HIM UP!

© Exchange Counselor Forms
The Pony Express 1973
P. O. Box 5906
San Jose, CA 95150

Form 3

Form #1 (continued)

EXCLUSIVE EMPLOYMENT OF BROKER TO EXCHANGE, SELL, LEASE OR OPTION

CALIFORNIA ASSOCIATION OF REALTORS® STANDARD FORM

1. The undersigned,_____
(PRINCIPAL), hereby grants to_____
a licensed real estate broker, hereinafter called "agent," the EXCLUSIVE AND IRREVOCABLE RIGHT commencing on _____
_____, 19_____ and terminating at midnight on_____, 19_____ to advise, offer, solicit, and negotiate for
the disposition of the Principal's right, title, and interest, through sale, lease, option or exchange on terms acceptable to Principal of
the real and personal property described as follows:_____

_____
_____
_____
_____
_____
_____
_____
_____

SUBJECT TO:_____
_____
_____
_____

2. Agent is hereby authorized to accept and hold on my behalf a deposit from any offeror pending Principal's acceptance. No offer shall be submitted to Principal unless signed by the individual offeror or his authorized agent.

3. I warrant that I am the owner of or can obtain and deliver marketable title to the property described above. Evidence of title to the real property shall be in the form of a California Land Title Association Standard Coverage Policy of Title Insurance to be paid for by_____.

4. Agent may ☐ may not ☐ place a for sale or exchange sign on the property.

5. Compensation to Agent: I hereby agree to pay Agent a fee of $ _____ upon any agreement for or transfer of title, during the term hereof or any extension thereof by Agent, or through any other person, or by me, or if said property is withdrawn from exchange, sale, lease or option without the consent of Agent, or made unmarketable by my voluntary act during the term hereof or any extension thereof.

(a) If within _____ days after expiration hereof, or any extension thereof, Principal enters into an agreement with anyone with whom Agent has had negotiations prior to final expiration, provided I have received notice in writing thereof before or upon expiration of this agreement or any extension thereof.

6. If action be instituted to enforce this agreement, the prevailing party shall receive reasonable attorney's fees as fixed by the Court.

7. Agent may represent all parties and collect compensation or commission from them provided there is full disclosure to all principals of such Agency. Agent may cooperate with sub-agents and may divide with other agents such compensation or commission in any manner acceptable to them.

8. Other Provisions:

_____
_____

9. I acknowledge that I have read and understand this Agreement, and that I have received a copy hereof.

DATED:_____, 19_____   _____, California

_____   _____
OWNER   OWNER

_____
ADDRESS   CITY   STATE   PHONE
10. In consideration of the above, Agent agrees to use diligence in the performance of his obligations.

_____
AGENT   ADDRESS   CITY   STATE

By _____
PHONE   DATE

For these forms address California Association of Realtors,
505 Shatto Place, Los Angeles 90020. All rights reserved.   **FORM EX-11**   (Rev. 4-76)
Copyright 1976 by California Association of Realtors.®

NO REPRESENTATION IS MADE AS TO THE LEGAL VALIDITY OF ANY PROVISION HEREOF IN ANY SPECIFIC TRANSACTION. IF YOU DESIRE LEGAL ADVICE, CONSULT YOUR ATTORNEY.

Form #2

Personal Data

Name			Age	Address						Date / /
Wife's Name			Age	Children's Age	M F	M F	M F	M F	M F	TOTAL
Occupation		Yrs.	Business Address				Phone - Bus.		Home	

NET WORTH

LINE No.		(1) CURRENT YEAR NET	(2) 1 YEAR AGO	(3) GAIN OR LOSS	(4) 2 YEARS AGO	(5) GAIN OR LOSS	
1	Cash In Banks						1
2	Savings Scd. IC6 L5						2
3	Stock Scd. IIC6 L13						3
4	Other Scd. IIIC6 L21						4
5							5
6	Real Estate Scd. IVC8 L32						6
7							7
8	Total Net Worth						8

ANNUAL INCOME & EXPENSE

9		(1)	(2)	(3)	(4)	9
10	Gainful Occupation Husband Gross		$			10
11	Gainful Occupation Wife Gross					11
12	Total Gainful Occupation			$		12
13	Interest Schedule IC9 L5	%	$			13
14	Dividends " IIC9 L13	%				14
15	Other " IIIC9 L21	%				15
16		%				16
17	Real Estate " IVC11 L32	%				17
18	Total Investment Income	100 %		$		18
19	Capital Gains					19
20	Total Income (Spendable)				$	20
21	Less Expense					21
22	Income Tax Federal $ (1) State $ (2)		$			22
23	Food	$				23
24	Clothing					24
25	Medical					25
26	Utilities					26
27	Miscellaneous		$			27
28	Personal Property Tax (Home - etc.)					28
29	Insurance					29
30	Personal Installment Payments P & I					30
31	Other					31
32	Total Annual Expense				$	32
33	Balance Available for Investment				$	33

34	INCOME TAX ALLOCATION		INVESTMENT ALLOCATION			34
35	Federal Income Tax L22(1)	$	ITEM	AMOUNT	TAX	35
36	Gainful Occupation L12	$	Interest %	$	$	36
37	Less Exemp. & Deduc.		Dividends %			37
38	Tot. & Tax on Same	$	Other %			38
39	Inc. Tax on Invest. (L 35 - L 38)		Real Estate %			39
40			Total 100 %	$	$	40
41						41

Addendum A

The statements and figures presented herein, while not guaranteed, are secured from sources we believe authoritative.

PREPARED BY _____

Form #3

INDIVIDUAL TAX ANALYSIS

NAME: ADDRESS: DATE:

WIFE'S NAME: CHILDREN NO: AGES: PREPARED BY:

LINE		(1) (2) PRESENT INCOME POSITION	(3) (4) PROPERTY	(5) (6) PROPERTY	LINE
1	GAINFUL OCCUPATION INCOME				1
2	Dividends				2
3	Interest				3
4	Annuities				4
5	Capital Gains Reportable				5
6	Other Income				6
7	TOTAL SECURITY INCOME				7
8	REAL ESTATE NET TAXABLE				8
9	TOTAL ORDINARY INCOME				9
10	Less: Personal Deductions & Exemptions				10
11	TOTAL TAXABLE INCOME				11
12	TOTAL TAX LIABILITY				12
13	Gainful Occupation Income (L1)				13
14	Less: Personal Deductions & Exemptions (L10)				14
15	Taxable Income, Gainful Occupation				15
16	TAX LIABILITY GAINFUL OCCUPATION				16
17	Gainful Occupation Income (L1)				17
18	Security Income (L7)				18
19	Total Gainful Occupation & Security Income				19
20	Less: Personal Deductions & Exemptions (L10)				20
21	Tax, Gainful Occupation & Security Income				21
22	TAX LIABILITY, GAINFUL OCCUPATION & SECURITY INCOME				22
23	Total Tax Liability (L12)				23
24	Less: Tax Liability, Gainful (L22) Occupation & Security Income				24
25	TAX LIABILITY REAL ESTATE				25
26	Tax Liability, Gainful Occupation & Security Income (L22)				26
27	Less: Tax Liability, Gainful Occupation (L16)				27
28	TAX LIABILITY SECURITY INCOME				28
29	Dividends (L2 ÷ L7)	% X L28	% X L28	% X L28	29
30	Interest (L3 ÷ L7)	% X L28	% X L28	% X L28	30
31	Annuities (L4 ÷ L7)	% X L28	% X L28	% X L28	31
32	Capital Gain (L5 ÷ L7)	% X L28	% X L28	% X L28	32
33	Other Income (L6 ÷ L7)	% X L28	% X L28	% X L28	33
34	Gainful Occupation Income (L1)				34
35	Security Income (L7)				35
36	Capital Gains not included in Line 5 above				36
37	Real Estate Gross Spendable				37
38	TOTAL INCOME				38
39	Less: Total Tax Liability (L12)				39
40	NET AFTER TAX				40
41	Overall Rate (L39 ÷ L38)	%	%	%	41

(Lines 29–33 marked TAX ALLOCATION)

For these forms, address California Association of Realtors, 505 Shatto Place, Los Angeles 90020.

(11-68)

The statements and figures presented herein, while not guaranteed, are secured from sources we believe authoritative.

FORM D

Form #4

HOME BUYER'S PROBLEM ANALYSIS

CALIFORNIA ASSOCIATION OF REALTORS® STANDARD FORM

(a check list to aid in determining the Buyer's qualifications and needs)

PERSONNEL DATA:

Name: (husband)_____ Phone (Office)_____

(wife)_____ (home)_____

Address: (home)_____

(work) (husband)_____ (wife)_____

Other Family Data: Boys_____ Cars_____

Girls_____ Boat_____

Relatives_____ Schools_____

Pets_____ Church_____

NEEDS:

Bedrooms_____ Separate Din. Rm._____

Baths_____ Din. Rm./Fam. Comb._____

Sq. Ft._____ Separate Fam. Rm._____

1 or 2 Story_____ Fam. Rm./Kitch. Comb._____

Style_____ Fireplace_____

Lot Size_____ Garage Capacity_____

Location_____ Unusual Needs_____

Possession_____ _____

FINANCES:

Capabilities: Down Payment Max.:_____Now

Or from Sale of Own Home_____

Monthly Payment:_____

(Including Taxes, Insurance)_____

(Excluding Taxes, Insurance)_____

Type Loan Needed_____

Other Equities: Amount, Details_____

Location_____

Trade-In Possibility Data:_____

EMPLOYMENT NOTES:

Husband: Company_____ Address_____

Position_____ How Long_____ Salary_____

Wife: Company_____ Address_____

Position_____ How Long_____ Salary_____

ADDITIONAL ITEMS:

How Came in Contact:_____

Other Data:_____

_____

_____

Form HBP—11

Form #5

CHECKLIST WORK SHEET

Vested Owner _____   Property Address _____

Address _____   Type of Property _____

City   State   Zip   Phone No.   Counselor

WHAT DOES THE PROPERTY OFFER?

1. Appreciation: Yes? ____ No? ____ How much? $_____ How soon? _____
        Why? _____
2. Income: How much now? $_____ How much in one year? $_____
3. Depreciation: Yes? ____ No? ____ How fast? _____
4. Tax Shelter: Yes? ____ No? ____
5. Pride of Ownership: Yes? ____ No? ____
6. Money by Refinance: $_____
7. Money by Additional Financing: $_____

WHAT WILL THE PROPERTY DO FOR SOMEONE ELSE'S CLIENT?

WHO WOULD WANT THIS PROPERTY?

1. Broker   2. User   3. Contractor   4. Attorney-Doctor
5. Widow   6. Older Couple   7. _____   8. _____

WHY IS THIS A GOOD OFFERING?

1. Does if need upgrading? ____ Repair? ____ (Deferred Maintenance)
2. Is local management available? ____ Who? _____
3. Is it large enough for professional management? ____
4. Have you a Profit and Loss Statement? ____ Is it signed by the owner? ____
5. Have you complete listing details? ____
6. Has a loan commitment been obtained? ____ Lender: _____
7. Complete area information? ____ Chamber of Commerce material? ____
8. Can it be converted to other uses? ____
9. Would conversion increase the income? ____
10. Could it be leased (cash rented), etc.? ____ Amount $_____
11. Comparable rents: _____
12. Is this property being used to best advantages? ____
13. Can it be expanded? ____
14. Must cash be generated in this transaction? ____ How much? _____
15. Can you justify all owners' and listers' "claims"? ____
16. Can all "claims" be put in writing and personally guaranteed? ____
         By whom? _____
17. Will this property have "esthetic" or buyers' appeal? ____

Form #6

18. What is this property's best single asset (benefit)? _____
19. Who is going to show the property? _____ Phone: _____
   a. Is the manager or "shower" negative?
   b. Are they going to help solve the problem or are they part of the problem?
   c. Have you counseled with the manager?
   d. Is this property and manager (or owner) ready to be previewed?
   e. Will it be necessary to send someone else out to the property "cold turkey" to analyze the manager or person showing the property?
   f. Do you have all of the phone numbers and other data required to show property on a minute's notice?

WOULD THIS LISTING BE BETTER SUITED IN THE LISTING PORTFOLIO OF ONE OF YOUR COMPETITORS?

COMPARABLES: (When Available)

	Address	Price	Loan	Disposition	Broker
1.					
2.					
3.					
4.					
5.					

CHECK LIST: (Items needed in my file)

___ Pictures	___ Prelim (Paid by Client)	___ Lien Holders Assumption
___ Maps	___ Counseling Sheet	___ Lien Holders Discount
___ Appraisal	___ Client Financial Data	___ Match Your File
___ Keys	___ Tax Bracket	___ Tax Counsel
___ Inventory	___ Discuss Formulas	___ Legal Counsel
___ Zoning	___ Closing Costs	___ Signed Agreements
___ Sign	___ Carry Back and How	___ Copy of Leases
___ Income Statement	___ Add Properties	___ Other Documents
___ Expense Statement	___ Refix Assumption Cost	___
___ Brochure	___ Neighbors	___

LIST OTHER EQUITIES THAT CAN BE ADDED:

© Exchange Counselor Forms
The Pony Express 1973
P. O. Box 5906
San Jose, CA 95150

Form 6

Form #6 (continued)

STATEMENT OF INCOME & EXPENSES
Apartment

Name of Resident Manager

Phone of Resident Manager

NAME OF OWNERS: _____ NAME OF PROPERTY: _____

ADDRESS OF PROPERTY: _____ CITY: _____ STATE: _____ ZIP: _____

TYPE OF PROPERTY: _____ AGE OF PROPERTY: _____

Is Professional Management Available? _____	INCOME FROM:
Name: _____ Phone: _____	(1) LEASES: $ _____
Address: _____ City: _____	(2) MO. TO MO. $ _____
State: _____ Zip: _____	DEPOSITS: $ _____

INCOME . 19_____ 19_____

	$	
Jan.	_____	_____
Feb.	_____	_____
March	_____	_____
April	_____	_____
May	_____	_____
June	_____	_____
July	_____	_____
Aug.	_____	_____
Sept.	_____	_____
Oct.	_____	_____
Nov.	_____	_____
Dec.	_____	_____
TOTALS	$ _____	$ _____

Average Vacancy: _____

Vacancy this date: _____

EXPENSES 19___ 19___ 19___ 19___

	$	$		$	$
Taxes R.E.	____	____	Custodial	____	____
Taxes P.P.	____	____	Telephone	____	____
Ins. Fire	____	____	Furn. Repl.	____	____
Ins. Liab.	____	____	Advertising	____	____
Util. Gas-	____	____	Fees & Lic.	____	____
Water Elec.	____	____	Pest Control	____	____
Rubbish	____	____	Legal	____	____
Yard Care	____	____	Accounting	____	____
Pool Care	____	____	Wk. Comp.	____	____
Elevator	____	____	MGT (on site)	____	____
Maintenance	____	____	MGT (prof.)	____	____
T.V. Cable	____	____	Lot Sweeping	____	____
Supplies	____	____	Snow Removal	____	____
Misc.	____	____	Misc.	____	____

GRAND TOTAL: $ _____ $ _____

Condition of Personal and Real Property: (i.e., Carpets, Drapes, Washer & Dryer, Painting, etc.):

☐ Excellent ☐ Good ☐ Fair ☐ Needs Upgrading Estimate Cost $ _____

Loan service as of _____ 19___ : Capital Improvements: _____

1st: $ ___	(Nature: ___).	___ Years.	___ % Interest. Monthly pmt: $ ___	. Tot. yrly. pmt.$ ___
2nd: $ ___	(Nature: ___).	___ Years.	___ % Interest. Monthly pmt: $ ___	. Tot. yrly. pmt.$ ___
3rd: $ ___	(Nature: ___).	___ Years.	___ % Interest. Monthly pmt: $ ___	. Tot. yrly. pmt.$ ___
4th: $ ___	(Nature: ___).	___ Years.	___ % Interest. Monthly pmt: $ ___	. Tot. yrly. pmt.$ ___

TRUST FUND: $ _____

Remarks: _____ Tax Bill Breakdown:

_____

_____ _____ Land

_____ _____ Improvements

_____ _____ Personal Property

_____ TOTAL

The income and expenses listed above are warranted to be the actual figures for the _____ month period ended _____ 19___. The undersigned understands that in reliance on the above listed figures, commitments and obligations may be made by one or more persons which would not have been made but for reliance on these figures.

Date: _____ 19___ Name: _____ Name: _____

(Signed by property owners representing correct information)

Mailing Address: _____ City: _____ State: _____ Zip: _____

Owner's Phone Number: _____ Broker: _____

EXCHANGE COUNSELOR FORMS
P. O. Box 5834
San Jose, CA. 95150

Form 5

Form #7

STATEMENT OF INCOME & EXPENSES
Farm

STATE_____
COUNTY_____
CO. SEAT_____

DATE_____
IRRIGATED_____
DRY LAND_____

NAME OF FARM_____ NEAREST TOWN_____ TOTAL ACRES_____
DIRECTION FROM TOWN_____ DISTANCE_____ ROADS_____ DISTANCE SCHOOL_____
HIGH SCHOOL_____ BUS_____ PHONE_____ DOMESTIC WATER_____
STOCK WATER_____ SOIL_____ AREA CULTIVATED_____ IRRIGATED_____
NON-IRRIGATED_____ SUB-IRRIGATED_____ ACRES ALFALFA_____ NATIVE_____
TOTAL TONE_____ PASTURE_____ CROPS NOW GROWING_____
_____ FOLLOWING CROPS ARE/ARE NOT INCLUDED IN SALE PRICE_____
IRRIGATION WELLS_____ DEPTH_____ POWER_____ NAME OF PUMP_____ CAPACITY OF PUMP_____
LAKES OR RESERVOIRS_____ FENCES_____ MAIN HOUSE CONST._____
NO. OF ROOMS_____ ROOF_____ FOUNDATION_____ BASEMENT_____
FLUES_____ ELECTRICITY_____ BATH_____ WATER SYSTEM_____
HEAT_____ CONDITION IMP_____ OTHER LIVING QUARTERS_____
_____ BARNS AND OUT BUILDINGS_____
NAME OF TENANT_____ ADDRESS_____
TERM OF LEASE_____ CROP OR SHARE RENT_____
WATER RIGHTS_____
WATER ASSESSMENTS_____
WHAT MINERAL RIGHTS GO?_____ TAXES_____
COMMENTS: (GENERAL IMPRESSION OF FARM) ADVANTAGES AND DISADVANTAGES (Use Separate Sheet, if necessary)

INCOME 19 19			EXPENSE		
SALE OF CROPS			OWNER OPERATED		IF LEASED BY TENANT
ALFALFA NO. OF TONS	SALE PRICE		FERTILIZER	% BY OWNER	
SUGAR BEETS-TONS PER ACRE	TOTAL PRICE		WATER ASSESS.	% BY OWNER	
CORN: YIELD	PRICE		R.E. TAXES		PERS. TAXES
WHEAT: YIELD	PRICE		INSURANCE		
BARLEY: YIELD	PRICE		MAINTENANCE		
BEANS: YIELD	PRICE		MACHINERY HIRED		
PASTURE INCOME			COST OF REPAIRS		
SALE OF LIVESTOCK			LABOR HIRED		
OTHER			ARTIFICIAL BREEDING		
OTHER	TOTALS		LIVESTOCK PURCHASED		
LOAN SERVICE AS OF		19	TOTAL		

1ST $_____ % INT._____ # YRS._____ ANNUAL PMT._____ ASSUMABLE_____ ?
2ND $_____ % INT._____ # YRS._____ ANNUAL PMT._____ ASSUMABLE_____ ?
3RD $_____ % INT._____ # YRS._____ ANNUAL PMT._____ ASSUMABLE_____ ?

The income and expenses listed above are warranted to be the actual figures for the_____ month period ended_____ 19____ . The undersigned understands that in reliance on the above listed figures, commitments and obligations may be made by one or more persons which would not have been made but for reliance on these figures.

Date:_____ 19____ Name:_____ Name:_____
(Signed by Property Owners representing correct information)
Mailing Address:_____ City:_____ State:_____ Zip:_____
Owner's Phone Number:_____ Broker:_____

EXCHANGE COUNSELOR FORMS
P. O. Box 5834
San Jose, CA. 95150

Form 11

Form #8

STATEMENT OF INCOME & EXPENSES
Motel and Hotel

BROKER _____   PRICE: _____

PROPERTY NAME _____   LOAN: _____

REFERRAL AFFILIATION _____   EQUITY: _____

PROPERTY ADDRESS _____ CITY _____ COUNTY _____ STATE _____

Owner_____ Phone _____ Mgr. _____ Motel Phone _____

Lot Size_____ Owned_____ Leased_____ Rm to Expand_____ Sewer_____ Hwy._____

Units_____ Singles_____ Doubles_____ Kitchens_____ Beds_____

Construction_____ Roof_____ Plaster_____ Floors_____

Age_____ Cond._____   ROOM INCOME: 19_____ 19_____

Operating EXPENSE: 19_____

(Room Tax Not Included)   (40 Units M/L) Aver. %

	ROOM INCOME			Operating EXPENSE	
Rates_____	Jan.	$_____	$_____	Sal. &Wages...13.50	$_____
Furniture_____ Own ☐ Lease ☐	Feb.	$_____	$_____	Exec.& Mgmt ...3.00	$_____
Carpeted_____	March	$_____	$_____	Payroll Tax & Ins 1.25	$_____
Room Phones_____ Dir. Dial	April	$_____	$_____	Laundry....... 3.50	$_____
Linens-Rented_____ Owned_____	May	$_____	$_____	Linen, China & Glass......... 1.00	$_____
Bath Tubs_____ Showers_____	June	$_____	$_____	Supplies (other) 2.75	$_____
Heating_____	July	$_____	$_____	Telephone 2.50	$_____
Air Cond.(Type)_____	August	$_____	$_____	Advertising & Prom 3.00	$_____
Drives_____	Sept.	$_____	$_____	Utilities....... 7.00	$_____
Pool_____	Oct.	$_____	$_____	Repairs & Maint. 5.50	$_____
Landscaping_____	Nov.	$_____	$_____	Pool Service Gardner	
Liv. Quarters_____	Dec.	$_____	$_____	Other Opr. Exp. 4.00	$_____
Furn. Included?_____	TOTAL	$_____	$_____	Garbage Franchise Fee	
Rest. ☐ Coffee Shop ☐ Lounge ☐	Misc.	$_____	$_____	Miscellaneous Taxes & Licenses 4.25	$_____
Own ☐ Leased ☐	TOTAL	$_____	$_____	Insurance.......1.90	$_____
				Equip. Rentals.. 2.25	$_____
				Total 55.40	$_____

Ice Machine_____

(OTHER INCOME (ANNUAL))

RECAP

Dispensing Machines_____	Restaurant	$_____	Gross $_____
Signs_____	Lounge	$_____	Less Expense $_____
	Vending	$_____	Balance $_____
T.V._____ Own_____ Lease	Telephone	$_____	Less Payments $_____
_____	Other	$_____	Net Spendable $_____
_____	Total Other		Equity Gain $_____
_____	Income	$_____	Total Gain $_____

Condition of Personal and Real Property: (i.e., Carpets, Drapes, Washer & Dryer, Painting, etc):

Excellent ☐   Good ☐   Fair ☐   Needs Upgrading ☐   Estimate Cost $_____

Loan service as of _____ 19____ : Capital Improvements _____

1st $_____	α $_____	/mo.____ % int.____ yrs. Tot. yrly. $_____	(Nature:_____	) Assum._____
2nd $_____	@ $_____	/mo.____ % int.____ yrs. Tot. yrly. $_____	(Nature:_____	) Assum._____
3rd $_____	α $_____	/mo.____ % int.____ yrs. Tot. yrly. $_____	(Nature:_____	) Assum._____
4th $_____	@ $_____	/mo.____ % int.____ yrs. Tot. yrly. $_____	(Nature:_____	) Assum._____
Lease $_____	@ $_____	/mo.____ yrs. Tot. yrly. $_____	(Nature:_____	) Assum._____

Remarks:_____

Tax Bill Breakdown:

_____ Land

_____ Improvements

Will Owners Provide Leaseback:_____   _____ Personal Property

Terms of Leaseback:_____   _____ Total

The income and expenses listed above are warranted to be the actual figures for the_____ month period ended _____ 19_____. The undersigned understands that in reliance on the above listed figures, commitments and obligations may be made by one or more persons which would not have been made but for reliance on these figures.

Date:_____ 19_____ Name_____   Name_____

(Signed by property owners representing correct information)

Mailing Address:_____ City_____ State_____ Zip_____

EXCHANGE COUNSELOR FORMS
P. O. Box 5834
San Jose, CA. 9515?

Form 13

Form #9

STATEMENT OF INCOME & EXPENSES
Ranch

DATE _____
STATE _____
COUNTY _____
CO. SEAT _____
ALTITUDE AT RANCH _____

CATTLE____ SHEEP____ MOUNTAIN____ PLAINS____
CARRYING CAPACITY
NO. OF COWS _____ HD _____ MO'S
NO. OF STEERS _____ HD _____ MO'S
NO. OF SHEEP _____ HD _____ MO'S

NAME OF RANCH_____ NEAREST TOWN_____ TOTAL ACREAGE_____
DIRECTION FROM TOWN_____ DISTANCE_____ ACRES DEEDED_____
STATE LEASE_____ ACRES AT $_____ PER YEAR_____ EXP. DATE_____
PRIVATE LEASE_____ ACRES AT $_____ PER YEAR – (WRITTEN–VERBAL) – EXP. DATE_____
TAYLOR GRAZING LEASE_____ ACRES AT $_____ PER YEAR – TERM_____ EXP. DATE_____
TAYLOR GRAZING PERMIT_____ HEAD AT $_____ PER HEAD – SEASON OF_____ TO_____
FOREST PERMIT_____ HEAD AT $_____ PER HEAD – SEASON OF_____ TO_____
NAME OF FOREST_____ LIKELIHOOD OF CUT (YES–NO) WHAT PERCENT_____ %
NAME OF RANGER OR SUPERVISOR AND ADDRESS_____
ACRES IN HAY_____ KIND_____ AVERAGE TONNAGE_____ QUALITY_____
ACRES FARMED_____ WHAT CROPS_____ AVERAGE YIELD_____
ACRES IRR. PASTURE_____ ACRES SUB-IRR. PASTURE_____ ACRES DRY PASTURE_____ ACRES WASTE LAND_____
PREDOMINANT RANGE GRASSES_____ CONDITION OF RANGE_____ WATER RIGHTS: NAME OF STREAM_____
NO. OF CU. FT._____ DATE OF PRIORITY_____ STREAM OR LAKES_____ MILES OF STREAMS_____
STOCK WATER: CREEK_____ SPRINGS_____ POUNDS_____ WINDMILLS_____
DISTANCE TO GRADE SCHOOL_____ BUS (YES–NO) DISTANCE TO HIGH SCHOOL_____ BUS (YES–NO)
KIND OF ROAD IN TO RANCH_____ MILES TO MAIN ROAD_____ NO. OR TYPE_____
IS THERE GOOD WINTER SHELTER_____ KIND_____ ANNUAL PRECIPITATION_____ DESCRIBE CLIMATE_____
WINTERS_____ SUMMERS_____ CONDITION OF FENCES_____ KIND_____ NO. OF PASTURES_____
IMPROVEMENTS [DESCRIBE FULLY – TYPE – CONDITION – WATER SUPPLY – BATH – ELEC. (YES–NO) SOURCE_____
[ARE BUILDINGS NEAT AND ATTRACTIVE (YES–NO) LAWNS (YES–NO) SHADE TREES (YES–NO)_____
EXPLAIN CARRYING CAPACITY AND BEST TYPE OF OPERATION_____
LIVESTOCK ON RANCH (INCLUDED – NOT INCLUDED) IN SALE PRICE - NO. OF CATTLE_____ NO. OF SHEEP_____
CLASSES AND AGES_____ STOCK FED_____ MONTHS_____ TO_____
TONS PER HEAD FED AVERAGE SEASON_____ % CALF CROP_____ % LAMB CROP_____ AVERAGE WEIGHT IN FALL_____
SHIPPING POINT_____ DISTANCE FROM RANCH_____ FREIGHT RATE TO (TRUCK–RAIL)_____ WHEN PURCHASED BY PRESENT OWNER_____
WHY IS RANCH FOR SALE_____
WILL 19____ HAY CROP BE INCLUDED IN SALE? (YES–NO) IF NOT, AT WHAT PRICE PER TON – $_____
REAL ESTATE TAXES $_____ PERSONAL TAXES $_____ ANY POISONOUS WEEDS_____ WHAT MINERAL RIGHTS GO_____
COMMENTS: (GENERAL IMPRESSION OF RANCH) (ADVANTAGES AND DISADVANTAGES) (Use Separate Sheet If Needed)

INCOME 19__ 19__		EXPENSE	
SALE OF CROPS		OWNER OPERATED	IF LEASED BY TENANT
ALFALFA NO. OF TONS	SALE PRICE	FERTILIZER	% BY OWNER
SUGAR BEETS–TONS PER ACRE	TOTAL PRICE	WATER ASSESS.	% BY OWNER
CORN: YIELD	PRICE	R.E. TAXES	PERS. TAXES
WHEAT: YIELD	PRICE	INSURANCE	
BARLEY: YIELD	PRICE	MAINTENANCE	
BEANS: YIELD	PRICE	MACHINERY HIRED	
PASTURE INCOME		COST OF REPAIRS	
SALE OF LIVESTOCK		LABOR HIRED	
OTHER		ARTIFICIAL BREEDING	
OTHER	TOTALS	LIVESTOCK PURCHASED	
LOAN SERVICE AS OF	19__	TOTAL	

1ST $_____	% INT._____	# YRS._____	ANNUAL PMT._____	ASSUMABLE_____	?
2ND $_____	% INT._____	# YRS._____	ANNUAL PMT._____	ASSUMABLE_____	?
3RD $_____	% INT._____	# YRS._____	ANNUAL PMT._____	ASSUMABLE_____	?

The income and expenses listed above are warranted to be the actual figures for the _____ month period ended _____ 19__. The undersigned understands that in reliance on the above listed figures, commitments and obligations may be made by one or more persons which would not have been made but for reliance on these figures.

Date:_____ 19____ Name:_____ Name:_____
(Signed by Property Owners representing correct information)
Mailing Address:_____ City:_____ State:_____ Zip:_____
Owner's Phone Number:_____ Broker:_____

EXCHANGE COUNSELOR FORMS
P. O. Box 5834
San Jose, CA. 95150
Form 10

Form #10

LAND AND LOT ANALYSIS

Broker _____   Comments _____

Salesman _____   _____

Office Address _____   _____

City, State & Zip _____   _____

Phone (AC _____) _____   _____

Property Address _____

City, County, State & Zip _____

Vested Owner _____	Price _____
Address _____	Terms _____
City, State & Zip _____	Will Subordinate? _____
Phone (AC _____) _____	Joint Venture? _____
Assessor's Parcel No. _____	Will Seller Provide Financing? ____
Current Tax Assessment _____	Option $_____ Terms _____
Other Special Assessments? _____	Gross Ac. _____ Net Ac. _____
Zoning _____ Zoning to Be _____	$_____ Per Ac.
Sewers _____ Water _____ Gas _____	$_____ Per Sq. Ft.
Electricity _____ Curbs/ Gutters __	$_____ Per Unit
Topography _____	Offer ($_____) Cash
Surroundings, Describe _____	Offer ($_____) Minimum Down
_____	Length of Escrow _____
_____	Conditions _____

APPLICABLE SITE DEVELOPMENT FEES:

Storm Drainage:	Acreage Fee	$	_____
	Other	$	_____
Sewer:	Acreage Fee	$	_____
	Connection Fee	$	_____
	Other	$	_____
Water:	Acreage Fee	$	_____
	Connection Fee	$	_____
	Other	$	_____
Park Fees:		$	_____
Bridge Fees:		$	_____
Annexation Fees:		$	_____
Any Other Fees:		$	_____
		$	_____

SHOW MAJOR CROSS STREETS BELOW:

SOIL TESTS: Available? _____
   If so, submit copy.
ENGINEERING STUDIES: Available? _____
   If so, submit copy.
APARTMENT SURVEY: Available? _____
   If so, submit copy.

SHOW NORTH DIRECTION BY ARROW.

ATTACH PLAT, PHOTOS AND AERIAL
PHOTOS OF PROPERTY, IF AVAILABLE.

EXCHANGE COUNSELOR FORMS
P. O. Box 5834
San Jose, CA. 95150

Form 14

Form #11

NOTE INFORMATION STATEMENT

© Exchange Counselor Forms
The Pony Express 1973
P. O. Box 5906
San Jose, CA 95150

Description of Note: ( ) Trust Deed _____
( ) Mortgage _____
( ) Personal _____

Beneficiary: _____ Address: _____

1st _____; 2nd _____; 3rd _____; Contract _____; Chattel (F.S.) _____

Current principal balance $ _____ Original balance $ _____

How long in existance? _____ How payable $ _____ per _____

Interest rate _____% Incl. _____ Prepaid _____ How long _____

Interest added (add on) _____; Other _____; Due Date _____

Payable by: Name _____   ___ Owner/Occupant
              Address _____   ___ Owner/Landlord
              City, State, Zip _____   ___ Broker/Salesman
              Phone _____   ___ Other

How was this note acquired? Gift ___; Carry back ___; Purchase ___; Created ___; Inherited ___.

Security: _____

Type of Property: _____

Address: _____

Approximate value of security $ _____ Additional Security: _____

Does this note contain an Alienation Clause? ____ If yes, give wording: _____

Approximate FMV of property at the time the note was created $ _____ __

Current balance of any prior existing encumbrances: First ____; Second ____; Other ____

Original amount $ _____ How payable $ _____ per _____

Remarks: _____

The information listed above is warranted to be the actual current status of the Note described herein. The undersigned understand that in reliance on the above listed figures, commitments and obligations may be made by one or more persons which would not have been made but for reliance on these figures.

Date: _____   Name: _____

Counselor: _____   Name: _____
                              Signed by the owner representing correct information.

Form 4

Form #12

PROPERTY ANALYSIS

Purpose: _____ Date: __/__/__

Name: _____

Location: _____

Type of Property: _____

Assessed Value:

Land	$ _____	_____ %
Improvement	$ _____	_____ %
Personal Property	$ _____	_____ %
TOTAL	$ _____	100%

Adjusted Cost Basis as of _____ $ _____

List Price $ _____ Market Value $ _____
Loans $ _____ Loans $ _____
List Price Equity $ _____ Market Value Equity $ _____

Existing Financing: Annual Payment Interest

1st	$ _____	_____	_____ %
2nd	$ _____	_____	_____ %
3rd	$ _____	_____	_____ %
Potential 1st	$ _____	_____	_____ %
2nd	$ _____	_____	_____ %

		%	2	3	Comments	
1	SCHEDULED GROSS INCOME					1
2	Less: Vacancy and Credit Losses					2
3	GROSS OPERATING INCOME					3
4	Less: Operating Expenses					4
5	Taxes					5
6	Insurance					6
7	Utilities					7
8	Licenses, Permits, Advertising					8
9	Management					9
10	Payroll, Including Payroll Taxes					10
11	Supplies					11
12	Services					12
13	Maintenance					13
14	Other					14
15						15
16						16
17	TOTAL EXPENSES					17
18	NET OPERATING INCOME Cap Rate List Price ___ % Cap Rate Market Value ___ %					18

ESTIMATE OF MARKET VALUE

				4	5	
19	INCOME APPROACH: Estimated Value Capitalized at Rate of ___ %					19
20	Cost Approach:					20
21	Sq. Ft. @ ___ Per Sq. Ft.					21
22	Sq. Ft. @ ___ Per Sq. Ft.					22
23	Sq. Ft. @ ___ Per Sq. Ft.					23
24	Less: Estimate of Accumulated Depreciation ___ %					24
25	Depreciated Value of Improvements					25
26	Plus: Site Improvements					26
27	Plus: Land ___ Sq. Ft. @ ___ Per Sq. Ft.					27
28	ESTIMATE OF MARKET VALUE BY COST APPROACH					28
29	MARKET DATA APPROACH: ___ @					29
30	FINAL ESTIMATE OF MARKET VALUE (CORRELATED)					30

INCOME ADJUSTED TO FINANCING

		1	2	3	4	5	
31	NET OPERATING INCOME (Line 18)						31
32	Less: Loan Payments	3rd Loan	2nd Loan	1st Loan	Total		32
33	Interest						33
34	Principal						34
35	Total Loan Payment						35
36	GROSS SPENDABLE INCOME	Rate: ___ % (Line 36 ÷ MV Equity)					36
37	Plus: Principal Payment						37
38	GROSS EQUITY INCOME	Rate: ___ % (Line 38 ÷ MV Equity)					38
39	Less: Depreciation	Personal Property		Improvements			39
40	REAL ESTATE TAXABLE INCOME						40

For these forms, address California Association of Realtors, 505 Shatto Place, Los Angeles 90020.

(11-68)

The statements and figures presented herein, while not guaranteed, are secured from sources we believe authoritative.

PREPARED BY: _____

FORM B

Form #13

228

INCOME PROPERTY STATEMENT
COMMERCIAL

PRESENTED BY_____

IMPROVEMENT:_____
ADDRESS:_____
CITY_____
( ) BLOCKS N-S OF_____
( ) BLOCKS E-W OF_____
SALES REPRESENTATIVE:_____
TELEPHONE_____ (Circle One)
SHOWING INSTRUCTIONS:_____ OWNER - MANAGER - TENANT
TELEPHONE_____KEY_____

(Picture of property or business card may be placed in above space)

SPECIAL FEATURES:

GENERAL INFORMATION:
LOT SIZE_____ ZONE____AGE____CONST._____ELEVATOR_____STYLE_____
LEGAL_____ PARKING_____STORIES____SEWER____HEAT_____AIR COND.____

EXISTING FINANCING: NO. YEARS
FIRST LOAN_____PYMT.____INT.____ORIG.____TO GO.____
LENDER_____LOCKED IN YES___NO___
SECOND LOAN_____PYMT.____INT.____DUE____ACCEL____
LENDER_____
OTHER LOANS_____PYMT.____INT.____DUE____ACCEL.____

INVESTMENT INFORMATION BASED ON:
FIRST LOAN_____PAYMENT._____INTEREST_____NO. YEARS____
LENDER_____COST $____
SECOND LOAN_____PAYMENT____INTEREST_____DUE____
LENDER_____
SELLER WILL CARRY:_____PAYMENT____INTEREST_____DUE____

SCHEDULED INCOME:

#	DESC.	TENANT	RENT	LEASE EXPIRES
			$	
			$	
			$	
			$	
			$	
			$	
			$	
			$	
			$	
			$	
			$	
			$	
			$	
			$	
			$	
			$	
	TOTAL MONTHLY INCOME	$		

OPERATING EXPENSES:

Taxes	$
Insurance F&L	$
License & Fee	$
Utilities:	
Water	$
Electricity	$
Gas	$
Management	$
	$
Trash	$
Gardener	$
Maintenance (Est.) ___%	$
Other	$
TOTAL	$

ASSESSED VALUE:

	Amount	Per Cent
Land	$	%
Improvement	$	%
Pers. Prop.	$	%
TOTAL	$	100%

INVESTMENT INFORMATION:

Price	$
Loan ( )	$
Down Payment	$
Scheduled Income	$
Vacancy Factor (Est.) ___%	$
Gross Operating Income	$
Operating Expenses	$
Net Operating Income	$
Less Payments	$
Gross Spendable	$
Furniture Reserve (Est.)	$
Carpet Reserve (Est.)	$
Adjusted Gross Spendable	$
Paid on Principal	$
Total Return	$
Earns _____% on Sale Price	
(Capitalization Rate)	
Spendable of ____% on Down Payment	
Earns ____% on Down Payment	
Purchase Price is ____ Times Gross	

Above information is from sources believed reliable but not guaranteed.

FORM # IPSC-11

For these forms address California Association of Realtors
505 Shatto Place, Los Angeles 90020. All rights reserved.
Copyright 1968 by California Association of Realtors.

Form #14

COMPARATIVE INVESTMENT ANALYSIS

NAME: _____ DATE ___ / ___ / ___

PURPOSE: _____

LINE No.		(1) PRESENT POSITION			(2) PROPERTY			(3) PROPERTY			(4) PROPERTY			(5) PROPERTY			(6) PROPERTY			
1	List Price																				1
2	Market Value																				2
3	Less: Total Loans																				3
4	Equity																				4
5	Plus: Available Cash																				5
6	Total Effective Equity																				6
7	Less: Transaction Costs																				7
8	NET EFFECTIVE EQUITY																				8
	CASH POTENTIAL																				
9	Cash From Owner																				9
10	Plus: Cash from PotentialLoan																				10
11	Total Cash Available																				11
12	Less: Transaction Costs																				12
13	NET CASH AVAILABLE																				13
	PROPERTY INCOME ANALYSIS																				
14	Gross Scheduled Income																				14
15	Less: Vacancy & Credit Losses																				15
16	Gross Operating Income																				16
17	Less: Operating Expenses																				17
18	NET OPERATING INCOME																				18
19	Capitalization Rate																				19
	OWNERSHIP ANALYSIS OF PROPERTY INCOME: TAXABLE INCOME																				
20	Net Operating Income																				20
21	Less: Interest Payments																				21
22	Less: Depreciation																				22
23	TAXABLE INCOME																				23
	SPENDABLE INCOME																				
24	Net Operating Income																				24
25	Less: Principle & Interest Payments																				25
26	GROSS SPENDABLE																				26
27	Less: Income Tax																				27
28	Less: Capital Improvements																				28
29	NET SPENDABLE ANNUALLY																				29
30	Per Month																				30
	EQUITY INCOME																				
31	Net Operating Income																				31
32	Less: Interest on Loans																				32
33	Less: Income Tax																				33
34	NET EQUITY INCOME																				34
35	Net Equity Income Rate		%			%			%			%			%			%		35
36	Plus: Equity Growth Rate %		%			%			%			%			%			%		36
37	TOTAL EQUITY RATE		%			%			%			%			%			%		37

For these forms, address California Association of Realtors, 505 Shatto Place, Los Angeles 90020.

The statements and figures presented herein, while not guaranteed, are secured from sources we believe authoritative.

PREPARED BY: _____

FORM C

Form #15

PACIFIC EXCHANGE & INVESTMENT COUNSELORS

Price:
Loans:
Equity:

HAVE:

ADDRESS:

PRICE:

LOANS:

EQUITY:

WHY DOES
NOT WANT:

SUGGESTED
SOLUTIONS:

REMARKS:

OWNER:

FEE:

COUNSELOR:

This information is from sources deemed reliable, but is not guaranteed by agent. Package is subject to price change, correction, error, omission, prior sale and withdrawal.

Form #16

MEETING CONTROL SHEET

SHEET NO.: _____
MEETING: _____
DATE: _____

	BROKER OR OWNER	DESCRIPTION	LOCATION	PRICE	LOAN	EQUITY	IDEAS				
1											
2											
3											
4											
5											
6											
7											
8											
9											
10											

EXCHANGE COUNSELOR FORMS
P. O. Box 5814
San Jose, CA. 95150

Form 7

Form #17

PRELIMINARY EXCHANGE PROPOSAL

F
R
O
M

_____

Date: _____

T
O

Subject: _____

MY CLIENT: _____

Type of Property: _____ Address: _____
: _____ : _____
: _____ : _____

Encumbrances: _____
_____
_____
_____

YOUR CLIENT: _____

Type of Property: _____ Address: _____
: _____ : _____
: _____ : _____

Encumbrances: _____
_____
_____
_____

TERMS AND CONDITIONS _____
_____
_____
_____

NOTE: Other data on properties outlined herein as per sheets attached and submitted herewith. Final terms and conditions, if any, to be in subsequent offer and/or escrow instructions.

This proposal is subject to prior disposition of the above properties, and shall expire on

(date) _____

Both Brokers agree to direct their immediate attention to this proposal and submit any additional data requested by either broker.

_____ _____
SUBMITTING COUNSELOR   DATE   BROKER RECEIVING OFFER   DATE

Remarks: _____
_____
_____

Form 1

Exchange Counselor Forms
The Pony Express 1973
P. O. Box 5906
San Jose, CA 95150

Approved: _____

Date: _____

Approved: _____

Date: _____

Form #18

EXCHANGE AGREEMENT

CALIFORNIA ASSOCIATION OF REALTORS STANDARD FORM

first party, hereby offers to exchange the following described property, situated in

County of _____, California:

For the following described property of

_____ second party, situated in

County of _____, California:

Terms and Conditions of Exchange:

The parties hereto shall execute and deliver, within_____days from the date this offer is accepted, all instruments, in writing, necessary to transfer title to said properties and complete and consummate this exchange. Each party shall supply Preliminary Title Reports for their respective properties. Evidences of title shall be California Land Title Association standard coverage form policies of title insurance, showing titles to be merchantable and free of all liens and encumbrances, except taxes and those liens and encumbrances as otherwise set forth herein. Each party shall pay for the policies of Title insurance for the property to be acquired ☐ conveyed ☐ .

Form #19

If either party is unable to convey a marketable title, except as herein provided, within three months after acceptance hereof by second party, or if the improvements on any of the herein named properties be destroyed or materially damaged prior to transfer of title or delivery of agreement of sale, then this agreement shall be of no further effect, except as to payment of commissions and expenses incurred in connection with examination of title, unless the party acquiring the property so affected elects to accept the title the other party can convey or subject to the conditions of the improvements.

Taxes, insurance premiums (if policies be satisfactory to party acquiring the property affected thereby), rents, interest and other expenses of said properties shall be pro-rated as of the date of transfer of title or delivery of agreement of sale, unless otherwise provided herein.

_____of_____Calif._____
            Broker   Address   Phone No.

is hereby authorized to act as broker for all parties hereto and may accept commission therefrom. Should second party accept this offer, first party agrees to pay said broker commission for services rendered as follows:-

_____

Should second party be unable to convey a marketable title to his property then first party shall be released from payment of any commission, unless he elects to accept the property subject thereto. First party agrees that broker may cooperate with other brokers and divide commissions in any manner satisfactory to them.

This offer shall be deemed revoked unless accepted in writing within_____days after date hereof, and such acceptance is communicated to first party within said period. Broker is hereby given the exclusive and irrevocable right to obtain acceptance of second party within said period. Time is the essence of this contract.

_____
_____
                                          _____
                                          _____
                                          _____
Dated_____19_____   _____

A C C E P T A N C E

Second party hereby accepts the foregoing offer upon the terms and conditions stated and agrees to pay commission for services rendered, to:-

_____of_____Calif._____
            Broker   Address   Phone No.

as follows:- _____

Second party agrees that broker may act as broker for all parties hereto and may accept commission therefrom, and may co-operate with other brokers and divide commissions in any manner satisfactory to them.

Should first party be unable to convey a marketable title to his property then second party shall be released from payment of any commission, unless he elects to accept the property of first party subject thereto.

_____
_____
                                          _____
                                          _____
                                          _____
Dated_____19_____   _____

FORM E 14   REVISED APRIL 1972

Form #19

EXCHANGE COUNTER OFFER

Dated:_____

The offer to exchange the real property known as_____

_____ for real property known as _____

_____

Dated_____, is not accepted in its present form, but
the following counter offer is hereby submitted:

_____
_____
_____
_____
_____
_____
_____
_____
_____
_____
_____
_____
_____
_____
_____
_____
_____

OTHER TERMS: All other terms remain the same.
RIGHT TO ACCEPT OTHER OFFERS:_____ reserves the right to
accept any other offer prior to_____ acceptance of this
counter offer and _____'s agent being so notified in
writing.
EXPIRATION: This counter offer shall expire unless a copy hereof
with _____ written acceptance is delivered to _____'s
agent within _____ days from above date.

X_____
X_____

....

Dated:_____

The undersigned accepts the above exchange counter offer.

X_____
X_____

Form #20

EXCHANGE RECAPITULATION

| PROPERTY 1 | MARKET VALUE 2 | EXISTING LOANS 3 | EQUITY 4 | CASH | | PAPER | | COMM. 9 | TRANS. COSTS 10 | NET EQUITY 11 | NEW LOAN 12 | OLD LOAN 13 | NET LOAN PROCEEDS 14 |
				GIVES (IN) 5	GETS (OUT) 6	GIVES 7	GETS 8						

FORM F

Form #21

HOMEWORK NEEDED BEFORE PRESENTING
PROPERTY PACKAGE TO THE MARKETPLACE

Various checklists regarding properties have been provided throughout this book. In addition to the "people" interviews and gathering information regarding motivation about the owners, their tax situations and their wants for exchange, we have to have a property package. The forms in this chapter can help organize information needed to properly market the client's property and identify the property best suited to solve his problem.

THE BACK-UP PACKAGE

After doing a homework investigation on the property and the owners, the property package may be ready to take into the marketplace.

The short description of the property and owner is entered on the "Package" form. (Form #16.) In addition, the broker should have the following information in his "back-up" package, a file that goes with him to each presentation of the property in the marketplace.

Back-up Package Checklist

☐ 1. Copy of exclusive listing agreement.
☐ 2. Plat map of the subject property.
☐ 3. Map of the entire area marked as to the location of the property.
☐ 4. Zoning regulations applicable to the subject property.
☐ 5. Copies of the most recent tax bills.
☐ 6. Copy of title report on acquisition or recent preliminary title report.
☐ 7. Photographs of the subject property.
☐ 8. Copy of recent appraisal report (if available).
☐ 9. Buyer's closing statement (on acquisition of property).
☐ 10. Statement of income and expenses (if applicable).
☐ 11. Bids on the management of the building(s).
☐ 12. Bids on insurance coverage.
☐ 13. Copy of termite damage report.
☐ 14. Bids on the cleaning or repair of deferred maintenance.
☐ 15. Itemized list of personal property and its age and value.
☐ 16. Security and rent deposit schedule.
☐ 17. Schedule of concessions to tenants (if any).
☐ 18. Rental or lease comparables.

☐ 19. Copies of notes, mortgages or trust deeds.

☐ 20. Any other item that should be included for a particular property.

Several copies of the back-up package should be made on the office copy machine. When any offer is received on the property, or if the broker makes an offer to another broker, a copy of the back-up package should be furnished to the interested party.

APPENDIX B

Glossary of Terms

ACCELERATION CLAUSE (Also called an "Alienation Clause")
A clause in a trust deed or mortgage giving the lender the right to call all sums owing him to be immediately due and payable upon the occurrence of a certain specified event, such as a sale, default or demolition.

ADJUSTED BASIS
See "Basis, Adjusted."

ADJUSTED GROSS INCOME
See "Income, Adjusted Gross."

AGREEMENT OF SALE
A written contract between buyer and seller in which they reach a meeting of the minds on the terms and conditions of the sale, but do not pass title. Sometimes called a land contract or contract of sale.

ALIENATION CLAUSE
See "Acceleration Clause."

ALLIGATOR
Slang. An investment that eats. Property that costs more to operate than it takes in.

ALL-INCLUSIVE DEED OF TRUST
See "Deed of Trust, All-Inclusive."

ALLOCATION OF BASIS
See "Basis, Allocation of."

ALLOWABLE DEPRECIATION
See "Depreciation, Allowable."

AMORTIZATION
Reduction of a loan through periodic payments in which interest is at a pre-determined rate and is charged only on the unpaid balance.

ANALYSIS OF A PROPERTY
A collection of, and summary of, all the known factors pertaining to a particular parcel of property for the purpose of forming an opinion as to its fair market value and future benefits.

APPRAISAL OF PROPERTY
An estimate of value of a specified parcel of property at a certain period of

time, after making a thorough analysis, usually in writing, and signed by an appraiser

ASSESSED VALUE
See "Value, Assessed."

ASSIGNMENT
A transfer to another party of the whole or portion of real or personal property, or certain rights thereto, or securities relative to real or personal property.

ASSUMPTION OF MORTGAGE, OR TRUST DEED
When a buyer takes title to real or personal property, and becomes the principal guarantor for the unpaid balance of the notes, and becomes primarily liable for the amount of any deficiency judgement, if applicable.

AUDITED GROSS INCOME
See "Income, Audited Gross."

AVAILABLE DEPRECIATION
See "Depreciation, Available."

AVOIDANCE OF TAXES
Legally acceptable procedure of planning transactions using the various regulations and tax court rulings to minimize the result taxes. See also "Evasion of Taxes."

BASIS, ADJUSTED
Adjusted cost of an asset.
An expression of value acceptable for tax purposes, upon acquisition by purchase, gift, bequest, exchange, termination of joint tenancy, termination of tenancy in common, and so forth.
Original cost *plus* allowable additions including capital improvements, certain carrying costs and assessments *minus* allowed depreciation and partial sales.
Book Value.

BASIS, ALLOCATION OF
The cost or other basis of property consisting of land, improvements and personal property that must be allocated to the separate units, usually in proportion to the RMV (Reasonable Market Value) of each.

BASIS, NEW ADJUSTED
Owner's basis in property acquired in an exchange. See also "New Basis."

BASIS, OLD ADJUSTED
Owner's adjusted basis in property being disposed of. See also "Old Basis."

BILL OF SALE
An executed written instrument given to pass title of personal property.

BLANKET ENCUMBRANCE
A single mortgage or trust deed which covers all of one or more parcels of real estate.

GLOSSARY OF TERMS

BOOK VALUE

See "Basis, Adjusted."

BOOT

The fair market value (FMV) of an asset, other than "like" real property, offered in lieu of cash in an exchange, i.e., trust deeds, land contracts, goodwill, services rendered, patents, patent rights, copyrights. In some cases, even real property may be considered as boot.

Note: IRS also includes cash as boot; however, exchangors keep cash separate from other boot in order to keep track of it.

CAPITAL ASSET

Real or personal, tangible or intangible property if it is NOT one of the following: (1) stock in trade (inventory); (2) property held for sale to customers in the ordinary course of the taxpayer's trade or business; (3) depreciable business property; (4) certain federal, state and municipal short-term, non-interest-bearing obligations issued on or after March 1, 1941, on a discount basis.

Capital asset examples: Goodwill, life estate, jewelry (inherited), deposit account in a bank, franchise, property held for the production of income, but not used in a trade or business of the taxpayer.

CAPITAL COST

Cost of improvement which has been made during the past year which tends to extend the useful life of the property or add to the facility. Must be amortized over the useful remaining life of the property or portion of the property to which it belongs. Actual division of all capital improvement expenditures made during prior years, by the number of years in which they were made, in order to establish the probable amount of similar capital expenditures for the coming year.

CAPITAL GAIN

Profit derived from the sale or exchange of capital assets. May be short term or long term.

CAPITALIZATION RATE

The percentage return shown on an investment when purchased in full fee. (Free and clear.)

$$\frac{\text{Net Operating Income} \times 100}{\text{RMV}}$$

The size of the "cap rate" is influenced by the conditions under which the particular investment is being operated, as well as the availability of funds, prevailing interest rates, risk and so forth.

CAPITAL LOSS

Loss suffered through the sale or exchange of a capital asset.

CASH

Cash money that the owner can add to the transaction, thus increasing his effective equity.

CASH METHOD OF REPORTING INCOME
Income is reported in the taxable year in which it is received, whether it is earned or not.

CASH SPENDABLE (INCOME)
Net cash spendable—or—cash remaining after all operating costs, including loan payments, capital costs, and income taxes attributable to the particular investment, have been paid.

Net operating income *less* loan payments LESS capital costs LESS federal and state income taxes.

Net spendable income.

CHATTEL MORTGAGE
A mortgage on personal property.

COMMUNITY PROPERTY
Real and personal property earned or accumulated after marriage through the joint efforts of husband and wife while living together.

CONDITIONAL SALES CONTRACT
A contract for the sale of property stating that delivery is to be made to buyer, title to remain vested in the seller until the conditions of the contract have been fulfilled.

CONSIDERATION
Anything of value given to induce one entering into a contract; money, trust deeds, services, or even love and affection.

CONTRACT PRICE
Term used in installment sales. (1) If property is *clear*, then contract price = selling price. (2) If property is *encumbered* and vendor's adjusted basis is greater than existing encumbrances, then contract price = owner's equity. (3) If property is encumbered and vendor's adjusted basis is *less* than existing emcumbrances, then contract price = owner's equity *plus* excess of mortgage over basis.

CORPORATION
A legal entity, created by law as a legal person having certain powers and duties of a natural person, together with the rights and/or liabilities, distinct and apart from those of the persons composing it. A corporation, however, never dies and only ceases to exist when, and if, it is dissolved through the proper legal process.

DEALER
A person who holds property primarily for sale to customers in the ordinary course of his trade or business.

DECLINING-BALANCE METHOD OF DEPRECIATION
See "Depreciation, Declining-Balance Method of."

DEDUCTIONS
Itemized standard deductions and minimum standard deductions. The

amount deducted from the *gross income* to arrive at the *adjusted gross income*.

DEED

A written instrument which, when properly executed and delivered, conveys title to real property.

DEED OF TRUST, ALL-ENCOMPASSING

See "Deed of Trust, All-Inclusive."

DEED OF TRUST, ALL-INCLUSIVE

A purchase-money deed which is subordinate to, but yet includes the encumbrance or encumbrances to which it is subordinated. Similar to a land contract, except that title actually is passed and may be guaranteed by title insurance. The seller remains as the trustor on the existing loan or loans. This includes:

All-encompassing Deed of Trust.

Wrap-around Deed of Trust.

Over-riding Deed of Trust.

DEFAULT

Failure to fulfill a duty or promise or to discharge an obligation, or to perform any act in an instrument in writing that has been agreed upon.

DEFICIENCY JUDGMENT

A judgment given when the security pledged for a loan does not satisfy the debt upon its default.

DEPRECIATION

The loss of value in property, brought about by age, physical deterioration, functional or economic obsolescence. See "Depreciation, Allowable."

DEPRECIATION, ALLOWABLE

That depreciation which is permitted by the Internal Revenue Service or other taxing authority, or that amount which MUST be taken annually by the investor as an expense item and charged against the adjusted basis when determining capital gains.

DEPRECIATION, ALLOWED

That depreciation which was actually taken annually and has been accepted by the Internal Revenue Service.

DEPRECIATION, AVAILABLE

See "Depreciation, Allowable."

DEPRECIATION, DECLINING-BALANCE METHOD OF

Where the improvement portion of an investment basis is depreciated by a fixed percentage of the remaining balance each year over the useful life of the improvements; i.e., 125 percent of straight line for used residential income property; 150 and 200 percent of straight line for *First Users only*.

DEPRECIATION, STRAIGHT-LINE METHOD OF

Where the improvement portion of the investment (less salvage value) is depreciated an equal amount each year over the useful life of the improvements.

DEPRECIATION, SUM-OF-THE-DIGITS METHOD OF

(Only available to *First User* owner.) Where the value of the improvement portion (less salvage value) of the investment is depreciated over the useful life of the property according to the following formula:

$$\frac{N + 1}{2} \times N = Denominator$$

(N = life term)

ECONOMIC LIFE

The period over which a property will yield a return on the investment over and above the return attributable to the land itself. See also "Useful Life."

ENCUMBRANCE

Pertains to the loan or loans which are against the property or are to be placed on the property. Also applies to anything else which affects the fee simple title to property, such as liens, easements, or restrictions of any kind. Liens are a special type of encumbrance which make the property security for a debt.

EQUITY

The difference between the fair market value and the existing loans on the property.

EQUITY BUILD-UP

The principal payment portion of the loan payments that goes to decrease the loan balances, and increase the owner's equity in the property.

EQUITY RETURN

The percentage relationship between the sum of the cash spendable income and the equity build-up to the owner's equity.

Gross equity return—figured with the cash spendable income *before* taxes.

Net equity return—figured with the cash spendable income *after* taxes.

ESTATE PLANNING

An investment program which is geared to the establishment of an estate in accordance with the wishes of the investor, and taking into account his age, educational background, marital status, hopes, aims, ambitions, managerial ability, and ability to stick to an organized plan of acquisition, and management of investments.

EVASION OF TAXES

Willful attempt to evade or defeat taxes; a felony punishable by fine of $10,000, imprisonment for not more than five years, or both. See also "Avoidance of Taxes."

EXCHANGE

Reciprocal transfer of property (investment).

GLOSSARY OF TERMS

EXCLUSIONS

Items specifically exempted by IRS from being classed as gross income, such as: Certain death benefits; gifts and inheritance; amounts received under accident and health plans; unemployment compensation; improvements by lessee on lessor's property; certain dividends from qualifying corporations.

EXECUTE

To complete, to perform, to make, to do, to follow out; to execute a deed; to make a deed, sign, seal and *deliver* same.

EXECUTOR'S DEED

A legal deed to real property given by an executor of an estate.

EXEMPTIONS

Items which IRS allows the tax payer as exemptions from the taxable income, due to marital status, number of dependents, age or blindness. See also "Deductions" and Exclusions."

FAIR MARKET VALUE

The broker's evaluation, after the collection and interpretation of all available data, of how much the property should reasonably be expected to bring, when offered in the open market for a reasonable length of time. See "Reasonable Market Value."

FIRST USER

Income producing property—Owner at the time that property is put to use and/or is available for rental.

Owner-user property—Owner at time property was originally put to use.

FIXED OPERATING EXPENSES

Those expenses relative to the operation of an investment which are fixed and are in no way affected by the quality of the management, i.e., taxes, insurance, utilities, pool service, rubbish removal.

GAIN, INDICATED

See "Indicated Gain."

GAIN, RECOGNIZED

See "Recognized Gain."

GROSS EFFECTIVE EQUITY

Equity PLUS available cash. See also "Net Effective Equity."

GROSS EQUITY INCOME

See "Income, Gross Equity."

GROSS EQUITY RETURN

See " Return, Gross Equity."

GROSS INCOME

See "Income, Gross."

GROSS RECEIPTS

Gross amount of receipts. May or may not be equal gross income. (In merchandising, gross receipts *minus* cost of goods sold = gross income. In real estate brokerage, gross receipt = gross income. In service type business, gross receipt = gross income.)

GROSS SCHEDULED INCOME
See "Income, Gross Scheduled."

GROSS SPENDABLE INCOME
See "Income, Gross Spendable."

GROUND RENT
Earnings of income from an investment attributable to the ground itself. "Economic Rent."

HOLDING PERIOD (IN A TAX-FREE EXCHANGE)
Dates back to the acquisition date of the original property.

IMPROVEMENT COST
The cost of improvement or repair which *does not extend* the useful life of the property but merely tends to maintain it. This may be deducted as an expense item.

INCOME, ADJUSTED GROSS
Gross income MINUS deductions. For a wage earner, gross income and adjusted gross income are one and the same.

A salesman may deduct all expenses attributable to earning his salary.

A business owner may deduct all ordinary business expenses. His net business income is his adjusted gross income.

An investor may deduct 50 percent of the excess of net long-term capital gains over net short-term capital losses to determine his adjusted gross income.

INCOME, AUDITED GROSS
The actual income derived from an audit of the records.

INCOME, GROSS
Ordinary income *plus* capital gains income. (In merchandising, gross income = gross receipt *minus* cost of goods sold. In service type business, i.e. real estate brokerage, gross income = gross receipts.)

INCOME, GROSS EQUITY
Return on equity before taxes; or net operating income *minus* interest on loans; or net operating income *minus* loan payments *plus* principal payments; or gross spendable income *plus* principal payments. See also "Income, Net Equity."

INCOME, GROSS SCHEDULED
Projection of rental income the owner hopes to receive during the coming year.

INCOME, GROSS SPENDABLE
Net operating income *minus* total loan payments (P+I). See also "Income, Net Spendable."

INCOME, NET EQUITY
Cash Spendable (after income taxes) *plus* equity build-up.

INCOME, NET OPERATING
Gross scheduled income *minus* vacancy allowance; or audited gross income *minus* operating expenses, but before any loan payments. The return on the investment if purchased for all cash.

INCOME, NET SPENDABLE
Net operating income *minus* loan payments (P+I) *minus* federal and state income taxes *minus* capital improvements. See also "Income, Gross Spendable."

INCOME, NET TAXABLE
Gross scheduled income *minus* vacancy allowance *minus* operating costs *minus* available depreciation *minus* interest on all loans.

INDICATED GAIN (Realized Gain)
The potential gain that would be recognized if the property were sold for cash.

INSTALLMENT SALE
A sale where the following conditions exist: (1) The payment of the purchase price must cover more than one taxable year; (2) the total down payment *plus* the principal portion of the loan payments in the year of the sale must not exceed 30 per cent of the *total selling price*.
Note: the excess of the mortgage over the adjusted basis of the property is considered as part of the down payment. (Relief of mortgage over basis.)
The payment by the buyer of any of the seller's existing obligations is also considered as part of the down payment, i.e., escrow expenses, delinquent taxes, and so forth.
The payment of a deposit in the year prior to the *consummation of the sale* is also considered as part of the down payment.

INTEREST PAYMENTS
The total interest payments during the year on all loans either now against the property or being projected against it.

JOINT AND SEVERAL NOTE
Note signed by one or more persons, the makers of which may be sued either jointly or individually for the full amount of the note.

JOINT NOTE
Note signed by two or more persons each having equal liability for payment.

LEVERAGE
The use of Other People's Money (OPM) in the form of loans to add to the investors own money for the purchase of a property. Ten Percent (10%) down payment plus a Ninety Percent (90%) loan is 90 percent Leverage.

LIQUIDATE
To convert property and/or other assets into money; to pay a debt in full.

LOAN CONSTANT
>The percentage of the unpaid balance of a loan which is represented by the sum of the *principal and interest* payments for the following year, which is needed to fully amortize a loan.
>
>For example a 6 percent loan amortized over 25 years has a loan constant of 7.732 per cent. Annual payments necessary to fully amortize a $100,000 loan in 25 years would therefore be $7,732 per year.

LOCKED-IN LOAN
>A loan which the borrower is forbidden by contractual agreement from paying off before a certain specified time has elapsed.

MOTIVATION
>Reason why property owner wants to sell or exchange his property.

NET EFFECTIVE EQUITY
>Gross effective equity MINUS selling costs.
>Equity PLUS available cash MINUS selling costs.

NET EQUITY INCOME
>See "Income, Net Equity."

NET EQUITY RETURN
>See "Return, Net Equity."

NET LOAN RELIEF
>In an exchange, loans relieved MINUS loans assumed. See also "Recognized Net Loan Relief."

NET OPERATING INCOME
>See "Income, Net Operating."

NET SPENDABLE INCOME
>See "Income, Net Spendable."

NET TAXABLE INCOME
>See "Income, Net Taxable."

NEW BASIS
>Basis of the new property in the hands of the new owner after acquisition of the property through purchase of exchange. Old basis *plus* loan assumed *plus* cash and/or boot paid *plus* recognized gain *minus* loan relief *minus* cash received MINUS boot received. See also "Basis, New Adjusted."

OLD BASIS
>Adjusted cost basis of the property being exchanged. See also, "Basis, Old Adjusted."

OPEN-END MORTGAGE
>One which provides for an increase in the unpaid balance in order to advance additional loan funds to the borrower up to the original sum of the note (at some future date).

OPERATING COST
> Actual expenses incurred in the operation of the property other than loan payments.
>
> Real estate taxes *plus* insurance *plus* management *plus* repairs *plus* maintenance *plus* utilities *plus* services *plus* licenses *plus* payroll *plus* materials used *plus* other actual expenses.

ORDINARY INCOME
> Taxable income other than capital gains income, subject to the full graduated tax rates.

OVER-RIDING DEED OF TRUST
> See "Deed of Trust, All Inclusive."

PLEDGE
> The depositing of personal property (i.e., stock, bonds) by a debtor with a creditor as security for a debt.

PRINCIPAL PAYMENTS
> The total principal payments during the year of all loans either now against the property or being projected against it.

PROJECTION
> An estimate of future performance and/or tax consequences resulting from either no charge or after a particular contemplated transaction.

PURCHASE—MONEY TRUST DEED
> A Trust Deed which is given by the buyer as part of all of the purchase price of a property.

PYRAMIDING
> An investment program designed to increase the investor's equities at the fastest possible rate. Leverage, depreciation, appreciation, inflation and income tax regulations are used to maximum advantage in the acquisition, holding, disposal and/or exchange of investments for other investments.

QUIT-CLAIM DEED
> A deed to relinquish whatever interest, if any, the *grantor* of the deed may have in the property.

REALIZED GAIN (Indicated Gain)
> Fair market value MINUS adjusted cost basis of the property; potential.

REASONABLE MARKET VALUE (RMV)
> See "Fair Market Value."

RECAPTURE
> Excess of accelerated depreciation over straight line—Section 1250. Depreciation on disposal of personal property—Section 1245. Of investment credit on disposal of certain property—Section 47. Involuntary conversion—Section 1033.

RECOGNIZED GAIN

That portion of the indicated gain which has been recognized by IRS as taxable in this particular transaction.

The lesser of (1) indicated gain, or (2) total other properties received in the exchange.

RECOGNIZED NET LOAN RELIEF

In an exchange, loan relieved *minus* loan assumed *minus* cash paid—or—net loan relief *minus* cash paid.

RECOURSE

By signing a note "without recourse," an endorser signifies that while he is transferring his property in the instrument, he does *not* assume the responsibility of an endorser.

REPLACEMENT COST

See "Reproduction Cost"

REPRODUCTION COST

Cost of replacing the improvements on a property MINUS an allowance for depreciation. See "Replacement Cost."

RETURN, GROSS EQUITY

Percentage return on owner's equity

$$\frac{\text{Gross equity income}}{\text{Owner's equity}} \times 100\%$$

RETURN, NET EQUITY

$$\frac{\text{Cash spendable (after taxes) PLUS equity build-up}}{\text{Owner's equity}}$$

SELLING COSTS

Broker's commission or fee PLUS escrow charges.

SPENDABLE FROM INVESTMENT

See "Cash Spendable." Take home pay from investment. Net spendable income.

STRAIGHT-LINE METHOD OF DEPRECIATION

See "Depreciation, Straight-Line Method of."

SUBJECT TO (MORTGAGE)

Grantee takes title but is not responsible for mortgage beyond the value of his equity in the property. No deficiency judgment. See also "Assumption of Mortgage, or Trust Deed."

SUBORDINATION CLAUSE

Clause in a lien permitting a subsequent lien (i.e., construction loan) to have priority over it.

SUM-OF-THE-DIGITS METHOD OF DEPRECIATION

See "Depreciation, Sum-of-the-Digits Method of."

GLOSSARY OF TERMS

TAX-FREE EXCHANGE
"Like for like" reciprocal transfer of property (business or investment); any "boot" received shall be taxable; properties being exchanged must NOT be held as stock in trade or primarily for sale.

TAX LIABILITY FROM INVESTMENT
Total tax liability LESS the tax liability from ordinary income.

TAX LIABILITY FROM ORDINARY INCOME
Tax liability based on tax rate schedules as applies to gross income MINUS deductions and exemptions.

TOTAL RATE
Equity rate PLUS growth rate.

USEFUL LIFE
The period of time over which the asset is expected to be useful to the taxpayer. Not necessarily the length of time the property will last, or will be economically feasible. Useful life is essential in determining the annual deduction for depreciation. See also "Economic Life."

VACANCY ALLOWANCE
The percentage factor, based upon experience of this particular property or similar properties, which represents the loss in annual income due to vacancies and uncollected rents.

VALUE, ASSESSED
The estimated value, for tax purposes, of real or personal property as determined by the assessor or particular taxing authority, usually the county, for the purpose or establishing the tax rate, including the allocation of land and improvements.

WANTS
What the owner is looking for in exchange for that which he now owns.

WRAP-AROUND MORTGAGE
See "Deed of Trust, All-Inclusive.

INDEX

INDEX

All references are to paragraph numbers.